The changing business environment in the Asia-Pacific region

As the Asia-Pacific region continues to undergo an accelerated process of change, relationships among the six ASEAN countries are shifting on many levels – between the two Koreas and China and Japan; between Japan and the rest of the region and between trading blocs. The contributions collected in this volume examine key aspects of those changes as well as their implications for foreign investors. Issues discussed include the changing role of Japan in the region, the emerging power of Hong Kong and China in the approach to 1997, and the process of democratization in Taiwan and South Korea.

Bringing together a variety of perspectives from international contributors, this volume presents the expertise that is vital for a correct interpretation of the changing relationships in the Asia-Pacific region.

Henri-Claude de Bettignies lectures on Asia business issues, organizational behaviour and ethics at INSEAD and is Visiting Professor of International Business at Stanford University.

International Thomson Business Press
Research in Asia-Pacific Business
Edited by Henri-Claude de Beltignies

This series presents selected papers given at the annual LUMH conference on Asia Pacific in Management Education in Europe, held at the INSEAD Euro-Asia Centre and sponsored by the Louis Vuitton Moët Hennessy Group. It covers key topics in management styles, business success, financial and economic growth, new markets, entrepreneurship, investment patterns, FDI and joint ventures, international relations and competition. Some titles focus on particular countries or groups of countries in the Asia-Pacific region, while others look more broadly at issues across the region. All reflect the highest quality of research on this vital region.

The changing business environment in the Asia-Pacific region

Edited by Henri-Claude de Bettignies

INTERNATIONAL THOMSON BUSINESS PRESS
I ⓣ P An International Thomson Publishing Company

London • Bonn • Boston • Johannesburg • Madrid • Melbourne • Mexico City • New York • Paris
Singapore • Tokyo • Toronto • Albany, NY • Belmont, CA • Cincinnati, OH • Detroit, MI

British Library Cataloguing-in-Publication Data
A catalogue record for this book is available from the British Library

First edition 1997

Phototypeset by Intype London Ltd
Printed and bound in Great Britain by St Edmundsbury Press, Bury St Edmunds, Suffolk

ISBN 0–415–12320–8

International Thomson Business Press
Berkshire House
168–173 High Holborn
London WC1 7AA
UK

International Thomson Business Press
20 Park Plaza
13th Floor
Boston MA 02116
USA

http://www.thomson.com/itbp.html

Contents

List of figures	vii
List of tables	ix
List of contributors	xi
Preface	xii
List of abbreviations	xiv
Introduction	xvi
Henri-Claude de Bettignies	

1 The changing morphology of the Asia-Pacific region   1
Dilip K. Das

**2 The normalization of economic relations in continental
north-east Asia: Recent developments and implications**   45
Friedrich von Kirchbach

3 The Asian trading bloc   71
Evelyne Dourille-Feer

**4 Recent changes in Korea and their possible economic
implications**   92
Didier Cazal

**5 Korea and north-east Asia economic cooperation:
The Tumen River 'golden delta' project**   112
Jin Park

**6 Investment strategies of European companies for east and
south-east Asia: Aiming at the centre or the periphery?**   136
Wolfgang Klenner

7 Post-Soviet east Asia: European responses and strategies   150
Gordon Daniels

8 **Japan and east Asia: The impact of economic links** 161
   Glenn D. Hook

9 **The rationale for strategic planning in the Asia-Pacific region: Implications for European corporations** 178
   Foo Check-Teck

10 **Time and strategic action: The Japanese case** 198
   Michael Hay and Jean-Claude Usunier

11 **Human resource management in foreign companies in Japan** 227
   Philippe Debroux

12 **The homecoming of the Overseas Chinese: Consequences and scenarios** 266
   Eric Bouteiller

13 **Translating Asian strategies into global strengths: The Philips and Thomson cases** 277
   Martin D. H. Bloom

14 **South-east and east Asia towards 2020: Exploring an image of Asia's future** 294
   J. R. Chaponnière

Index 311

List of figures

1.1 The changing morphology of the Asia-Pacific region   4
1.2 Asia-Pacific countries' shares in world exports 1965–90   28
1.3 Asia-Pacific exports of manufactures as a share of
    total world exports of manufactures: 1965–90   31
2.1 Map of north-east Asia   47
2.2 Trade flows in continental north-east Asia   53
2.3 FDI into Yanbian Prefecture, Jilin, by country of origin:
    Jan 1991–June 1992   60
3.1 Japanese bilateral trade balance with the
    United States, EEC and south-east Asia   74
3.2 Asian trade flows: 1970 and 1991   78
3.3 Evolution of Japanese exports by region   79
3.4 Japanese exports to ASEAN by sectors: 1991   80
3.5 American and Japanese investment in Asia: 1991 stock   81
3.6 Trade links between India and Asia: 1970 and 1991   87
5.1 The location of the TRADP   113
5.2 The Tumen zone   114
5.3 The site of Hunchun   116
5.4 The three categories of the TRADP   118
5.5 How the Tumen River project will benefit Japan   127
5.6 The Tumen River as Japan's central gateway to the
    continental economy   128
10.1 Japanese *makimono* time pattern   216
12.1 Chinese population in the Far East in 1991   266
12.2 Overseas Chinese and their neighbours: 1990   267
12.3 Chinese population and share of GNP: 1990   268
12.4 Foreign trade Greater China-United States   270
12.5 US trade deficit with Greater China   270
13.1 Philips in Asia   278

13.2 Philips in Asia (as percentage of total Philips
     Group activity)   278
13.3 Matsushita Electronics (profits as percentage of sales)   280
13.4 Thomson Consumer Electronics: 1990 (regional balance
     as percentage of total)   284

List of tables

1.1 GDP and GNP of Asia-Pacific countries 5
1.2 Comparative average annual GNP growth rates: 1965–90 22
1.3 Comparative GDP at constant prices: 1965–90 22
1.4 GDP and GNP growth: 1965–90 23
1.5 Exports as percentage of GDP 24
1.6 Real growth rate of exports: 1965–90 25
1.7 Export expansion from Asia-Pacific economies: 1965–90 27
1.8 Comparative export performance: 1965–90 29
1.9 Export of manufactures from Asia-Pacific economies: 1965–90 30
1.10 Comparative performance in export of manufactures 32
1.11 Portfolio investment in and by the Asia-Pacific economies: 1965–91 34
1.12 Gross domestic investment average annual growth rate 35
1.13 Structure of production 36
1.14 Share of value-added in manufacturing industries 38
2.1 Basic indicators on continental north-east Asia: 1990/1 48
2.2 Orders of magnitude of intra-regional trade flows in north-east Asia 55
2.3 Growth rates of intra-regional trade flows in north-east Asia 56
2.4 Importance of trade with neighbouring countries for Chinese border provinces: 1989/90 65
3.1 Demand contributions to Japanese economic growth 73
3.2 Japanese ODA: 1989/90 75
3.3 Japanese economic outlook for 1992 76
3.4 GDP growth rate in Asian NIEs and ASEAN countries 77
3.5 Japanese direct investments: first half fiscal 1992/first half 1991 82
3.6 FDI approvals in south-east Asia: 1986–9 82

3.7   GDP growth rate for Pacific countries   84
3.8   Chinese economic indicators   85
3.9   Major FDI in China: first half 1992   85
5.1   Tumen outlays   119
5.2   Economic complementarities   120
9.1   Profile of ASEAN sample   180
9.2   CEO perceptions of global performance context   182
9.3   The degree of predictability within each environment
      to which the corporation is exposed   184
9.4   Comparing with the norm within the industry   185
9.5   Benefits of formal planning   187
9.6   Problems associated with formal planning   189
9.7   CEO assessment of strategic planning system
      capability to help the corporation cope with environmental
      changes   190
9.8   Assessment of strategic planning performance   192
10.1 Time orientation, time horizons, levels of strategy,
      organizational needs and their temporal issue   203
11.1 Number of years stationed/planned for CEOs in Japan   237
11.2 Number of foreign expatriates in Japanese subsidiaries   237
11.3 Hours worked by employees of foreign firms in Japan   239
11.4 Comparative situation of the welfare system   240
11.5 Criteria for selecting the local personnel   242
11.6 Origins of mid-career local managers   245
11.7 Training programmes offered by the companies   249
11.8 Localization of management   249
11.9 Extent of influence by the headquarters of foreign
      companies   251
13.1 Philips in Asia   279
13.2 Philips in Asia (as percentage of total Philips
      Group activity)   279
13.3 Philips in Asia (employment by country)   279
13.4 Thomson Consumer Electronics: 1990   279
14.1 Asian GNP per capita: 1976   294
14.2 Forecast of population growth in Asia: 1990 and 2025   300
14.3 Scenarios for growth in Singapore: 1990–2020   302
14.4 GDP in the Asia-Pacific region and Western powers:
      1990 (in US$ billion and on PPP basis)   303

List of contributors

Martin Bloom is Associate Fellow at the RIIA, London
Eric Bouteiller is Chargé de Mission at the HEC Eurasia Institute, Jouy-en-Josas, France
Didier Cazal is Professor of Strategy at Groupe EIA, Marseille, France
J. R. Chaponiere is a researcher at the Centre Asie, IREPD, Grenoble
Foo Check-Teck lectures at the Nanyang Technological University, Singapore
Gordon Daniels is Reader in Modern History at the University of Sheffield
Dilip Das is Visiting Professor at INSEAD Euro-Asia Centre
Evelyne Dourille-Feer is Chargé de Mission at the Centre d'Etudes et d'Information Nationales, France
Michael Hay is Professor at the London Business School
Glenn Hook is Director of the Centre for Japanese Studies at the University of Sheffield
Wolfgang Klenner is Professor at the University of Ruhr, Bochum
Jin Park is a Lecturer in Politics at the University of Newcastle East Asia Centre
J.-C. Usunier is Professor at the Université Pierre Mendès France
Friedrich von Kirchbach is Senior Economic Research Officer at the International Trade Centre, UNCTAD/GATT

Preface

Scholarship on the Asia-Pacific region is growing throughout the world, yet it remains relatively modest in extent given the area's tremendous strategic importance. Within Europe, in particular, research on Asia is still far from meeting our need for a better understanding of the region's dynamics. We are still inadequately equipped to anticipate Asia's evolution and the consequences of this for the rest of the world.

In founding the Euro-Asia Centre at INSEAD in 1980, I enjoyed the support of a group of enlightened corporate leaders who shared my concern over Europe's lack of insight into Japan and the Asia-Pacific region. The Centre represents an effort to create and disseminate knowledge likely to be of use to decision-makers, helping to build competencies through which Western and Asia Pacific businesses can move towards a better handling of their interdependence. It also seeks to promote networks of personal and institutional relationships, fostering an on-going, mutually rewarding climate of cooperation.

It is in this context that the present series of books has been developed, to present the work of the Euro-Asia Centre's faculty, and the proceedings of conferences, symposia, and public forums organized by the Centre both in Asia and the West.

Initially, the series will present the proceedings of the annual LVMH (*Louis Vuitton Moët Hennessy*) Conference on Asia Pacific in Management Education in Europe, held at the Euro-Asia Centre each year in early spring.

This Conference has been made possible thanks to the support of the highly successful international group LVMH, a world leader in luxury goods, for which sector the Asia Pacific region is becoming the world's largest market. The LVMH Group is, of course, keenly aware of the need to promote research on the dynamics of the Asia

Pacific region, and has supported the present conference annually since it was first held in 1985.

The initial purpose of the Conference was to bring together Asia specialists and other scholars interested in aspects of Asian studies, to discuss their findings and share their research interests, thus developing closer ties and promoting cooperation between scholars and the many research centres with an interest in Asia. The Conference aimed to encourage the sharing of teaching materials, and to foster academic exchange between professors engaged in developing an understanding of Asia and its future, and in developing the particular skills needed to do business in Asia. Over the years, the LVMH Conference has grown in size and now brings together about a hundred scholars from some fifteen countries for two days of lively exchange on a chosen theme. Recently, the Conference has also invited executives from Asian and Western corporations, eager to exchange views and ideas with the academic community. Their presence has enhanced the gathering and the debate it elicits.

The present series will, initially, present an edited selection of papers from the most recent LVMH Conferences (since 1993).

I would like to express my thanks to the LVMH Group for their support. This series will, I hope, make a modest but useful contribution to our understanding of the Asia-Pacific region – the world's fastest-growing economic pole, and one whose future impact we can ill afford to ignore.

Henri-Claude de Bettignies

List of abbreviations

ADP	Asian Development Bank
AFTA	Asian Free Trade Agreement
ANCER	Australia–New Zealand Closer Economic Relations Trade Agreement
APEC	Asia-Pacific Economic Cooperation Forum
API	Asia Pacific Institute
ASEAN	Association of South-east Asian Nations
CEO	Chief executive officer
CEPII	Centre d'Etudes Prospectives et d'Informations Internationales
CIS	Commonwealth of Independent States
CRT	Cathode-ray tube
DPRK	Democratic People's Republic of Korea
EAEC	East Asian Economic Caucus
EC	European Community
EPB	Economic Planning Board
FDI	Foreign direct investment
FOB	Free on board
GATT	General Agreement on Tariffs and Trade
GDP	Gross Domestic Product
GNP	Gross National Product
ICOR	Incremental Capital Output Ratio
KIEP	Korean Institute for International Economic Policy
LDP	Liberal Democratic Party (Japan)
NAEF	North-east Asian Economic Forum
NAFTA	North American Free Trade Area
NEARDA	North-East Asia Regional Development Area
NIEs	Newly Industrializing Economies (east Asia)
NMP	Net material product
OC	Overseas Chinese

OECD	Organization for Economic Cooperation and Development
OEM	Original Equipment Manufacture
OPTAD	Organization for Pacific Trade and Development
PABX	Private automatic branch exchange
PAFTA	Pacific Free Trade Area
PAFTAD	Pacific Trade and Development Conference
PBEC	Pacific Basic Economic Council
PECC	Pacific Economic Cooperation Conference
PMC	Programme Management Committee
PPP	Purchasing power parity
PRC	People's Republic of China
ROK	Republic of Korea
SEZ	Special Economic Zone
SWOT	Strengths, weaknesses, opportunities and threats
TEDA	Tumen Economic Development Area
TRADP	Tumen River Area Development Programme
TRAMCA	Tumen River Area Management Company
TREZ	Tumen River Economic Zone
UNCTAD	United Nations Conference on Trade and Development
UNDIESA	United Nations Department of International Economic and Social Affairs
UNDP	United Nations Development Programme
VCR	Video cassette recorder
VTR	Video tape recorder

Introduction

Henri-Claude de Bettignies

For attentive observers of the Asia-Pacific region, change is accelerating in some foreseen directions, but also in some unexpected ones. We need to pause, to reflect, to try to understand the significance of what is currently happening, and its likely consequences.

Thanks to the Louis Vuitton Moet Hennessy (LVMH) Group we have been able to do just that, bringing together in Fontainebleau over 100 scholars concerned with the future of the region, willing to share their research efforts, keen to build networks and to enrich European management education's capital of knowledge, research and teaching materials on the Asia Pacific region. This volume makes available the papers presented at the 8th LVMH Conference, held at the Euro-Asia Centre on the INSEAD campus, in February 1993. The theme of the conference was 'Changing Relationships in the Asia-Pacific Region. Implications for European Corporations'. We wanted to go beyond knowledge, beyond understanding, to anticipate what was likely to happen, from an assessment of the current dynamics (if not turbulence) of the region. As I said at the opening of the conference, 'The so-called collapse of the bubble in Japan, for example, is likely to have a major long-term impact beyond its current consequences for the Japanese socio-economic environment or on Japanese FDI it is essential for us to assess the essence of this change, and the very process of change itself. There is much to be gained from an insight into such processes. If Japanese earnings are to decrease, if management practices are evolving, if the political system is trying effectively to transform itself, if Japan redefines its role in the Asia-Pacific region, we need to integrate this transformation process into our understanding of Japanese dynamics and to draw the implications at both strategic and operational levels in our corporations.

As China flexes its muscles, attempting to monitor (if it cannot control) its fast economic growth, and muddling through the impossible task of managing the potentially explosive regional gap, it is essential for us to interpret correctly the clues given by its diplomacy. During 1996 Beijing reassessed its relationship with Russia (Yeltsin's visit), Japan (Emperor Akihito's historic trip), Korea and Vietnam: what role does China see itself playing in the region? The task of managing its domestic socio-economic and political problems does not prevent Beijing from demonstrating certain diplomatic orientations which must be correctly interpreted.

Korea is also furthering its democratisation process, giving itself significant short-term economic pain, and may well be driven to rethink its own scenarios and the possible timing of reunification. Korean society is also experiencing profound change, with inevitable implications for Korea's relations with its neighbours and partners.

The papers in this volume explore these dimensions – among several others – and are organised into six groups, essentially along regional lines. From the dynamics of the Asia Pacific region, to perspectives on its multiplicity of changing relationships, we explore south-east and east Asia, together with a special section on Japan and a discussion of external and internal influences in the region.

The volume starts with a very comprehensive review of the region in which Professor Dilip Das reads the past and, from an analysis of the current economic dynamics, gives his personal scenario. He identifies five units of analysis and defines the multicausality of the region's fast development. Professor Das carefully nuances the role of government in each country or cluster of countries and does not underestimate the relevance of cultural characteristics as having 'decisive ramifications'. Dilip Das illustrates well the role of Japan in the region (at its 'hub') and shows that it will remain dominant in spite of the current Japanese difficulties. He emphasises the transition from 'Communism to consumerism' and gives convincing data to illustrate the new role played by the NIEs.

From this survey of the region, we move to north-east Asia, with Friedrich von Kirchbach and Zhang Ruijin, who bring a very useful review of recent development at the mouth of the Tumen river and its surrounding region (some 1,500 square kilometres in total). In the continental area between China, North Korea and Russia, the normalisation of economic relations is a key factor, with much potential. The UNDP has encouraged a process of regional cooperation which the authors see as a breakthrough. The rapid growth, fuelled by cash and barter trade at national, border and individual level is however fraught with many difficulties and much ineffectiveness. The trade and investment flows between South Korea and China are, the authors feel, bound to remain the most dynamic factors in this poorly documented part of Asia. Von Kirchbach and Ruijin also see Japan retaining its position at the economic epicentre of the north-east Asian region, with solid prospects for closer economic relations with the mainland countries.

The paper on south-east Asia by Evelyne Dourille-Feer analyses the development of a potential Asian trading bloc. Will the 'flying geese' metaphor last, particularly when the Japanese model is ageing? The author is sceptical, as the economic 'glue' holding the geese together 'becomes insufficiently binding'. Evelyne Dourille-Feer stresses a dominant theme throughout the conference namely great confidence in the lasting dominance of Japan and the growing importance of China in the trading pattern of the region. She also sees India as somewhat isolated from the dynamics of east and south-east Asia.

The section on changes in east Asia offers two very different papers. Didier Cazal discusses the economic implications of the recent changes in Korea and analyses the consequences of the political process on the economy, both at macro and corporate levels. He gives us his view of the thorny business/government relationship, and mentions several nagging problems adversely affecting the business environment. It is clear from Didier Cazal's paper that no understanding of the Korean situation can be achieved without an insight into the complex relationship between the political and the economic issues, both at the domestic and international level.

Jin Park also looks into the Tumen River 'golden delta' project. The magnitude of the project, and the scale of the resources necessary for its success invite the author to give – in the short term – a 'nuanced' assessment of its future. He sees the project as an excellent opportunity for South Korea to expand its economic, cultural and political influence in Yanbian (where long-established cultural links already exist). Japan takes a pragmatic and incremental approach and perhaps, as von Kirchbach and Ruijin would probably agree, this is most realistic in the short term.

Wolfgang Klenner asks how European corporations should enter the regional market – via the centre or the periphery? Clearly, the initiative is in the hands of the business community rather than the politicians. Klenner is the only contributor to emphasize the role of human resources (both expatriate and local staff) among the conditions for success in the region. He rightly suggests that European companies often take a less practical approach than the

Japanese or the Overseas Chinese. Pinpointing the disadvantages of European firms in the region, he concludes that they have no choice, they must invest if they want to remain competitive globally.

Gordon Daniels gives us an interesting assessment of the consequences of the transformation of the Soviet Union. Europe should remain very attentive to what is taking place in post-Soviet southeast Asia, as traditional patterns of interaction with the former Soviet Union undergo significant change, with important consequences for the region's dynamics.

Glen D. Hook proposes a new way to look at the evolution of Japan's relations with the region. His political and economic analysis is explicit with regard to the challenges facing Japan in Asia. Hook also explores the question of a military pro-active Japan and raises important considerations.

Foo Check Teck, in his presentation on corporate strategy, invites European corporations to take a planned yet flexible approach to strategic management based on real cross-cultural understanding. Furthermore, he encourages a 'contextualised, contingency-based perspective of management, while not scrapping formal strategic planning entirely'.

In their paper, Michael Hay and Jean-Claude Usunier continue to explore the cultural or cross-cultural area in the context of 'time concepts' and strategic planning. This is a very well documented, stimulating paper which will provide food for thought for anyone operating businesses on a global basis.

Philippe Debroux offers a rich paper capitalising on his long experience of human resource management in Japan. Foreign companies having operations in Japan will find Philippe Debroux's report very useful in understanding the changes taking place in that country today.

Eric Bouteiller analyses an increasingly-studied phenomenon, the role of the Overseas Chinese and their importance in the development of China. Eric Bouteiller encourages Europeans to establish partnerships with Overseas Chinese as part of a long-term strategy in Asia.

Martin D. H. Bloom takes us into two extremely interesting cases of European companies in Asia (Philips and Thomson). His 'clinical' approach provides a rich assessment and understanding of different logics and strategies.

The final paper, by Jean-Raphael Chaponnière is the sort of forward-looking piece that one hopes to hear at an international conference on 'change'. Optimistic and nuanced, he presents alterna-

tive visions which integrate both the economic and political dimensions in common with many scholars attending the LVMH
Conference. His paper illustrates well our effort to understand
change in this vital region, and to at least try to anticipate it.

1 The changing morphology of the Asia-Pacific region

Dilip K. Das

THE ECONOMIC TAKE-OFF

For medieval Europe, the Asia-Pacific region was a cornucopia of exotic products and culture. Today, it is a land of effervescent economic growth, whose rise can be traced back to the early 1960s, when the Japanese economy came into its own. Since then, several fundamental and far-reaching economic changes have taken place in the region and a new era of economic expansion has begun, outpacing all other regions in terms of economic growth over the last three decades. Throughout the 1960s, Japan's GNP grew by more than 10 per cent per annum. Japan went on to export its way successfully out of all the exogenous economic disturbances of the 1970s, and was followed by the 'four dragons' whose economic achievements were eventually to even this. Other south-east Asian countries, and China, followed close on the heels of the dragons. One country's economic growth helped others in the region, generating almost self-perpetuating economic expansion. These 'pioneering' countries concentrated their energy on economic growth, pursued pragmatic macro-economic policies, and embarked on programmes of spiralling industrialization, very quickly forming the most dynamic economic region in the world. They demonstrated to the rest of the world that vigorous economic growth can be attained without miraculous intervention. Herman Kahn, with some prescience, noted that the Asia-Pacific economies were fast becoming the focus of world economic power. The epicentre of international economic dynamism has migrated throughout history, from its ancient origins in the Mediterranean, to north-west Europe, and then to the north Atlantic. During the post-war period it has moved again, to the Asia-Pacific region (Kahn 1979) – a fact now widely acknowledged, with scholars and international commentators citing 'the Pacific century' as a matter of course (Vogel 1984; Linder 1986; Gibney 1992). In what follows, we trace the growth of the Asia-Pacific economies from poverty to international economic stardom, analyse the economic characteristics of each sub-region, and delve into the causal factors underlying their hyper-growth and economic transformation.

THE REGION DEFINED

The Asia-Pacific economies have long been the subject of active interest and animated discussion among economists, industrialists, bureaucrats and politicians. Since the mid-1960s, when Professor Kiyosyhi Kojima set out his concept of an Asia-Pacific region, the area has been variously defined, with each definition including its proponent's favourite country group, policy coverage and institutional arrangements. Kojima envisaged a two-tier region which included the five industrialized countries, namely the United States, Canada, Australia, New Zealand and Japan, as the core group. The developing countries of the region were of secondary importance and were to be the secondary partners in the regional economic grouping. He posited a Pacific Free Trade Area (PAFTA) in 1966, involving mutual elimination of tariffs among the member economies while retaining them for non-members. Other country groupings, and hence acronyms, have developed over time: The Pacific Free Trade and Development Conference (PAFTAD) had a strong economic bias while the Organization for Pacific Trade and Development (OPTAD) was to be an OECD-like organization, championed by Sir John Crawford and Subiro Okita; the Pacific Economic Cooperation Conference (PECC) brought together academics, businessmen and government officials for an informal exchange of views on regional and international economies, and now produces several economic and statistical publications on the Asia-Pacific region; the Pacific Basin Economic Council (PBEC) examined the issues of business in local Asia-Pacific communities, and the East Asia Economic Caucus (EAEC) was proposed by ASEAN (the Association of South-East Asian Nations) to unite the latter economically with Japan, China, Taiwan, Hong Kong, South Korea, Vietnam, Myanmar and the Pacific island nations (Japan declined to commit itself to the idea, however). Finally, the Asia-Pacific Economic Cooperation forum (APEC), which was floated by the former Australian Prime Minister Bob Hawke in 1989, and initially received unenthusiastic support from Japan, had grown by 1992 into a formal body of 15 regional members, namely the United States, Canada, Mexico, Japan, Australia, New Zealand, China, Hong Kong, Taiwan, South Korea, Thailand, Indonesia, Malaysia, Singapore and the Philippines. By the time of its fourth meeting in 1992, membership problems were still not settled. Why, for example, should Mexico be a member when several nations in Indochina, and the Pacific islands, are not?

Against the background of this surfeit of definitions and regional groupings, I am venturing to propose my own:

- Japan, the largest and pivotal Asia-Pacific economy;
- Australia and New Zealand, two well-established prosperous economies;
- South Korea, Taiwan, Hong Kong, Singapore, four newly indus-trializing economies;
- Indonesia, Malaysia, Thailand, the Philippines, and the ASEAN-4, the first three of which are among the better-performing developing economies;
- China, a large developing economy that has recorded high growth rates throughout the 1980s.

These groupings, based on economic norms, bring together those economies of east and south-east Asia and the western Pacific which with minor exceptions have experienced dynamic growth in the immediate past because of their liberal, pragmatic and market-oriented macro-economic policies, their outward-oriented indust-rialization strategy and their efficient resource allocation by way of rational prices; they are also all countries whose governments are consciously committed to economic growth. All of these economies demonstrate complementarity in terms of natural resources, tech-nology and market size, and all have cooperated dynamically and shown deepening interdependence since the early 1980s. The econ-omies of the eastern pacific are excluded. Their inclusion would alter the focus of this compact, mutually cooperative, interactive, and therefore symbiotic group, making it sprawling and cumber-some, both functionally and conceptually. This is not to say that the eastern Pacific economies will not interact closely with those of the Asia region, as the US and Japan already do. But they will relate to the Asia-Pacific group without belonging to it and will remain active external participants.

As seen in Figure 1.1, the Japanese economy, by virtue of its financial prowess, technological lead and the strength of the yen, and by virtue of the fact that it is the largest economy of the region, will be the epicentre of this economic grouping. It is an important

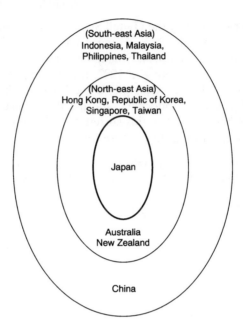

Figure 1.1 The changing morphology of the Asia-Pacific region

determinant of the prosperity of the Asia-Pacific region. A lot of what Japan does will determine the future direction of the regional economy. The four newly industrializing economies of east Asia, and the two industrialized economies of Australasia, interact more closely with Japan than with the ASEAN-4 and China, making the Asia-Pacific region a compact, three-tier growth pole of the international economy. In the foreseeable future, it promises to be as dynamic as the other two growth poles of the international economy, namely the European Community (EC) and the two north Atlantic economies, the United States and Canada.

VIVE LA DIFFERENCE

The rich diversity of the Asia-Pacific region is demonstrated by its sheer size, population, GDP and other indicators. China alone has a huge land area of over 9.5 million square kilometres and a population of 1.1 billion. The region also includes micro-states, covering less than 1,000 square kilometres and with populations of under 10 million. Japan, the largest economy of the region, is an economic super-power with a per capita income of US$25,430 (Table 1.1).

Table 1.1 GDP and GNP of Asia-Pacific countries

	GDP in 1990 ($ million)	GDP as proportion of total regional GDP (%)	GNP per capita in 1990
Japan	2,942,890	66.8	25,430
Korea	236,400	5.4	5,400
Taiwan	144,820	3.3	7,997
Hong Kong	59,670	1.3	11,490
Singapore	34,600	0.8	11,160
Indonesia	107,250	2.4	570
Malaysia	42,400	0.9	2,320
Thailand	80,170	1.8	1,420
Philippines	43,860	1.0	730
Australia	296,300	6.6	17,000
New Zealand	42,760	0.9	12,680
China	364,900	8.2	370
Total	4,396,060	100.0	

Source: World Bank 1992. Data for Taiwan comes from CEPD 1992.

At the other extreme, small economies such as the Philippines, New Zealand, Malaysia and Singapore have a GDP of less than US$50 million. The Philippines, Indonesia and China are classed as low-income economies, with per capita incomes of US$730, US$570 and US$370, respectively. Japan, with 67 per cent of the regional GDP, dominates the regional economic stage to an overwhelming extent. China and Australia are the second and third largest economies, accounting for 8.2 per cent and 6.6 per cent of regional GDP respectively.

Some Asia-Pacific countries are very densely populated, others sparsely so. Most are a contiguous whole, but Indonesia and the Philippines are archipelagos, together having over 20,767 islands, ranging from small reefs to areas roughly the size of France, Japan, Korea and Taiwan are ethnically homogenous societies, while Malaysia, Indonesia, Singapore and Hong Kong are multiracial and multicultural.

When growth began in the region, during the early 1960s, Japan was reconstructing its war-ravaged economy, China was in the throes of revolutionary turmoil, Korea and Taiwan were abjectly poor. At this point Australia and New Zealand were prosperous countries, although they were far from being matured industrial economies.

Thus, while the majority of Asia-Pacific countries developed from low levels of economic activity, others grew from an already strong base. There is striking disparity in natural resource endowments among the countries of the region. This diversity has been harnessed to deepen economic interdependence and maintain high growth. As described above, Japan posted high growth rates in the 1960s. In the 1970s and 1980s, Japanese growth slowed, while the four Asian newly industrializing economies (NIEs) and the ASEAN-4 began to register high growth rates in their turn. The expansion of trade and investment in the region during the 1980s further stimulated growth in the NIEs and the ASEAN-4. In addition, rapid growth in China during the 1980s was achieved through active economic interaction with the market economies of the region, which, in turn, contributed to regional growth. An interesting economic symbiosis has developed among the regional economies, with Japan providing capital, technology and markets, and Australia, New Zealand, the NIEs and the resource-rich ASEAN-4 drawing in natural resources and providing capital and exports of manufactured goods. The stark complementarity of the Chinese and Japanese economies has been sharply evident, and has, in fact, facilitated collaboration between the two.

PIONEERING GROWTH

The Asia-Pacific region, particularly Japan and the NIEs, has established itself as a trail-blazer in the arena of economic growth. No serious student of rapid economic growth and industrialization today can afford to ignore Japan and the NIEs. However, the achievements of the Asia-Pacific economies were neglected by academics during the 1960s. Myrdal's *magnum opus* published in 1968, heralded the south Asian countries as the economies of the future, and prototypes for rapid economic growth (Myrdal 1968). The world was enthralled by the superficial intricacies of their five-year plans, and by the vigour and direction that their governments strove to impart. The NIEs did not come under scrutiny until the publication of the Asian Development Bank's report in 1971. This was an influential work that defined the new thinking on Asia-Pacific economies. The superlative performance of Japan and the NIEs challenged the received wisdom on economic growth and initiated a new orthodoxy. Adam Smith and classical economists could only partly explain their performance. Standard theories about the rise of capitalism and industrialization, *à la* Garnaut, seemed almost as obsolete as pre-Galilean astronomy.

The Asia-Pacific economies expanded faster than those of any other region in the world. During the post-war period they were swept by four waves of economic dynamism – first, in Japan in the 1950s, followed by the NIEs in the 1960s. The third wave struck the ASEAN group in the 1970s, while the fourth struck and transformed the Chinese economy during the 1980s. Over the post-war period, five economies in the Asia-Pacific region achieved the exceptionally rare feat of doubling their GDP in a decade. These were: Japan, South Korea, Taiwan, Hong Kong and Singapore. During the 1980s, China – through active reform of its domestic economy and interaction with the region's market economies – became the sixth economy to achieve this distinction (Garnaut 1988). Thailand has long maintained high growth rates, and is heading in the same direction. While other countries in the Asia-Pacific region were experiencing rapid economic expansion, Australia and New Zealand gradually achieved the status of matured, industrialized, albeit small economies, growing at a sedate pace.

There are considerable differences, of course, in the economic policies of the Asia-Pacific countries, with the *laissez-faire* of Hong Kong on one hand, and South Korea's interventionist industrial policy on the other. However, there are several basic similarities in macro-economic policy, as well as common determinants of rapid growth. The Asia-Pacific economies have recorded the highest rates of domestic savings in the world, with government policies and fiscal incentives contributing to this. Real interest rates were positive and, from an international perspective, high, and the government sector also made direct contributions to saving, particularly in South Korea, Taiwan and China. High savings rates were one factor contributing to strong investment performance; external capital was another. Several Asia-Pacific economies supplemented domestic savings with external capital inflows whenever the resource gap seemed large. With the exception of the Philippines, these countries were careful to jeopardize their external stability. High savings leading to high investment soon became a virtuous cycle – since a large proportion of national income was continually invested, capital stock expanded rapidly. Several Asia-Pacific economies kept a firm grip on their financial markets and forced them to serve the needs of the industrial sector during the initial phases of growth.

High investment certainly leads to technological upgrading and to expansion of capital stock. It thus helps to explain better growth performance, but only partly. The classical view that factor input determines economic growth is now considered limited. Studies such as Denison *et al.* (1962) and Otani and Villanueva (1988) have shaken the classical view. Capital formation was not wholly satisfactory as an exploration of cross-country differences in growth rates. Cross-country comparisons, while confirming some correlation between high investment ratios and high growth rates, nonetheless, report weak correlation coefficients. In addition, there is the unanswered riddle of the direction of causality. A major part of growth performance is attributed to total factor productivity, generated by all-encompassing, albeit ill-defined, 'residual factors'. These include the human factor (and Lee Kwan Yew's 'vital intangible', i.e. the people's determination to pull their country up by its own bootstraps), macro-economic policy and improvements in resource allocation, institutional and structural characteristics, absorption of technology, efficiency of investment or incremental capital output ratio (ICOR), provision of public goods, management and entrepreneurship and the like.

Let us, therefore, turn to the residual factors in the context of the Asia-Pacific region. The first outstanding characteristic shared by the Asia-Pacific economies is their outward-oriented growth process, or the growing ratio of foreign trade to GDP and domestic expenditure. International economic orientation has contributed both to growth and stability. Economies that are internationally insolvent or have binding international liquidity constraints cannot grow. They are also highly vulnerable to debt traps. Rising exports of manufactures from the Asia-Pacific countries helped diversify export structures away from primary exports and thereby steadied their terms of trade. Outward economic expansion also establishes a second virtuous cycle, linking trade expansion to the technological upgrading of the domestic industrial sector. Exporting firms are gradually able to import advanced capital goods embodying state-of-the-art technology. Trade exposes them to the newest techniques and helps them focus on the art of the possible. These firms realize the importance of the technological edge they must have to stay competitive in the international markets. The brisk expansion of trade provided them with opportunities to specialize according to comparative advantage which, in turn, encouraged the exploitation of scale economies as well as the maintenance of high-capacity utilization (Balassa and Williamson 1990). Asia-Pacific economies from Japan to the ASEAN-4 have been able to capture these dynamic gains from trade in addition to the static gains that were provided by improved resource allocation. Although only Hong Kong was a free-trading economy, other governments on various occasions supported the expansion of their manufacturing sectors, including manufacturing exports. Import tariffs were occasionally slapped on consumer imports, for balance-of-payments reasons, although the bias introduced by these tarrifs was largely offset by export subsidies. Policy neutrality was more or less maintained.

Second, in order to stimulate export-oriented industrialization, Asia-Pacific countries used both credit subsidies and financial repression (as in South Korea) and fiscal subsidy (as in Taiwan). The former had its side effects, however. With capital costs subsidized, the favoured sectors tended to become capital-intensive and large-scale. In addition to providing loans at below the market rates (possibly to buy government debt at low interest rates), banks were forced to suppress deposit rates which were discouraging savings in the financial sector. Conversely, a fiscal subsidy on the output or exports of a favoured industry does not have these side effects. Besides, the cost of fiscal subsidies is hidden in low deposit rates but explicit in the tax structure (Bradford and Branson 1987).

Third, economic growth in the Asia-Pacific region was accompanied by rapid change in the structure of production. The agricultural sector declined as the importance of manufacturing and service sectors grew, and exports reflected this change. Structural changes continued steadily and by the 1970s the developing economies of the Asia-Pacific region had made considerable progress in industrialization. Their economies had acquired a significant level of capital intensification.

Fourth, prudent and cautious macro-economic management was another hallmark of these generally low-inflation economies. During the 1980s, seven Asia-Pacific countries enjoyed an average long-term inflation rate of 5 per cent or less. The best performers were Japan (1.5 per cent), Malaysia (1.6 per cent) and Taiwan (2.2 per cent). The Philippines and New Zealand were the poorest performers having average inflation rates of 14.9 and 10.5 per cent respectively. The World Bank associated higher growth with lower price distortions. The *World Development Report 1983* contained a price distortion index for 31 countries. It was prepared using measures of distortion of foreign exchange pricing, factor pricing and product pricing, and demonstrated that in the 1970s countries with higher government-induced distortions grew slowly. The *World Development Report 1985* showed that large price distortions also lead to slower export growth and increased debt-servicing difficulties. Although distortions did exist (as in Korea), the Asia-Pacific economies were generally identified with low levels of price distortions. In spite of this, these economies implemented numerous reforms in their industrial and trade policies, as well as in their financial systems. During the 1980s, several of them adopted macro-economic reforms that were conducive to growth. Some (Japan, Taiwan and Korea) had to adjust to external surpluses, while others (Australia, New Zealand, Indonesia, Malaysia and Thailand) had to adjust to external deficits. The adoption of reform measures drove these economies to liberalization and efficiency-enhancing macro-economic policies. Australia and Thailand were the exceptions in this regard, since while making structural adjustments they were forced to impose controls on capital movement, but in general governments in the region saw an opportunity to liberalize their economies while making macro-economic adjustments. The freeing of market forces helped achieve the optimal allocation of resources on the given production possibility curve in these economies and the dynamic gains resulting from their international economic orientation helped move this curve outward.

Fifth, Asia-Pacific governments were strongly committed to fostering economic growth – which was given higher priority than social and welfare objectives – intervening directly in economic affairs to that end. Yet they were less intrusive in terms of resource allocation than were the governments of other developing economies, and did not stifle market forces. Government policy in all these economies, including Indonesia after 1965, rejected public ownership of the means of production together with centralized planning. These economies discovered early on that a healthy private sector can bring dividends. The market orientation of these economies facilitated the operation of price mechanisms, so that resources were able to move with relative ease from less to more productive uses. Reliance on markets for resource allocation also facilitated adjustments to domestic and external economic shocks. An exemplary case of collaboration between the market and government can be seen in the phasing out of industries that were losing comparative advantage in Japan and the NIEs. These governments did not suffer from the 'soft state' syndrome and were authoritarian in varying degrees, with the result that rent-seeking groups were unable to influence or dominate them, even though such groups have had a powerful influence on policy-making in other market economies. The Asia-Pacific economies were able to pursue their goals in a more determined manner without frittering away their creative energy.

Sixth, much is made of the cultural values of Asia-Pacific societies as promoters of economic growth. Formal education, personal discipline, and a thrifty attitude are highly valued, and are central to the philosophy, generally known as Confucianism. This cultural tradition is common to both north-east and south-east Asia, although it is more prevalent in the former than in the latter. A strong emphasis on thrift, higher education, and the promotion of a meritocracy, are clearly relatable to a capacity to sustain high levels of growth. Individual and social disciplines impart social cohesion and a readiness to accept change. Individuals and families react passively to the short-term price of change, recognizing its long-term promise and potential. They tend to rationalize the short-term pain, and in the process create an environment of political stability, essential for stable economic growth. In addition, the Sinic societies – China, Japan, Korea – have for centuries shown intense respect for bureaucracy and officialdom. This has made it possible for modern governments to get away with 'soft authoritarianism'. An almost religious regard for education, scholarship and learning has also played a vital role. In the Confucian world, wisdom and virtue are as one – a belief that has helped create skilled and well-educated workforces in the region. All of these societal characteristics have decisive economic ramifications.

The rise of the Asia-Pacific countries to economic prominence has given new relevance to the rhetorical question posed by Simon Kuznet in the preface of his seminal work, published in 1966: were economic principles devised and followed in the West suitable for universal application, or were they culture-bound, with no meaning or relevance outside the societies in which they were created (Kuznet 1966)? In its quest for productive efficiency, the West emphasized individualism, and successfully harnessed the forces of scientific creativity and technological innovation. In contrast to this, the Asia-Pacific societies traditionally emphasized human relations, group cohesion and harmony. When they embarked on their own processes of industrialization and economic growth, they borrowed technology from the West through various modes of technology transfer, but married these machines to their own more people-centred cultures, achieving unparalleled economic growth. The combination of Western technology with an Eastern ethos produced laudable economic results (Tai 1989). And while this mix is not a sufficient condition for economic growth, its success nonetheless implies that if Western individualism was appropriate for the pioneering period of industrialization, it is likely that post-Confucian 'collectivism' is better suited to the modern age of mass industrialization and mass production (MacFarquhar 1980). The east Asian model has emerged as the first alternative to the rational Western model born at the dawn of the industrial revolution.

A little-known tendency of the post-Confucian countries, namely Japan, Taiwan, Hong Kong, Singapore and Korea, is that they are singularly meritocratic, with decisive economic ramifications. Their entrenched belief in a society ranked by merit, and by inherent genetic differences, is essentially Platonic, reflecting Plato's categories of people as 'gold', 'silver' or 'brass' (Dore 1987). Meritocracy begins with school children, continues through universities, and is enshrined in bureaucracies, both public and private. At all levels, high performers are repeatedly separated from the 'also-rans'. The system assumes that people legitimately deserve material rewards, prestige and power by virtue of their capabilities. Meritocracy identifies the high achievers, separates the wheat from the chaff, and rewards the deserving. Academic achievements, although important, are not the only determinants of success in a career. Other qualities such as drive, determination and dynamism also play an important role. Individuals of above-average academic ability are also judged for these qualities, and will be more quickly promoted. Meritocracy, then, allows the best possible use of human resources and contributes to institutional efficiency, which is then translated into economic performance. Compare this to the lack-lustre economic performance of other, non-meritocratic societies, for example in southern Asia. Despite a wealth of natural resources, these countries lack the necessary meritocratic culture that would best exploit both these and their workforces' capabilities.

Japan, the Asia-Pacific region's pioneer economy, is geographically so close to the other Asia-Pacific economies that such proximity – and propinquity – inevitably influences its neighbours. Japan's neighbours benefit both tangibly and intangibly: they can benefit easily and cheaply from the exchange of goods and services, including financial services, and they are far more likely to exchange ideas with, and emulate, the pioneer of their own geographical region than another equally alluring but more remote role model.

SUB-REGIONAL TRANSFORMATIONS
Japan

In the early 1950s, the Japanese economy had a dualistic structure, and depended heavily on US military procurement orders. The

Engel coefficient for urban households in the mid-1950s was 45 per cent, i.e. almost half of disposable income was being spent on food (Kosai 1986). This is characteristic of a developing economy. The Japanese economy's first good year was 1955, when it recorded a 10 per cent growth rate in real terms. This date is cited as the beginning of *suryo* or quantitative prosperity. Industry consciously began to bridge the technology gap that existed between Japan and other industrialized economies, and began to develop export sectors. The earliest successes were seen in shipbuilding. Export success gradually began to spread to other sectors and with that, domestic consumption and investment began to boom. The sudden rise in plant and equipment investment during the latter half of the 1950s brought about a sea change in the economy, and by 1959 Japan had entered a period of prosperity known as the *iwato* boom. The upswing of the business cycle lasted for 42 months, and had an all-pervading effect on the economy. Japan found itself on the crest of a techno-logical revolution. Fast-moving growth and modernization processes facilitated the development of consumer durable sectors such as automobiles, electronic machines and appliances. The international economy was entering an era of mass production in several key consumer durable industries, and world-wide demand for such prod-ucts was strong. The establishment of the General Agreement on Tariffs and Trade (GATT) promoted free trade, which was to benefit Japan immensely.

The institutional competitiveness of Japanese exports continued to increase thanks to well-conceived domestic and international strategies, based on properly laid-down objectives, clear ideas on how to achieve them, and government provision of the necessary institutional support. Success or otherwise on international markets is explained by differences in countries' growth-productivity-resource orientation, on the one hand, and distribution-security-opportunity orientation on the other (Scott 1985). Japan fell into the former category. Although business and government collabor-ated closely and purposefully, the vital ingredient was the growth and productivity orientation of both. The growth-oriented outlook of the large corporations was strengthened and nurtured by fierce domestic competition. The *kaisha* were also supported by a well-planned government strategy turning them into formidable inter-national competitors (Abegglen and Stalk 1985). Their growth-pro-ductivity orientation was based on dynamic comparative advantage (Higashi and Lanter 1990). Japan's export production was domi-nated by large firms because they had greater financial, personnel and material resources than small or medium-sized firms, and could absorb the effects of export price changes while deciding whether to slash prices or to shift into new products or businesses.

After the mid-1960s, Japan maintained its growth momentum and steadily caught up with the other industrialized economies. Measures of total factor productivity growth show that it outperformed all the major industrial economies during the period 1966–73 (Balassa and Noland 1988). Japan fell behind France and Germany from 1973–85, but remained well ahead of the United States. However, Japan constantly maintained its lead in capital formation, with a growth rate roughly double that of the other major industrial economies. By 1980, Japan had become a force to reckon with in industrial development, technological advancement, trade, and managerial and organizational capability. By the mid-1980s it emerged as the world's second largest economy, third largest trader and largest creditor. Towards the end of the decade it also became the largest donor and largest foreign investor (Das 1992).

Australia and New Zealand

These are two small, land-rich, better-off, industrial economies and, like Japan, members of the OECD (Organization for Economic Cooperation and Development). They have high per capita incomes and moderate growth rates. Their pattern of trade reflects their highly favourable endowment of land. Measured in terms of the volume of GDP, Australia is larger than Sweden and Switzerland, but smaller than Spain. Its per capita GNP is comparable to Italy and the Netherlands. The GDP of New Zealand is comparable to that of Ireland, while its per capita GNP is close to that of Belgium. Both countries are sparsely populated. A rich natural resource base, together with domestic and external capital, and a long history of economic growth have laid the foundations for high living standards. Yet the two nations have found it hard to sustain their relative position among the affluent countries. Since they have traditionally relied on agriculture and extractive industries for a great proportion of their export earnings, they have found it progressively more difficult to create wealth comparable to that being generated by the former industrial, and now technological societies. Natural resources and primary products are still a large part of their foreign trade. Australia is a large exporter of coal, wool, wheat, beef and mineral ores, while New Zealand exports are dominated by meat, dairy products, wool and forestry products. Thus, these two economies depend heavily on exports of primary products for their foreign exchange earnings. Much like developing countries, they export primary goods to finance their imports of capital goods. Both economies have been recipients of foreign direct investment (FDI), bringing with it technology and managerial skills. They are reliant on the other OECD economies, and on FDI, for access to the lastest technology. During the last three decades, in terms of growth rate and general economic performance, Australia has been far more dynanic than New Zealand.

The two economies have witnessed three distinct eras: first, the emigrant colonialism of the pre-war period when they were providers of food and raw materials to industrial societies, particularly Britain. Second, after 1945, the slow transition towards economic independence began. The traditional dependence on Britain in both trade and finance ended. This phase was marked by extensive government intervention in all aspects of the economy, and by the introduction of financial controls and exchange restrictions. The third phase can be dated from the late 1970s, when the two economies began to adjust to the international economy and discovered their place in the Asia-Pacific region.

Both economies have experienced periods of concern, faced with restrictions on their commodity and foodstuff exports to traditional markets in Europe and north America, due to the intensification of protectionistic policies since the mid-1970s. Their exports failed to keep pace with the growing import bills, and they tended to give in readily to protect their domestic manufacturing sectors, often at high costs. Japan's rise as a major industrial power had profound implications for both nations. With its voracious need for industrial raw materials, Japan became a major trading partner for Australia and New Zealand, and was quick to spot a large market for its manufactured and durable consumer goods in these two regional neighbours. Economic interdependence and common strategic interests have brought the three economies closer together and the mutual affinity is likely to grow. During the 1980s, South Korea also became a significant trading partner for Australia and New Zealand and economic ties were substantially strengthened with China, Taiwan and the ASEAN-4. In the process, the Australasian economies have successfully carved a regional niche for themselves. Their future growth prospects largely depend on their success in increasing efficiency at home, as well as growth in the regional and international economies.

The two countries entered the New Zealand Australia Free Trade

Agreement in 1965, and signed the Australia–New Zealand Closer Economic Relations Trade Agreement (ANCER) in 1983. The new agreement aims at lifting the restrictions on all goods traded across the Tasman (although a small number of products were specifically set aside for later consideration). The objectives of the earlier agreement were less ambitious – seeking progressively to liberalize trade in specified goods. ANCER was set up with the aim of eventually establishing a trans-Tasman free trade zone by phasing out all tariff, quantity and other restrictions on trade between the two partners. Subsequently, the agreement was extended to free up trade in services and to consider ways of harmonizing business laws (Australian Government Publishing Service 1986). Both partners benefited from ANCER, although New Zealand more so than Australia. This is partly accounted for by the fact that Australia is a much more important trading partner for New Zealand than New Zealand is for Australia (Australian Government Publishing Service 1989).

Asian Newly Industrializing Economies (NIEs)

The success of the four NIEs has attracted a great deal of professional and popular interest. They have been extensively studied and the literature on their economic growth and its rationale is vast. As indicated earlier, although the four dragons began to breathe fire in the 1960s, their achievements were not recognized until the early 1970s. The publication of *Industry and Trade in Some Developing Countries* (Little *et al.* 1990) was an important step in this direction. These four economies took a leaf out of the book of Japan's economic success and pursued an export-oriented strategy, deliberately promoting exports of manufactured goods in keeping with their comparative advantage. They saw wisdom in shunning import-substitution after the initial stages of growth, and exploited dynamic gains from trade, reaping the benefits of their comparative advantage. The result was an exemplary economic performance. They recorded very high rates of GDP growth which were in turn associated with their high rate of export volume growth. Poorly endowed with natural resources, their exports were initially concentrated on traditional and labour-intensive manufactured products, eventually progressing to capital- and technology-intensive manufactured goods. By the early 1990s, they had begun to make forays into knowledge-intensive product markets.

The NIEs all displayed certain common characteristics at the beginning of their hypergrowth. These included a well-educated and disciplined labour force, a competent bureaucracy, a social and governmental commitment to economic growth, a market-oriented domestic economic strategy, and a dominant private sector (although we should note that the small public sector was also seen as an efficient performer) (Amsden 1989; Chang and Singh 1992). In addition, the international economic environment of the 1950s and 1960s was aptly suited to the outward-oriented growth strategy of the NIEs. This unusual combination of factors assisted their brisk take-off into high and sustained growth.

The high level of human capital raised the technological level of the NIEs within a very short time-span. The NIEs maintained significant growth rates in savings and capital accumulation. However, other developing economies failed to take off despite comparable rates of savings and investment. What else had the NIEs done to achieve their extraordinary success? While most other developing economies remained wedded to ideologically-oriented development doctrines promoted by institutions such as UNCTAD, and stressed basic social needs, income distribution (before growth and production) and other objectives, the NIEs were influenced by the resurgence of neoclassical economics in the 1960s and adopted clear, pragmatic neoclassical policy lines. Sound macro-economic policies and, in general, high-quality economic management, were among the basic reasons for their economic success. Their economic strategy and management were characterized by pragmatism and flexibility. Conversely, the outcome of ideologically-oriented economic policies and poor-quality economic management can be seen in the shoddy performance of south Asian developing economies, which has continued decade after decade.

Mainstream neoclassical economics, and the Western model of free enterprise, both preclude governments from running their economies and spurn government intervention. However, three of the NIEs' governments were omnipresent in the handling of their economic affairs, Hong Kong being the only exception. However, intervention in this case did not replace markets, but guided them. It sought not to subdue or distort the market, but to conform to it – a practice little understood in the context of Western-style capitalism. The soft authoritarianism of these governments determined the NIEs' basic direction without smothering market forces and destroying domestic competition. This strategy supported the survival of the fittest kind of industrialization and thereby improved the efficiency of resource allocation. Instead of being counterproductive, this kind of government intervention enhanced economic efficiency because governments adopted policies to compensate for the weaknesses of the free enterprise system. The negative externalities were identified and taken care of by the governments. For instance, an important externality for developing countries is the cost of selling in the world market. The developing country exports have to counter the quality bias, and individual enterprises cannot bear the cost of countering the bias and creating a market niche without government support. Another area that benefits from government intervention is that of the market cost of labour, which often tends to be higher than the social cost of labour. Thus, in the NIEs, intervention lubricated business rather than thwarting it.

Lastly, it is their emphasis on private enterprise and on fostering domestic and international competition that has contributed to the NIEs' resilience. Private sector enterprises, without competition, would have resulted in private monopolies which would in turn have been as pernicious as public sector ones. The experience of the NIEs supports the dictum that competition is value-creating.

The ASEAN-4

In the oft-cited metaphor of the 'flying geese' – with Japan as the 'leading bird' in a formation of Asia-Pacific economies, followed by the NIEs – the ASEAN-4 come last. This sub-group has learned a great deal from the economic and technological experience of the economies that preceded it in the 'flying geese' formation, and has been able to replicate their performance to a considerable degree. ASEAN has also gained immensely from economic cooperation with them. Particularly noteworthy, in this context, is Malaysia's 'look east' campaign, encouraging business to 'learn from Japan'. ASEAN was established in a low-key manner in 1967, initially without any economic ambitions. However, steps towards economic cooperation were soon being taken, and the federation of ASEAN Chambers of Commerce and Industry was established in 1971, for cooperation among private enterprises.

Although they are geographically neighbours, economic ties between the ASEAN-4 were initially tenuous. They were well endowed with natural resources and, therefore, were suppliers of industrial raw materials and foodstuffs. Their exports were strongly specialized in primary products. With rapid industrialization, significant structural change occurred during the 1970s. Manufactured exports grew, receiving impetus from the huge expansion in world trade that took place in the early 1970s. With the exception of Indonesia, each of the ASEAN countries increased the share of manufactured goods in total exports. Trade expansion enabled these countries to establish extensive links with a wide range of other nations, especially the industrialized economies. Being essentially land-based, the ASEAN-4 were also careful not to neglect their agricultural sectors. Consequently, per capita food production rose steadily. Indonesia recorded the minimum rate of growth of food production.

The economic philosophy of the ASEAN-4 has generally been one of pragmatic flexibility, bending with international economic developments and responding to external changes with economic prudence. At an early stage in their industrialization process they began to show a healthy respect for outward-looking strategies. This strategy is known to create pressure for the adoption of better monetary, exchange rate and labour policies. Their macro-economic management is considered to be of high quality (Arndt 1989). The ASEAN countries have increasingly allowed market forces to drive their economies, and this, coupled with their outward orientation, has enhanced their functional efficiency, and the efficiency of resource allocation. Also, it is generally agreed that external factors significantly influenced the growth process in the ASEAN-4 (Chintayarangsan *et al.* 1992).

Owing to recession, the early 1980s were lean years for these economies, but their average growth rate for the decade as a whole was the highest for any region in the world. They attracted a good deal of FDI due to rapid growth and prudent economic management. A major part of FDI went into high-tech industries. By the early 1990s, Malaysia had become the largest exporter of integrated circuits in the world. ASEAN's eagerness to emulate the NIEs and Japan is obvious.

China

During the economic restoration period of 1950–7, the Chinese economy grew at an average of around 8 per cent per annum, but this brisk growth abruptly collapsed with the 'Great Leap Forward' of 1958–60. However, despite reversals and the chaotic decade of the Cultural Revolution (1966–76), China's economic performance was not abjectly dismal. Long-term average output grew by over 5 per cent per annum, although the per capita rise was much lower. Initially, growth in output was achieved solely by increasing the labour force. The high rate of savings helped build capital, but the ICOR was also high and the efficiency of investment remained low. China could not help being impressed by the achievements of neighbouring Japan and the NIEs, and identified the economic bene-fits potentially attainable from dismantling its myriad price and quantity controls, establishing a market economy and adopting open trade policies. By the end of the Cultural Revolution, the realization that the complex economic system was detrimental to both efficiency and output was complete. 1976 was ear-marked for the initial implementation of measures promoting economic reform and eco-nomic opening. The reform measures were first introduced gingerly, but then decisively after the Third Plenary meeting of the Eleventh Communist Party Central Committee in December 1978, an epoch-making moment in modern Chinese economic history, and the begin-ning of a sweeping set of economic reforms, popularly known as the 'open door' policy.

Several liberalization and open market reform measures were initiated in the early 1980s, and these were reinforced in a stronger wave of reforms in 1984. The former import-substituting industriali-zation strategy was almost abandoned. Commitment to reform was steady, and elements of the successful formula adopted by Japan and the NIEs were eagerly institutionalized. Society supported the new economic ideology and accepted the use of markets for the allo-cation of resources in lieu of the central planning authority. The operation of market forces was first felt in the rural economy, and then after 1984 in the urban economy. The opening of the economy enabled the absorption of much-needed technology from abroad as well as the inflow of FDI (World Bank 1985, 1989). The conse-quences of liberalization and reforms were clearly visible in China's growth rate. Real GNP grew by an average of almost 9 per cent per annum from 1978–91, a rate that doubles the size of the economy every eight years. Thus, liberalization and reforms paid off hand-somely. The economy acquired a great deal of momentum and by the early 1990s was bursting with life. When the republics of the former USSR next door were close to bankruptcy, China had over US$40 billion in foreign exchange reserves and was attracting plenty of FDI. More than US$1 billion-worth of Chinese funds were floated in the West in the early 1990s, and investors' response was highly favourable (*The Economist* 10 November 1992: 13–14). China has tried to integrate with the surrounding Asia-Pacific economies, especially with Japan.

Hindsight reveals that in spite of its answering commitment to economic reforms, China's course has zig-zagged. A steady course is nonetheless essential, because the centrally-planned sections of the economy were operating poorly even in the early 1990s. Officially, one-third of the state-owned enterprises were money-losers, and twice as many were in fact in the red. Fortuitously, half of China's industrial output at this point was accounted for by firms that were not state-owned, but run by market-sensitive lower-tier governments, private individuals and foreign investors. In addition, problems related to poor infrastructure continue to dog the economy. The 14th National Congress of the Chinese Community Party (October 1992) attempted to institutionalize the open market reforms politically, and turn China into a 'socialist market economy'. During the Congress the following operating principles were set out: macro-economic tools are better instruments of economic control; planning should cover nothing more than strategic targets; infrastructure investment should be the government's prerogative; government should no longer manage industrial enterprises; bureaucracy must be shrunk, as must employment in state enterprises; more attention should be paid to the services sector for absorbing surplus labour (Byrnes 1992). This is the famous thesis of patriarch Deng Xiaoping and represents the current proclivities of the managers of the Chinese economy. Japan will serve as a key model for the relationship between government and industry as China switches to a market economy (Mitsumori and Meshino 1992). Indications are that the 'reform revolution' continues apace, and that in the short-term consumerism will supplant Communism.

ECONOMIC ASCENSION

The long-term growth rate is a good indicator of economic dynamism because it eliminates short-term variations, and reveals whether growth was a sustained feature or a mere period-specific event caused by some favourable internal or external developments. The average GNP growth of the Asia-Pacific economies from 1965–90, and that of other country groups, is given in Table 1.2. The group average for the Asia-Pacific region was 4.6 per cent. No other country group has shown performance comparable to that of the Asia-Pacific region. The second best performing group, the OECD economies, has an average GNP growth rate of 2.4 per cent, which is half the Asia-Pacific growth rate.

The brisk growth rate of the Asia-Pacific economies led to more than fourfold economic expansion of their GDP in real terms from

Table 1.2 Comparative average annual GNP growth rates: 1965–90 (percentage)

Japan	4.1
ANIEs	7.1
ASEAN-4	3.6
Australia and New Zealand	1.5
China	5.8
Asia-Pacific region	4.6
Sub-Saharan Africa	0.2
South Asia	1.9
Middle-East and north Africa	1.8
Latin America and the Caribbean	1.8
OECD countries	2.4
United States	1.7

Source: World Bank 1992. Data for Taiwan comes from CEPD 1992.

Table 1.3 Comparative GDP at constant prices: 1965–90 (in 1987 $ billion)

	1965	1970	1980	1989
Asia-Pacific countries	919 (13.6)	1515 (17.6)	2473 (20.6)	3759 (25.3)
United States and Canada	2597 (38.6)	3030 (35.2)	4016 (33.4)	5271 (35.4)
European Community of 12	2252 (33.5)	2821 (32.7)	3771 (31.3)	4548 (30.6)
World	6719 (100.0)	8618 (100.0)	12030 (100.0)	14867 (100.0)

Note: Figures in parentheses stand for percentage of total world GDP.

Source: International Economic Data Bank, Australian National University, Canberra.

1965–89 (Table 1.3). The north American and western European economies, constituting the other two growth poles of the global economy, doubled their respective GDPs over the same period, and world GDP increased just over twofold. This growth pattern enhanced the weight of the Asia-Pacific region in the international economy. Its GDP was 13.6 per cent of the total world GDP in 1965. By 1989, its share rose to 25.3 per cent, while both the pre-established growth poles lost ground. Rapid economic expansion has established the Asia-Pacific region as the third growth pole of the international economy. However, as seen in Table 1.4, it is

Table 1.4 GDP and GNP growth: 1965–90 (percentage)

	GDP as a proportion of world GDP				Average annual growth rate of GNP per capita over 1965–90
	1965	*1970*	*1980*	*1989*	
Japan	10.0	13.5	14.9	17.7	4.1
Korea	0.3	0.4	0.6	1.1	7.1
Taiwan	0.2	0.3	0.5	0.8	8.5
Hong Kong	0.1	0.1	0.2	0.4	6.2
Singapore	0.1	0.1	0.1	0.2	6.5
Indonesia	0.3	0.3	0.4	0.6	4.5
Malaysia	0.3	0.4	0.6	1.0	4.0
Philippines	0.2	0.2	0.3	0.3	4.4
Thailand	0.2	0.2	0.3	0.4	1.3
Australia	1.2	1.3	1.2	1.4	1.1
New Zealand	0.2	0.1	0.1	0.1	1.9
China	0.8	1.1	1.4	2.3	5.8
Regional average	13.6	17.6	20.6	25.3	4.6

Source: International Economic Data Bank. Australian National University, Canberra.

still the smallest of the three in terms of the volume of GDP. The future need not be a repetition of the past, and economic growth during the 1990s may slow down. The explanatory phase of the business cycle that began in Japan in November 1986 ended in 1991. Several indexes began to show 'plateau condition' and the corporate earnings rate hit ceiling. Notwithstanding the slow-down of the Japanese economy, no one expects the region to lose its momentum. It will, therefore, continue to catch up with the other two growth poles.

As seen in Table 1.4, there were marked intra-regional differences in economic expansion. The mantle of greatest dynamism fell on the NIEs because their long-term (1965–90) average GNP growth rate was 7.1 per cent. Taiwan and Korea recorded an outstanding 8.5 and 7.1 per cent respectively. China, as noted earlier, did not do poorly, as this indicator shows, recording a respectable 5.8 per cent long-term average. Japan followed with 4.1 per cent. By the early 1980s Japan had become a matured industrial economy and its growth rate had stabilized at a lower level than that of earlier decades. In addition, it suffered from the *endaka* recession in the mid-1980s (Das 1992). Among the ASEAN-4, the Philippines were

Table 1.5 Exports as percentage of GDP

	1965	1970	1980	1989
Japan	5.2	6.6	10.8	14.2
ANIEs	18.0	26.4	50.1	72.1
ASEAN-4	26.6	26.7	31.0	35.8
ANZ	11.9	13.4	15.4	17.7
China	6.8	8.2	10.8	15.2
Regional average	8.5	9.2	15.2	21.2

Source: International Economic Data Bank, Australian National University, Canberra.

still a languorous economy, pulling the long-term average of the group down to 3.6 per cent. The other three members averaged 4 per cent or higher. Since this group was a late boomer, their decadal average for the 1980s was close to 10 per cent, although the Philippines were, again, the exception. Australia and New Zealand recorded a sedate 1.5 per cent average annual growth over this period. Table 1.4 also shows that between 1965 and 1989, the NIEs' share of world GDP quadrupled, soaring from 0.7 per cent of the world GDP in 1965 to 2.5 per cent in 1989. South Korea, Taiwan and Hong Kong all quadrupled their respective shares. China raised its share by a multiple of 2.9 and the ASEAN-4 by a multiple of 2.3. Japan came close to doubling its share of world GDP. Australia and New Zealand's shares remained stable.

Starting from a low economic level, several countries of the Asia-Pacific region achieved per capita income levels comparable to the poorer countries of the European Community. In 1990, South Korea surpassed Portugal in per capita income and Taiwan went ahead of both Greece and petrol-rich Saudi Arabia. Singapore and Hong Kong were better off than Spain and almost as rich as New Zealand, with living standards not very far behind those of Italy and Britain. Malaysian per capita income was 71 per cent higher than that of Turkey.

The Asia-Pacific economies have continued to develop their policy of openness. If export, as a proportion of GDP, is taken as a measure of openness (Table 1.5), then the performance of the NIEs is quite outstanding. In just one-quarter of a century exports soared from 18 per cent of GDP to 72.1 per cent. The ASEAN-4 also did well but their endeavours accounted for were concentrated in the latter half of the 1970s and the 1980s. In 1989, exports accounted for 35.8 per cent of the ASEAN GDP. The NIEs and the ASEAN-4 became the most open economies in the world. Australia and New

Table 1.6 Real growth rate of exports (measured in constant 1987 dollars) 1965–89 (percentage)

Japan	9.9	
Korea	18.7	
Thailand	9.5	15.5
Hong Kong	11.1	
Singapore	11.3	
Indonesia	5.4	
Malaysia	8.2	7.0
Philippines	5.5	
Thailand	9.6	
Australia	5.1	4.9
New Zealand	4.2	
China	8.0	
Average for Asia-Pacific countries		10.1
United States and Canada		5.9
European Community of 12		5.6
Developing countries		5.6
World		6.0

Source: International Economic Data Bank, Australian National University, Canberra.

Zealand, like other industrial economies, were already fairly open in the mid-1960s, and have since slowly opened their economies further. As the statistics indicate, China's opening-up began in earnest after the adoption of the 'open door' policy during the 1980s. Japan's economy has also continued to open. For the region as a whole, progress in this direction seems steady and appears to have accelerated after the 1970s.

The openness of an economy is inevitably closely associated with its export growth rate and its economic integration with other regional and non-regional economies. Supporting this observation, NIEs recorded the highest long-term real growth rate in exports. From 1965–89, their exports grew annually at an average rate of 15.5 per cent (Table 1.6). ASEAN came next with a group average of 7 per cent, although Indonesia and the Philippines lagged behind because they were slow to open and have remained, therefore, the least open economies in the group. Note that all these economies began developing their exports from a very low level and that the statistics do tend to hide the low base effect. Japan recorded an export growth rate of 9.9 per cent, the long-term average being adversely influenced by languid performance during the 1980s. The average growth rate of exports for the Asia-Pacific region was 10.1 per cent, which is almost twice as high as that for the United States, the European Community, and other developing countries. Thus, the region's export performance was outstanding, its outward-orientation richly rewarded. Was the trade-related dynamic growth of the Asia-Pacific countries externally driven or internally generated? Were the demand-side variables, or the supply-side factors, the principal determinants of dynamic export growth? James Riedel went to considerable length, in his statistical investigation, to answer these queries and concluded that international trade expansion worked only as 'the handmaiden' of growth for the Asia-Pacific region, and not as the 'engine of growth'. He found evidence suggesting that it was the supply-side rather than demand factors that were primarily responsible for the region's dynamic export performance (Riedel 1984) and he categorically rejected the premise that the export performance of the region was externally driven.

Such an aggressive export performance resulted in steep rises in the volume of exports from the region, doubling to US$37 million between 1965 and 1970, and futher increasing to US$291 million by 1980, an eightfold increase in one decade (Table 1.7). In 1990, exports from the region reached US$715 million, which is again two and a half times the level of one decade ago. In 1965, the Asia-Pacific countries accounted for a puny 11.4 per cent of total world exports. This proportion did not rise much in 1970, but in 1980 they accounted for 15 per cent of total world exports. In 1990, this proportion was as high as 22 per cent. Japan has traditionally dominated exports from the region. In 1965, it accounted for 42.6 per cent of total exports from the region. In 1970, the corresponding proportion rose to 52.1 per cent and further to 66.1 per cent in 1980. Japan's domination of regional exports continued, then, to increase.

However, the situation was reversed in 1990 when Japan's share dropped to 40.1 per cent of the total exports of the Asia-Pacific region. Other large exporters in the region are China, Taiwan, South Korea and Singapore.

Between 1965 and 1990, Japan doubled its share in world exports and accounted for 8.81 per cent of the total (Figure 1.2). The NIEs expanded their share of world trade from 1.4 per cent of the total to 6.6 per cent, while the ASEAN-4 expanded their share from 1.9 per cent to 2.7 per cent over the same period. These dramatic jumps should be interpreted carefully. The small base effect is obvious

Table 1.7 Export expansion from Asia-Pacific economies 1965–90

	1965		1970		1980		1990	
	Exports (million $)	*As Percentage of total world exports*	*Exports (million $)*	*As Percentage of total world exports*	*Exports (million $)*	*As Percentage of total world exports*	*Exports (million $)*	*As Percentage of total world exports*
Japan	8,452	4.87	19,319	6.61	129,542	6.67	286,768	8.81
Korea	175	0.10	830	0.28	17,446	0.90	64,837	1.99
Taiwan	450	0.26	1,428	0.49	19,837	1.02	67,040	2.06
Hong Kong	880	0.51	2,037	0.70	13,672	0.70	29,002	0.89
Singapore	981	0.57	1,554	0.53	19,375	1.00	62,627	1.62
Indonesia	722	0.42	1,055	0.36	21,909	1.13	25,553	0.78
Malaysia	1,206	0.69	1,687	0.58	12,939	0.67	31,505	0.97
Philippines	766	0.44	1,060	0.36	5,751	0.30	9,134	0.28
Thailand	607	0.35	685	0.23	6,369	0.33	23,002	0.71
Australia	2,971	1.71	4,482	1.53	21,279	1.10	35,973	1.10
New Zealand	979	0.56	1,203	0.41	5,262	0.27	9,045	0.28
China	1,643	0.95	1,768	0.60	17,481	0.90	80,529	2.47
Regional average	19,831	11.42	37,108	12.69	290,863	14.98	715,016	21.96

Source: International Economic Data Bank, Australian National University, Canberra.

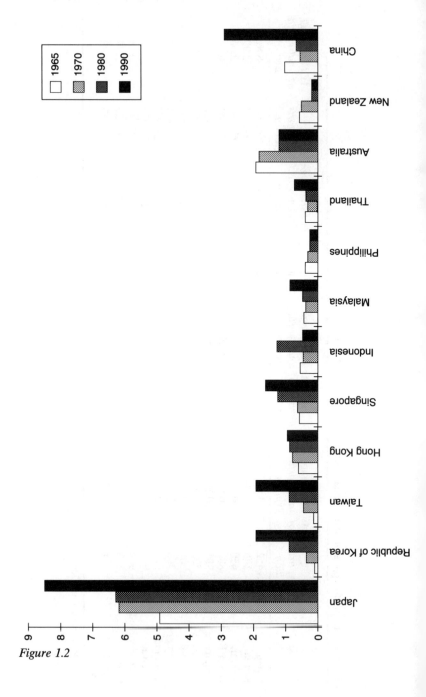

Figure 1.2

Table 1.8 Comparative export performance: 1965–90 ($ million)

	1965	1970	1980	1990
Asia-Pacific countries	19,831	37,108	290,863	715,016
	(11.42)	(12.69)	(14.98)	(21.96)
United States and Canada	35,110	58,775	275,992	496,522
	(20.22)	(20.10)	(14.22)	(15.25)
European Community of 12	65,885	116,125	687,847	1,349,580
	(37.94)	(39.70)	(35.43)	(41.45)
World	173,650	292,475	1,941,181	3,255,825
	(100.00)	(100.00)	(100.00)	(100.00)

Note: Figures in parentheses stand for percentage of total world trade.
Source: International Economic Data Bank, Australian National University, Canberra.

for these two sub-groups. China succeeded in raising its share of world trade by a multiple of 2.6. Conversely, Australia's and New Zealand's shares slipped drastically from 2.3 per cent to 1.4 per cent, due to a lack of export drive in the two nations.

Table 1.8 indicates that the Asia-Pacific economies have gained in international trade at the expense of the United States and Canada. The European Community has also strengthened its position. Until the mid-1970s, the Asia-Pacific region did not hold a position of significance on the international trade scene, although individual regional countries were doing well. However, largely because of the extraordinarily good performance of the NIEs, Thailand and China during the 1980s, the region has now gained a high profile on the international trade scene.

Initially, labour-intensive and resource-based products dominated Asia-Pacific exports. This is how industrialization begins. However, soon these economies began to export light manufactured products. Manufactured goods are high value-added goods, and their exports are an important indicator of the competitive strength of a country's industrial sector and economic maturity in general. In 1965, the Asia-Pacific region accounted for a mere 10.85 per cent of the total world manufactures exports (Table 1.9). In 1990, this proportion stood at 24.78 per cent – one-quarter of total world manufactures exports. In the early years these exports were heavily dominated by Japan. For instance, in 1965 Japan accounted for 73 per cent of manufactured exports from the region, and for 74.4 per cent in 1970. However, by 1980 other countries in the region were participating more actively and Japan accounted for only 61.1 per cent of the

Table 1.9 Export of manufactures from Asia-Pacific economies 1965–90

	1965		1970		1980		1990	
	Export of manufactures (million $)	As % of total world exports of manufactures	Export of manufactures (million $)	As % of total world exports of manufactures	Export of manufactures (million $)	As % of total world exports of manufactures	Export of manufactures (million $)	As % of total world exports of manufactures
Japan	7,704	7.92	18,024	9.92	124,028	11.32	279,436	11.63
Korea	104	0.11	635	0.35	15,686	1.43	60,675	2.53
Taiwan	187	0.19	1,087	0.60	17,441	1.59	62,112	2.59
Hong Kong	823	0.85	1,954	1.08	13,194	1.20	27,784	1.16
Singapore	336	0.35	474	0.26	10,452	0.95	38,315	1.60
Indonesia	27	0.03	15	0.01	533	0.05	9,061	0.38
Malaysia	73	0.07	125	0.07	2,464	0.22	17,263	0.72
Philippines	43	0.04	80	0.04	2,118	0.19	5,905	0.25
Thailand	19	0.02	55	0.03	1,788	0.16	14,783	0.62
Australia	432	0.44	846	0.47	5,588	0.51	13,004	0.54
New Zealand	53	0.05	132	0.07	1,062	0.10	2,255	0.09
China	752	0.77	797	0.44	8,517	0.78	64,693	2.69
Regional average	10,552	10.85	24,224	13.33	202,872	18.51	595,289	24.78

Source: International Economic Data Bank, Australian National University, Canberra.

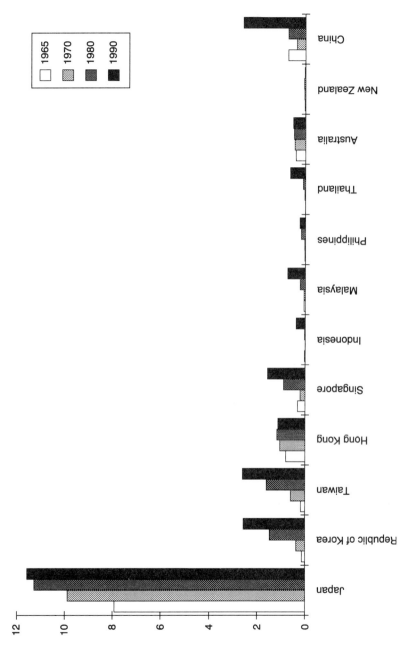

Figure 1.3 Asia-Pacific exports of manufactures as a share of total world exports of manufactures: 1965–90

Table 1.10 Comparative performance in export of manufactures ($ million)

	1965	1970	1980	1990
Asia-Pacific countries	19,831 (11.42)	37,108 (12.69)	290,863 (14.98)	715,016 (21.96)
United States and Canada	35,110 (20.22)	58,775 (20.10)	275,992 (14.22)	496,522 (15.25)
European Community of 12	65,885 (37.94)	116,125 (39.70)	687,847 (35.43)	1,349,580 (41.45)
World	173,650 (100.00)	292,475 (100.00)	1,941,181 (100.00)	3,255,825 (100.00)

Note: Figures in parentheses stand for percentage of total world trade in manufactures.

Source: International Economic Data Bank, Australian National University, Canberra.

total. In 1990, this proportion had further plummeted to 46.9 per cent, due to active manufactures export drives by China, Taiwan, South Korea and, to a lesser extent, Singapore and Hong Kong. From 1965–90, the NIEs raised their share of world markets in manufactured goods from 1.5 per cent to 7.9 per cent, while the ASEAN-4 increased theirs from 1.6 per cent to 2.9 per cent. As with exports, the low base effect is obvious for these two sub-groups. Australia and New Zealand did not capture markets in manufactures in 1990 to any greater extent than they had in 1965. Conversely, China, after a poor performance until 1980, succeeded in raising its market share by three and a half times during the decade of the 1980s (Figure 1.3).

The growing participation of the Asia-Pacific economies in international trade in manufactures is apparent from Table 1.10. Their significance grew considerably during the 1980s. At the beginning of the decade, the Asia-Pacific economies and the north American growth pole were neck and neck in terms of volume of manufactured exports. However, by 1990, the Asia-Pacific region had left north America far behind, with almost 70 per cent more exports. The European Community has maintained its position of strength, essentially due to intra-trade manufactures.

Japan, Taiwan and South Korea have emerged as net foreign investors in the international economy. Of these, Japan is, of course, the largest. According to *International Financial Statistics*, the net FDI made by Japan in 1980 was a skimpy US$2.1 billion. This soared to US$46.3 billion in 1990, and at this point Japan was the largest foreign investor in the world. In 1991, Japanese FDI fell to US$29.4 billion because of financial turmoil in Japan. South Korea recorded a tiny net foreign investment of US$7 million in 1980. This amount rose to US$105 million in 1990 and to US$241 million in 1991. Taiwan also became a substantial net investor during the latter half of the 1980s, with investments touching US$5.3 billion in 1990.

Table 1.11 shows that Japan turned into a net exporter of capital through portfolio investment in 1983. Taiwan, South Korea, Malaysia and Singapore also began to make relatively small portfolio investments abroad during the latter half of the 1980s. China began to do so in 1989, although investments were not substantial until 1991.

We can, then, safely assert the emergence of the Asia-Pacific region as the third growth pole of the international economy. Unprecedented growth in GDP, fast-moving export expansion (especially manufactures), expansion in FDI and portfolio investment, and other economic achievements all point to the region's importance on the international economic stage. The economic dynamism of the Asia-Pacific economies is rejuvenating the global economy. Some countries see new threats rather than new opportunities in the phenomenon of the Asia-Pacific growth. Such countries suffer from severe constraints on factor mobility and have a limited ability to take initiatives to make the necessary structural adjustments.

STRUCTURAL AND INDUSTRIAL TRANSFORMATION

As mentioned earlier, economies in the Asia-Pacific region consistently maintained high rates of investment. The only exception to this rule is the Philippines which was unable to maintain its investment during the 1980s due to non-economic reasons (Table 1.12). The NIEs were the highest investors, recording average investment rates of 12.8 per cent for the period 1965–80 and 5.8 during the 1980s. The ASEAN-4 (excluding the Philippines) recorded 10.5 per cent and 6.2 per cent in the 1980s. China recorded an average of 10.7 for the first period, equal to that of the ASEAN group, while for the 1980s it recorded an average of 13.7 per cent – the highest rate of investment not only in the Asia-Pacific region, but in the world as a whole. Australia and New Zealand, particularly the latter, increased their rate of investment during the 1980s. The average rate of investment for the Asia-Pacific region from 1965–80 was 9.5 per cent, and 9.0 per cent during the 1980s. Both of these averages are higher than those for any other region in the world. The 1980s were a difficult period and several regions recorded negative growth

Table 1.11 Portfolio investment in and by the Asia-Pacific economies: 1965–91 ($US million)

	1965	1970	1975	1980	1981	1982	1983	1984	1985	1986	1987	1988	1989	1990	1991
Japan	80	250	2,590	9,430	7,670	840	-2,900	-23,960	-41,750	-102,040	-91,330	-51,750	-32,530	-14,490	35,450
Korea	0	0	0	40	60	15	188	333	982	301	-113	-482	-29	811	..
Taiwan	:	?	?	45	85	145	41	-50	-46	69	-371	-1,711	-902	-1,006	45
Hong Kong	?	?	?	?	?	?	?	?	?	?	?	?	?	?	?
Singapore	0	0	-2	13	-48	-29	-49	-151	175	-549	252	-293	324	287	232
Indonesia	0	0	0	46	47	315	368	-10	-35	268	-88	-98	-173	0	0
Malaysia	88	-28	268	-11	1,131	601	668	1,108	1,942	30	140	-448	-107	-255	170
Thailand	0	13	1	96	44	68	108	155	895	-29	346	530	1,486	-38	110
Philippines	..	3	27	4	3	1	7	-3	5	13	19	50	280	-50	..
Australia	128	456	417	1,896	673	2,399	1,183	736	2,144	1,188	4,325	5,834	377	1,970	4,842
New Zealand	0	0	0	0	0	0	0	0	0	0	0	0	88	30	..
China	..	..	..	..	..	41	20	83	742	1,567	1,051	876	-180	-241	-7,558

Source: International Economic Data Bank, Australian National University, Canberra.

Table 1.12 Gross domestic investment average annual growth rate

	1965–80	1980–90
Japan	6.9	5.7
Korea	15.9	12.5
Taiwan	12.9	3.4
Hong Kong	8.6	3.6
Singapore	13.3	3.6
Indonesia	16.1	7.1
Malaysia	10.4	2.9
Thailand	8.0	8.7
Philippines	7.6	–2.5
Australia	2.7	3.0
New Zealand	0.8	4.4
China	10.7	13.7

Source: World Bank 1992. Data for Taiwan comes from CEPD 1992.

in their investment. Latin America recorded negative growth of 2 per cent, and sub-Saharan Africa −4.3 per cent. The developing economies of Europe recorded a growth rate of −0.1 per cent over this period. Another feature of investment was that while there was a resource gap for many countries in the region before 1980, forcing them to borrow from external sources, during the 1980s several countries not only financed investment out of their own savings but also generated surplus overinvestment. The principal surplus-generating countries were Japan, Taiwan, Hong Kong, Singapore and China.

Growing investment leads to the accumulation of physical capital and thereby to transition from a less-developed to a more-developed economy. The implicit assumption is that the ICOR is not inimical. The central feature of this transition is the transformation of the production structure and, therefore, the GDP composition. The structural changes occur in the following sequence: first, the share of industry in total output rises, while the share of the agricultural sector shrinks, both in relative and absolute terms. Second, with continued rises in investment and income, the share of the services sector begins to expand largely at the expense of the manufacturing sector. Three causal factors lie behind this transition. First are changes in comparative advantage resulting from the ongoing accumulation of physical and human capital. Second, Engel's law posits decline in relative expenditure on food and necessities, with

Table 1.13 Structure of production

	Agriculture		Industry		Manufacturing		Services	
	1965	1990	1965	1990	1965	1990	1965	1990
Japan	10	3	44	42	34	29	46	56
Korea	38	9	25	45	18	31	37	46
Taiwan	26	4	30	46	21	37	44	49
Hong Kong	2	0	40	26	29	18	58	73
Singapore	3	0	24	37	15	29	74	63
Indonesia	51	22	13	40	8	20	36	38
Malaysia	28	..	25	..	9	..	47	..
Thailand	32	12	23	39	14	26	45	48
Philippines	26	22	27	35	20	25	47	43
Australia	9	4	39	31	26	15	51	64
New Zealand	..	9	..	27	..	19	..	64
China	38	27	35	42	28	38	27	31
Regional average	24	11	30	37	20	26	47	52

Source: World Bank 1992. Data for Taiwan comes from CEPD 1992.

rising income and a concomitant increase in the share of manufactured products and services. Third, an economy's choice of macro-
economic policies, and its trade orientation also influence the structural transformation (Chenery and Syrquin 1975). As seen in Table
1.13, the relative contribution of the agricultural sector has contracted considerably in the Asia-Pacific region from 1965–90. In Japan
the agricultural sector contributed only 3 per cent of GDP in 1990.
In South Korea and Taiwan the relative contribution of this sector
was also reduced considerably, while in Hong Kong and Taiwan it
disappeared. In the ASEAN countries the relative decline of the
agricultural sector was significant, with the familiar exception of
the Philippines, where the relative decline was only marginal. In
Australia the agricultural sector shrank further, while in New Zealand it still contributed 9 per cent to GDP in 1990. In China there
was a marked reduction, but the agricultural sector still contributed
over one-quarter of GDP. Being a highly populous country, China
has to maintain a substantial agricultural sector, although its relative
contribution will continue to decline. For the region as a whole,
the contribution of the agricultural sector fell by more than half,
which implies that the regional economic structure was inclining
more towards industrial and services activities.

In Japan, the relative contribution of the industrial and manufacturing sectors has declined because, at its stage of development, the
services sector usually becomes more important and grows faster.
The Japanese service sector's contribution to GDP grew by 10 per
cent from 1965–90. In South Korea and Taiwan, however, industrial
and manufacturing activities expanded along with the services sector.
All three sectors expanded at the expense of the agricultural
sector. Hong Kong recorded a decline in its industrial sector, and
became virtually a service economy. However, in Singapore the
contribution of the industrial sector expanded at the cost of the
services sector, whose contribution to GDP declined by 11 per cent.
Rapid industrialization in the ASEAN-4 countries as a whole is
evident from the considerable expansion of the industrial and manufacturing sectors. Their relative contribution to GDP virtually
doubled. The Philippines was, again, the exception, with slow
industrial growth.

Like Japan, Australia has grown to become a services-dominated
economy. The relative contribution of its services sector has
expanded at the cost of other sectors. Like the ASEAN-4, China
industrialized fast and its efforts are visible in the change in distribution of its GDP over the 1965–90 period. The relative contribution
of the manufacturing sector rose by 10 per cent. For the region,
the manufacturing and services sectors have expanded, while the
agricultural sector has declined in importance.

Although statistics for the latter half of the 1980s are incomplete,
Table 1.14 illustrates the progress of various sub-sectors in
industrialization during the 1980s reasonably well. Countries having
high levels of per capita value-added in manufacturing, such as
Japan, Australia, New Zealand, Singapore and Taiwan, show a
higher proportion of value-added in machinery and capital-intensive
industries. In Japan, the combined share of machinery and capital-
intensive industries reached 65 per cent. Conversely, countries
having relatively low per capita value-added in manufacturing, such
as Indonesia, Malaysia, Thailand, the Philippines and China, have
a higher proportion of value-added in labour-intensive and food-
processing industries. The resource-abundant countries show a
higher concentration in resource-processing and food-processing
industries. Among the NIEs, Singapore has a high concentration in
the machinery and capital-intensive industries. This is a country-
specific example of concentration. Hong Kong is characterized by
its emphasis on labour-intensive manufacturing.

Both South Korea and Taiwan briskly expanded their machinery

Table 1.14 Share of value-added in manufacturing industries (percentage)

	Year	Resource processing	Food processing	Labour intensive	Capital intensive	Machinery
Japan	1980	17.2	9.7	12.5	24.4	36.2
	1988	15.2	10.0	9.8	23.6	41.4
Korea	1980	19.9	17.3	23.3	20.5	19.0
	1988	17.1	11.8	21.0	19.3	30.0
Taiwan	1980	24.5	12.5	26.9	21.4	20.6
	1988	24.1	10.3	16.0	22.9	26.6
Hong Kong	1980	11.7	5.3	47.0	11.3	24.7
	1988	11.7	6.4	47.6	8.9	25.9
Singapore	1980	24.7	5.1	10.3	11.6	48.3
	1988	11.6	5.8	5.9	20.2	56.4
Indonesia	1980	14.4	30.3	23.5	18.3	13.5
	1988	14.6	26.5	26.8	21.9	10.1
Malaysia	1981	23.6	23.7	18.0	11.5	23.2
	1987	19.4	19.6	16.5	21.4	23.0
Thailand	1982	16.3	54.1	12.0	8.3	9.3
	1986	15.6	35.6	24.0	8.6	7.2
Philippines	1980	17.8	31.0	17.1	22.9	11.1
	1987	19.8	43.5	13.6	15.4	8.6
Australia	1980	19.1	18.6	14.4	23.9	24.0
	1987	19.5	20.4	15.8	23.0	21.0
New Zealand	1981	17.4	27.7	20.3	16.2	18.4
	1986	22.3	26.9	18.6	14.9	17.3
China	1980	12.3	12.4	22.2	25.1	27.9
	1986	20.7	11.9	18.4	22.2	26.9

Source: Gleaned from Table 1.4, MITI 1992.

sectors over the 1980s. The share of value-added in labour-intensive and food-processing industries declined in both countries, while those in machinery and capital-intensive industries exceeded 50 per cent. Among the ASEAN-4, Malaysia has a 46 per cent concentration in machinery and capital-intensive groups. The doubling of the share of value-added in capital-intensive industries has a lot to do with this. As opposed to this, Malaysia's natural resource production and food production shares fell rapidly. In Thailand, Indonesia and the Philippines the share of food-processing industries has traditionally remained large due to abundant food resources in these countries. However, in Indonesia and Thailand the share of this group declined over the 1980s and that of labour-intensive industries has risen. It should be remembered that a great deal has happened in Thailand since 1986, the last year for which the statistics are included. The share of value-added in capital-intensive and machinery sectors in China is close to 50 per cent. These two sub-sectors were large and state-controlled (MITI 1992). In most Asia-Pacific countries the industrial sector has climbed several rungs on the ladder of comparative advantage. With steadily rising investment and increasing stock of physical and human capital, the ability of these economies to export new products and compete successfully in the international markets has markedly increased.

Along with physical capital, human capital has also accumulated fast in the region. Japan and the NIEs have attained high general literacy levels and the result is remarkable human capital endowment in the labour force. These countries have also trained a good number of scientists and engineers and have ensured an indigenous capacity for technological adaptation – this being essential for successful industrialization. In the ASEAN-4 countries the situation is far from uniform. The Philippines has a strong educational tradition but trains inadequate science- and technology-related personnel. Thailand has made impressive strides in the past in this regard. In Malaysia, as much as 30 per cent of its adult population is illiterate, although the number of college graduates in various disciplines has soared impressively. Among the ASEAN countries, Indonesia's educational achievements are the least impressive. ASEAN generally has the lowest average proportion of technically-trained people in the Asia-Pacific region, slowing down the efficient adaptation of technology from abroad in the future (Noland 1990). In urban China the labour force is not as well trained as in the NIEs, and the economy is also expected to face bottlenecks of science- and technology-related personnel.

CONCLUSION

Over the last three decades, the Asia-Pacific region has developed into the third growth pole of the international economy. Scholars began to speculate on the dawn of a Pacific century. During this period, several informal groupings and forums involving various combinations of the Asia-Pacific countries have emerged, although they are far from institutionalizing these arrangements in the manner of an Asian OECD. No matter how the region is defined, the Japanese economy has to be its hub. A great deal of diversity exists in the economic and social indicators of these countries. The Asia-Pacific region has established itself as a trail blazer in the area of economic growth. Six regional economies doubled their output in a decade. Their dynamic trade-oriented growth posed an intellectual challenge. They appear to present an alternative model of development, a model that is more relevant, and therefore more successful, than the standard neoclassical model in which the world has so far trusted. There are considerable differences in the macro-economic policies pursued by these countries, yet there are also several basic points in common. All have recorded high savings and investment rates, and adopted outward-oriented economic strategies after an initial spell of import-substitution. This led to a change in the structure of production as well as that of trade. High export growth along with unusually rapid structural change in manufactured trade suggests that economic policy played a decisive role, shifting the specialization of production towards higher value-added goods. Supply push and export promotion strategies were among the key elements underpinning dynamic transitional growth. Other causal factors included lower levels of price distortions, the adoption of pragmatic liberalization measures, market orientation, a high commitment to economic growth on the part of both governments and society, and a broadly Confucian cultural orientation. Proximity to Japan, the pioneer regional economy, stimulated the other regional economies both directly and indirectly. Despite striking similarities in the growth process, each economy or group has followed its own characteristic growth path, yet the final result, for the majority, was the same.

The brisk growth rate led to more than fourfold economic expansion of GDP for the Asia-Pacific region in real terms from 1965–89. North America and the EC, which comprised the other two growth poles of the global economy, doubled their respective GDPs over the same period. This growth pattern enhanced the weight of the Asia-Pacific region in the international economy. To be sure, there were marked intra-regional differences in economic expansion. The mantle of greatest dynamism fell on the NIEs. These countries opened their economies considerably. The NIEs and the ASEAN-4 have, in fact, become the most open economies in the world. In a region which was in general highly successful in export expansion, these two country groups also recorded the highest long-term average export growth rates. This trade-related dynamic growth was principally supply-driven, although demand-side factors did assist. Following a steep rise in the volume of its exports, the Asia-Pacific region accounted for almost one-quarter of total world exports by 1990. In terms of volume, Japan dominated regional exports, although this domination declined markedly over the 1980s. China, Taiwan, South Korea and Singapore developed as substantial exporters in their own right. Exports of manufactured products have special significance because they represent the competitive strength of the industrial sector. In the mid-1960s, the region accounted for 11 per cent of total world exports of manufactures, and almost the whole of this was from Japan. By 1990, the region accounted for as much as one-quarter of total world exports of manufactures, with Japan no longer dominating, although it retained its position as the largest exporter of manufactured products in the region. Exports from China, Taiwan, South Korea and, to a lesser extent, from Singapore and Hong Kong had expanded significantly. In terms of the value of manufactured exports, by 1990 the Asia-Pacific region had left north America far behind. Japan, Taiwan and South Korea have emerged as net foreign investors. These countries, along with Malaysia and Singapore, and, to a lesser extent China, have also begun to make portfolio investments abroad.

The economic structure of the region has undergone considerable transformation. The relative contribution of agriculture to GDP has contracted considerably in favour of industry and services sectors. In as many as five regional economies, the services sector has become dominant. Countries having high levels of per capita value-added in manufacturing, such as Japan, Australia, New Zealand, Singapore and Taiwan, showed a higher proportion of value-added in machinery- and capital-intensive industries, while others recorded a marked expansion in food-processing and labour-intensive sectors. In addition, the last three decades have seen a considerable accumulation of human capital endowment in the region's labour force.

Bibliography

Abegglen, J. C. and Stalk, G. (1985) *Kaisha: The Japanese Corporations*, New York: Basic Books Inc.

Amsden, A. (1989) *Asia's New Giant*, New York: Oxford University Press.

Arndt, H. W. (1989) 'Industrial Policy in East Asia', *Industry and Development* 22, United Nations Industrial Development Organisation, Vienna.

Asian Development Bank (1971) *Southeast Asia's Economy in the 1970s*, London: Longman.

Australian Government Publishing Service (1986) Fourth Report of the Senate Standing Committee on Industry and Trade, Canberra.

—— (1989) 'The Impact of the Australia-New Zealand Closer Economic Relations Trade Agreement', Research Report 29, Canberra: Bureau of Industry Economics.

Balassa, B. and Noland, M. (1988) *Japan in the World Economy*, Washington D.C.: Institute for International Economics.

Balassa, B. and Williamson, J. (1990) *Adjusting to Success: Balance of Payments Policy in the East Asian NICs* (revised edition), Washington D.C.: Institute for International Economics.

Berger, P. L. and Hsiao, H. H. M (eds) (1988) *In Search of an East Asian Development Model*, New Brunswick: Transaction Books.

Bradford, C. I. and Branson, W. H. (1987) 'Pattern of Trade and Structural Change' in C. I. Bradford and W. H. Branson (eds), *Trade and Structural Change in Pacific Asia*, Chicago: Chicago University Press.

Byrnes, M. (1992), 'China Faces Sweeping Changes', *The Financial Review*, 24 October.

CEPD (Council for Economic Planning and Development) (1992) *Taiwan Statistical Data Book 1992*, Taipei: CEPD.

Chang, H. J. and Singh, A (1992), 'Public Enterprises in Developing Countries and Economic Efficiency', UNCTAD Discussion Paper 48, August.

Chenery, H. B. and Syrquin, M. (1975), *Patterns of Development 1950–70*, London: Oxford University Press.

Cheng, T. and Haggard, S. (1987), *Newly Industrializing Asia in Transition: Policy Reform and American Response*, Berkeley, CA: Institute of International Studies.

Chintayarangsan, R., *et al.* (1992) 'ASEAN Economies: Macro-Economic Perspective', *ASEAN Economic Bulletin*, March: 353–75.

Corbo, V. *et al.* (1985) *Export Oriented Development Strategies: The Success of Five Newly Industrialising Countries*, Boulder, CO: Westview Press.

Das, D. K. (1992) *The Yen Appreciation and the International Economy*, London: Macmillan Press.

Denison, E. F. (1962) *The Sources of Economic Growth and the Alternatives before US*, New York: Committee for Economic Development.

Dore, R. (1987) *Taking Japan Seriously*, London: The Athlone Press.

Garnaut, R. (1988) *Asia's Giant*, Adelaide: University of Adelaide.

Gibney, F. (1992) *The Pacific Century*, New York: Maxwell Macmillan International.

Higashi, C. and Lanter, G. P. (1990) *The Internationalization of the Japanese Economy*, Boston: Kluwer Academic Publishers.

Kahn, H.(1979) *World Economic Development: 1979 and Beyond*, London: Croom Helm.

Kosai, Y. (1986) *The Era of High-Speed Growth*, Tokyo: University of Tokyo Press.

Kuznet, S. (1966) *Modern Economic Growth: Rates, Structure and Spread*, New Haven: Yale University Press.

—— (1971) *Economic Growth of Nations: Total Output and Production Structure*, Cambridge, Mass., Harvard University Press.

Lau, L. J. (ed.) (1990) *Models of Development: A Comparative Study of Economic Growth in South Korea and Taiwan*, San Francisco: Institute for Contemporary Studies Press.

Linder, S. B. (1986) *The Pacific Century*, Stanford: Stanford University Press.

MacFarquhar, R. (1990) 'The Post-Confucian Challenge', *The Economist*, 9 February: 67.

Ministry of Internation Trade and Industry (MITI) (1992) 'Vision for the Economy of the Asia-Pacific Region in the Year 2000 and Tasks Ahead', Tokyo, 20 August (mimeo).

Mitsumori, K. and Meshino, K. (1992), 'China Maps Capitalist Road on Japan's Economic Model', *The Nikkei Weekly*, 19 October.

Mutoh, H. *et al.* (1986) *Industrial Policies for Pacific Economic Growth*, Sydney: Allen and Unwin.

Myrdal, G. (1968) *Asian Drama: An Enquiry into the Poverty of Nations*, New York: Pantheon Books.

Noland, M. (1990) *Pacific Basin Developing Countries*, Washington D.C.: Institute of International Economics.

Otani, I. and Villanueva, D. P. (1988) 'Determinants of Long-term Growth Performance in Developing Countries', IMF Working Paper 88/97, 7 November.

Riedel, J. (1984) 'Trade as the Engine of Growth in Developing Countries Revisited', *The Economic Journal* 373, March; 56–73.

Scott, B. R. (1985) 'National Strategies: Key to International Competitiveness', in B. R. Scott and G. C. Lodge (eds), *US Competitiveness in the World Economy*, Boston: Harvard Business School Press.

Smith, M. *et al.* (1985), *Asia's New Industrial World*, London: Methuen.

Tai, H. C. (1989) 'The Oriental Alternative', in H. C. Tai (ed.) *Confucianism and Economic Development*, Washington D.C.: The Washington Institute Press.

Vogel, E. F. (1984) 'The Advent of the Pacific Century', *Harvard International Review*, March.

World Bank (1985) *China: Economic Structure in International Perspective*, Washington D.C.: World Bank.

—— (1989) *Economic Prices for Project Evaluation in China*, Washington D.C.: World Bank.

—— (1992) *World Development Report 1992*, Washington D.C.: World Bank.

Woronoff, J. (1986) *Asia's 'Miracle Economies': Korea, Japan, Taiwan, Singapore and Hong Kong*, New York: M. E. Sharpe.

2 The normalization of economic relations in continental North-East Asia
Recent developments and implications

Friedrich von Kirchbach

INTRODUCTION

Until recently, north-east Asia was one of the few 'white' regions on the world map. Arguably, nowhere else in the world could one find such heterogeneous neighbours as the people, cultures and economies of the five countries bordering the Sea of Japan, namely the two Koreas, Japan, Russia and China.[1]

The rapid changes in this region after the end of the Cold War, and the growing interest in regional economic cooperation and integration, have transformed continental north-east Asia from a *terra incognita* into a popular topic subject for academic research, international conferences and technical cooperation. Trade among the five coastal countries of the Sea of Japan has jumped to about US$70 billion in 1991, or more than one-quarter of transatlantic trade.

This chapter examines the extent of recent changes in this region, and their implications from an economic and business point of view. The central question is: to what extent have economic relations in the region been normalized? How much headway has been made on the scale from complete isolation (intra-Korean relations in the past) to economic integration? To what extent has the improvement in relations between the countries under review contributed to the emergence of a more cohesive economic area, which would justify a regional approach?

The analysis focuses on the development of trade within continental north-east Asia in the context of the larger economic and political process of normalization. The development of intra-regional trade is a sensitive indicator of economic integration between neighbouring economies.

Some business implications are discussed in the final section of the chapter: to what extent will Western companies have to develop a closer interest in the region?

DEFINITION AND CHARACTERISTICS OF NORTH-EAST ASIA

Definitions of north-east Asia invariably differ. This chapter focuses on the continental area, which has as its centre the three-country triangle between China, North Korea and Russia at the mouth of the Tumen River, with a radius of about 1,500 kilometres. The area as a whole includes North and South Korea, Primorski, Khabarovsk and Amur regions in the Russian Far East, and three Chinese north-eastern border provinces of Heliongjiang, Jilin and Liaoning (see Figure 2.1).

In economic and geographical terms, this definition has a number of advantages. It includes the three north-east Chinese provinces, which form a certain entity, although the inclusion of the three Russian regions mentioned above is more arbitrary: these are the three regions bordering north-east China, and they include a large share of the population and economic activity of the Russian Far East. Most importantly, they are the three Russian regions that stand to benefit the most from improved economic relations in the region.

This geographical focus complements existing studies of cross-border integration, as seen in other Chinese border provinces – Guangdong with Hong Kong, Fujian with Taiwan, Yunnan with Myanmar, Guanxi with Vietnam, and Xingjiang with Kazakhstan. Moreover, it does not overlap with the 'Chinese Economic Area', consisting of China, Hong Kong and Taiwan, which has already achieved a high degree of integration, with intra-regional trade amounting to more than one-third of total trade (Jones *et al.* 1992).

Mongolia has been left out due to its small population and limited economic weight. The situation of Mongolia has, in fact, more in common with that of the Chinese province of Inner Mongolia, and other western Chinese provinces.

This chapter examines in particular the changes in the region's three socialist countries, since it is essentially these that shed new light on our regional concept of north-east Asia.

Continental north-east Asia, according to the above definition, has an area of about 2.3 million square kilometres – about half of which is on the Russian side. Heilongjiang is the largest of the three Manchurian provinces, more than twice as large as the Korean peninsula. The region has some 170 million inhabitants, including

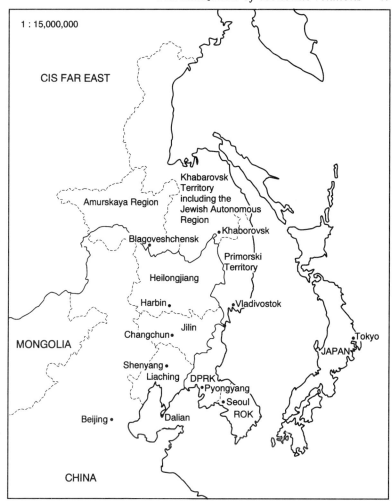

1 : 15,000,000

CIS FAR EAST

Khabarovsk
Territory
including the
Jewish Autonomous
Region

Amurskaya Region

• Khaborovsk

• Blagoveshchensk

Primorski
Territory

Heilongjiang

Harbin •

• Vladivostok

Jilin

Changchun •

MONGOLIA

• Tokyo

JAPAN

Shenyang •

Liaching

DPRK

• Pyongyang

Beijing •

• Dalian

• Seoul

ROK

CHINA

Figure 2.1 Map of north-east Asia

around 100 million Chinese, 65 million Koreans and 5 million Russians (Table 2.1).

The region's GNP in US dollars, according to official statistics, is generated mostly in South Korea (85 per cent). If one adjusts per capita income in China to a more realistic level of, say, US$1,200 (*The Economist* 28 November 1992: 5), South Korea's share of regional GNP can be estimated at around 67 per cent, and Manchuria's share at around 27 per cent.

Table 2.1 Basic indicators on continental north-east Asia: 1990/1

	Area (1,000 sq km)	Population (million)	GNP ($ billion)	GNP/capita (nominal $US)	GNP/capita ppp[a] ($US) (1989)
North-east China	802	99	42	425	2,656[b]
Heilongjiang	469	35	13	370	
Jilin	187	25	8	320	
Liaoning	146	39	20	520	
Russian border area	1,255	5	17	3,200[a]	6,270[c]
Amurskaya Region	264	1	3		
Primorski Ter.	166	2	7		
Khabarovsk Ter.	825	2	6		
Korea peninsula	220	65	306	4,707	
DPRK	121	22	23[d]	1,064[d]	2,172
Rep. of Korea	99	43	283	6,500	6,117
Continental North-east Asia	2,277	170	365	2,152	
Japan	378	124	3,141	25,430	14,311
Indochina	750	79	13	170	
ASEAN	3,054	316	272	860	

Note: GNP figures for China, DPRK, Russia and Indochina exclude services.
[a] ppp: purchasing power parity
[b] for all of China
[c] for all of Russia
[d] official data, on the high side

Source: China Statistical Yearbook 1991; Russia Far Eastern Economic Yearbook 1991; The Far East and Australasia 1993; UNDP Human

Although the population of continental north-east Asia is only about half that of ASEAN, it has a higher GNP than the latter grouping, due to the weight of South Korea. Continental north-east Asia is clearly larger in area, population and GNP than Indochina or even the Baht bloc, if Thailand is included. Although its population is larger than that of Japan, the combined (nominal) GNP of continental north-east Asia is only 12 per cent of that of Japan.

PROGRESS ON THE NORMALIZATION OF ECONOMIC RELATIONS

Until the late 1980s, continental north-east Asia was the scene of one of the world's largest military build-ups. Alliances in the region were based on military and political strategies. This applied to Sino-Soviet relations, as well as to Sino-South Korean, Soviet-South Korean, and intra-Korean relations. Since the political collapse of central and eastern Europe, the region has seen rapid changes in bilateral relations. Within less than four years, its diplomatic landscape has been fundamentally transformed.

Political normalization has taken place in four stages. First, Gorbachev's 1989 visit to Beijing, after three decades of mutual isolation and animosity. By the end of 1992, the two countries has signed several agreements on regional security, border issues and economic and technical cooperation.

Second, the establishment of diplomatic relations between the Soviet Union and South Korea in 1990, followed by mutual state visits at presidential level and a series of economic agreements (including a major credit line from South Korea to Russia).

Third, the important progress in intra-Korean relations, with several visits at prime ministerial level, and the lifting of the ban on intra-Korean trade. And finally, the establishment of diplomatic relations between China and South Korea in 1992.

In turn, border disputes have been either resolved or down-graded on the political agenda. China and Russia have compromised on the notorious border issues of the past. The process of political normalization in continental north-east Asia is increasingly driven by economic rather than traditional political and ideological interests.

Interest in political normalization has become broader-based and more pragmatic. In China and Russia, there has been a notable shift in power and initiative from central government, to provincial and local authorities. According to some observers, this holds true even for the new Rajin Sonbong Free Economic and Trade Zone in North Korea.

The triple objectives of diffusing political tensions in the region, reducing military expenditure and benefiting from economic collaboration are valid for each of its constituent countries, although of course in different proportions. The north-eastern provinces of China are keen to overcome their traditional inward orientation and emphasis on heavy industry, and to emulate the success of the southern provinces. The open-city status acquired by Hunchun, and planned for Changchun and Harbin, are cases in point. So are China's efforts to push forward with the development of the Tumen delta.

In North Korea, external pressures combine with the growing role of a younger generation in the economic administration. Cut off from a lifeline of credits, cheap oil and political recognition from its northern neighbours, North Korea stands with its back against the wall. A cautious, limited degree of regional cooperation is seen as the only way out of its present, unsustainable political and economic isolation.

The Russian border provinces are seven time zones away from Moscow. There is a widespread feeling that Moscow is leaving the Russian Far East out in the cold. Former subsidies from western Russia are no longer forthcoming. The military installations – once the backbone of the Primorski region – are lying idle. A new economic mainstay has to be found. A reorientation towards the Asia-Pacific rim is the most logical choice, and there is particular interest in collaborating with American, Japanese and South Korean firms. As the inflow of foreign investment and the development of sustainable trade (except for the traditional items of fish and timber) remain at a low level, the development of trade with China on a barter basis is an attractive, though second-best, alternative.

For South Korea, the economic benefits of a thaw in regional politics are obvious: China and Russia offer a natural resource endowment, labour reserves and markets of significant interest to the South Korean economy. Among the large-scale conglomerates (or *chaebols*), expansion into continental north-east Asia is a top priority for the next years. Moreover, regional cooperation offers a framework facilitating the rapprochement with North Korea. The lesson of German reunification has not been lost on South Korea, in the sense that its 'Nordpolitik' now stresses the importance of the economic stabilization of North Korea, with a view to reducing the staggering cost of eventual reunification.

The recent developments clearly augmented regional stability and form a basis for the first efforts towards regional cooperation. The Tumen River Area Development Programme, under the auspices of the United Nations Development Programme (UNDP) represented a breakthrough: for the first time, representatives from all the countries in the region came together to discuss the possibility of regional economic development and multilateral cooperation in trade, investment, environmental protection and technology.

While the above factors lend support to the continuation of the normalization process, the potential obstacles at the political level should not be ignored. These include the succession issue in China, the delicate balance between the centrifugal and centripetal forces of north-east China and the Russian Far East, and the succession problem and potential implosion of North Korea.

Against this background, political collaboration in continental north-east Asia continues to be project- and issue-oriented, rather than global and institutionalized; short-term rather than long-term; and cautious, with a fair amount of mutual distrust.

PROGRESS IN THE NORMALIZATION OF INTRA-REGIONAL TRADE

Types of trade

In order to understand the present patterns of trade in continental north-east Asia, it is essential to distinguish between different types of trade.

First, there is the distinction between cash and barter trade. In 1992, China and Russia decided to conduct all future foreign trade with each other and with North Korea as cash, rather than barter trade. This decision, however, has not been implemented in practice. The bulk of Sino-Russian trade, Sino-North Korean trade and Russian-North Korean trade continues to be conducted as barter trade, for a number of reasons relating to foreign exchange availability, the condition of the banking sectors and the greater flexibility of barter trade arrangements. Trade with South Korea is conducted on a cash basis.

Second, a decision has to be made according to the type of trader involved. In principle, one may distinguish between three forms of trade: national, border and individual.

National trade of a number of key products, such as energy and minerals, is conducted on a monopoly basis by the limited number of national foreign trade companies. In practice, this trade is highly centralized and managed from the respective capitals – Beijing, Moscow and Pyongyang. It applies in particular to goods that are subject to national export licensing requirements. Goods may originate in any part of the exporting country and go to any part of the importing country. From a north-east Asian perspective, according to the above definition, this is often a kind of transit trade.

Border trade is handled by foreign trade companies and other authorized enterprises from the border provinces and regions. It involves primarily goods produced and consumed in the border areas. For example, 80 per cent of the total exports under the trade regime of Heilongjiang and Jilin provinces represent goods produced in these provinces. Border trade has a major impact on the economic development of the region. There is a special regime to support the development of border trade. In China, for instance, tariffs on border trade amount to only 50 per cent of normal tariffs. Traders in the border regions find that they have greater flexibility under the border trade regime, to adapt rapidly to the specific demand and supply patterns, and to find solutions to trade restrictions in the bordering areas.

Individual trade consists of the transactions of individual entrepreneurs travelling to neighbouring countries and selling and buying goods. These transactions are not recorded in trade statistics. They have grown rapidly in recent months, and are thought to be far from negligible.

The following combinations of payment terms (cash and barter) and forms (national, border and individual trade) are the most frequent:

- National trade, which is largely but not exclusively conducted as barter trade by the leading national foreign trade companies.
- Border trade, which is conducted by provincial and district firms authorized to be involved in foreign trade, and which is almost exclusively conducted as barter trade.
- Individual trade on the part of visitors, using a variety of imaginative forms of transaction and payment.

Quantitative indicators on intra-regional trade

At present, the trade orientation of continental north-east Asia is low in comparison to Asian standards. Export ratios (i.e. exports divided by GNP or NMP) were around 9 per cent for Jilin province

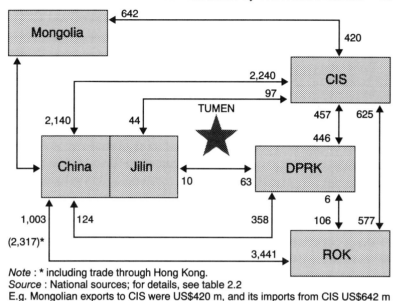

Figure 2.2 Trade flows in continental north-east Asia

(compared to 18 per cent for China as a whole), around 7 per cent for North Korea and around 8 per cent for Primorski (compared to around 5 per cent for all of Russia).

In the past, the geo-economic advantages of continental north-east Asia have been clearly underutilized. Based on the centrally-planned economic system of the three neighbouring countries (China, North Korea and the Russian Federation), integration into the international division of labour has been low. This has restrained the pursuit of economic complementarities and comparative advantages.

In fact, the three-country triangle at the mouth of the Tumen River Area is at the centre of a series of concentric circles, which are increasingly trade-oriented towards the outside world (see Figure 2.2). In the past, there has been very little intra-regional trade in the immediate border area of Khasan District in Primorski, Hunchun City in Jilin province and Raijin/Sonbong District in North Korea. Trade between the Russian and Chinese border provinces of the Tumen River and North Korea has been slightly more active: Jilin's bilateral trade with North Korea, and the CIS, excluding individual trade, amounted to US$214 million in 1991, plus some

US$900 million in bilateral trade between North Korea and CIS in 1991 (data for trade between Primorski and Jilin or North Korea are not available).

Trade among all countries of continental north-east Asia, except for North Korea and Mongolia, has been of an order of magnitude ten times larger: Sino-CIS trade and Sino-South Korean amount to some US$4.4 billion each, and CIS – South Korean trade amounts to US$1.2 billion.

In the outermost circle, intra-regional trade in Asia (including the NIEs, Japan, China and ASEAN) amounted to some US$280 billion in 1990, thereby exceeding intra-north-east Asian trade by a factor of 30. Intra-regional trade in Asia has become more important than trade with north America or western Europe. In other words, Asian firms find their most important buyers and suppliers within Asia.

The geographical position of the Tumen River delta in the middle of these concentric circles is the basis for its significant potential for trade development. At present, intra-regional trade accounts for just 6 to 7 per cent of the total trade of the countries under review (see Table 2.2). This is low in view of existing complementarities. It is also low by international comparison: the corresponding share for total Asian trade is around 30 per cent, not to mention the even higher shares for Europe (be it western or central Europe). China's border trade with the CIS and North Korea in 1991 remained at US$286 million on the export side and US$216 million on the import side, less than 0.5 per cent of national trade.

Overall trade among north-east Asian countries is picking up rapidly. This applies in particular to trade between the two Chinese provinces of Jilin and Heilongjiang, and Russia. It also holds true for South Korean trade with other countries in the region, which has increased at double-digit growth rates (see Table 2.3).

Product composition of intra-regional trade (see von Kirchbach 1993)

Sino-Russian trade

Thanks to its diversified industrial structure, China has a wide range of international competitive products to offer for export to Russia. This applies not only at national level, but also to the supply and demand situation in the border provinces, i.e. Heilongjiang, Jilin and Liaong, on the Chinese side, and the import demand in the Russian Far East.

Table 2.2 Orders of magnitude of intra-regional trade flows in north-east Asia (US$ million)

Exporting country	Importing country								
	China	DPRK	Russia	ROK	Mongolia	Sub-total	Share (%)	Japan	Total exports
China	—	358 (90E1)	2,239 (90E1)	3,441 (91I2)	30 (90E1)	6,068	9.8	12,024 (90I3)	62,901 (89E1)
DPRK	124 (90I1)	—	457 (91I4)	106 (91I2)	n.a.	687	35.4	298 (90I3)	1,940 (89E5)
Russia	2,140 (90I1)	446 (91E4)	—	557 (91I2)	642 (91E4)	3,805	7.7	3,356 (90I3)	49,390 (90E6)
ROK	2,317 (91E7)	6 (91E2)	625 (91E2)	—	5 (91E2)	2,953	4.1	12,356 (91E2)	71,870 (91E2)
Mongolia	11 (90I1)	n.a.	420 (91I4)	0.4 (91I2)	—	431	54.4	8	793 (89E2)
Sub-total	4,592	810	3,741	4,124	677	13,944	7.5	28,042	186,084
Share (%)	8.6	28.4	5.7	5.1	56.3	6.8		12.0	
Japan	6,131 (90E3)	176 (90E3)	2,564 (90E3)	21,120 (91I2)	10 (90E3)	30,001		—	287,040 (90E3)
Total imports	53,345 (90I1)	2,850 (89I5)	65,510 (90I6)	81,525 (91I2)	1,202 (89I2)	204,432		234,588 (90I3)	

Note: The information in brackets indicates first the year to which the data refer, second whether data have been reported by the exporting (E) or importing (I) country; the last number refers to the sources as listed below.

Sources:

1 China Statistical Yearbook 1990. Trade between Heilongjiang Province and the former USSR reached reportedly Swiss Francs 1.2 billion in 1989 (Intertrade, May/June 1991: 24). This implies that about 20 per cent of total bilateral trade is handled by this province.

2 Korea Foreign Trade Association.

3 OECD Monthly Trade Statistics, Series A, November 1991.

4 Business International, Doing Business in Central and Eastern Europe, Full-year data figure extrapolated from 1st half 1991.

5 Economist Intelligence Unit, North Korea Country Report, 3, 1991.

6 IMF, Direction of Trade Statistics, Yearbook 1991, and quarterly issues.

7 Data provided by Chinese Authorities, including US$ 1.3 billion of trade through Hong Kong.

Table 2.3 Growth rates of intra-regional trade flows in north-east Asia
(percentage per annum)

Exporting country		China	DPRK	Importing country Russia	ROK	Mongolia	Japan	Total exports
China	89/90		−6	53	33	145	7	18
	90/91		n.a.	−25	52	n.a.	n.a.	n.a.
DPRK	89/90	−32		9	n.a.	n.a.	5	n.a.
	90/91			n.a.	761	n.a.	n.a.	n.a.
Russia	89/90	4	−6		−6	−2	17	−11
	90/91	24	n.a.		56	−47	2	−27
ROK	89/90	34	n.a.	150		267	−6	4
	90/91	71	367	20		9,303	−2	11
Mongolia	89/90	30	n.a.	9	373		n.a.	n.a.
	90/91	n.a.	n.a.	−47	−81		n.a.	n.a.
Japan	89/90	−24	−7	−12	6	n.a.		10
	90/01	n.a.	n.a.	−35	14	n.a.		n.a.
Total	89/90	−10	n.a.	−2	14	n.a.	17	
imports	90/91	n.a.	n.a.	−48	17	n.a.	n.a.	

Source: National trade statistics compiled by ITC.

At present, consumer goods constitute north-east China's main
export to the Russian Far East. Food products play a leading role
and will continue to figure importantly in bilateral relations in view
of the agricultural surplus in north-east China and the deficits in
the Russian Far East. The proximity of the Russian market, combined with the logistical problems of transporting north-east China's
agricultural produce to southern China, make the Russian Far East
an attractive target market.

Fresh and canned meat and maize alone accounted for more than
half of Jilin's border trade exports to the CIS in 1991. In addition,
a large variety of other food items, such as fruits, vegetables,
potatoes and beer, will continue to be traded bilaterally as economic
relations between the two countries normalize further. Garments
and consumer durables such as radios and TVs are also likely to
continue to be of major interest in Sino-Russian exports, in view of
the supply and demand situation in the two countries.

In the future, however, it is likely that the share of investment
and intermediate goods in Russian imports from China will increase.
Production capacity in industry and agriculture in Russia will have
to be enlarged and modernized. In turn, Russian exports – both on
a cash and barter basis – will have to be used to supply not only
goods for consumption, but also investment goods. The interest of
Russian buyers in Chinese capital goods and technology, in particu-

lar for light industries, is obvious, and was clearly evident at the third Harbin Border and Local Trade Economic and Trade Fair in June 1992.

The identification of promising Russian export products is more difficult, basically because the national export offer is more limited, particularly if only products from the Russian Far East are taken into consideration. In fact, the availability of competitive products from Russia is the major bottleneck factor in bilateral trade relations.

The traditional export items – fish and timber – continue to be of significant interest to north-eastern China. Both industries have considerable potential for product diversification and for the development of new forms of cooperation.

Chinese import demand for Russian fertilizers by far exceeds present Russian export levels. Russian fertilizer exports could certainly be increased if larger quantities were made available, and Russia's high export tax reconsidered.

As far as agricultural machinery is concerned, there appears to be good potential for intra-industry trade between the two countries. There is considerable Chinese interest in heavy agricultural machinery from Russia, and interest in lighter equipment from China in Russia. As trade ties between the two countries normalize and develop, this type of intra-industry trade is bound to increase, as it has done in other industrializing and industrialized regions.

Boris Yeltsin's December 1992 visit to Beijing confirmed the potential for Sino-Russian technological cooperation, particularly in the context of major Russian-built industrial projects initiated in the 1950s, and in nuclear power development. Arms, including possibly an aircraft carrier, are likely to become Russia's top export to China.

One of the major issues in Sino-Russian bilateral relations is the need to diversify from trade to more complex forms of economic cooperation. Bilateral investment and joint ventures need to be undertaken to exploit existing complementarities. Growth sectors for joint ventures may include forestry (for which the Russian Far East has the resources, and China has well-developed downstream industries), agriculture (for which China has successfully adapted cultivation and technology to suit the region's climatic and soil conditions) and trade support services (where Chinese investment and joint ventures in wholesale and retail distribution are picking up, and where cooperation in financial institutions would be desirable).

Sino-North Korean trade

Unequal size, and the outward orientation and diversity of the Chinese and North Korean economies, make for considerable imbalance in the number of priority products in bilateral trade.

Jilin's and Heilongjang's exports to North Korea include a wide variety of products. Chief among these at present are coking coal from Heilongjiang (1 million tons in 1991), maize, meat and vegetables from Jilin and, to a lesser extent, garments and textiles, chemical products and tyres. The international competitiveness of Chinese producers in these product lines, coupled with the geographical proximity, suggest that these export items will continue to rank high in bilateral trade with North Korea, at least to the extent that they can be financed by North Korean exports.

Due to the low degree of specialization in the North Korean economy, exports to China (and other countries, for that matter) are likely to continue to be primarily resource-based in the short and medium term. This is compounded by the fact that, in comparison to China, North Korea does not have an absolute advantage in wage costs or technology. Nor does the present agricultural production provide for any major exportable surplus. In the short and medium term, North Korean exports to China will therefore continue to consist of items such as fish and crustaceans, logs, metals, minerals and steel products. In addition, selected manufactured products will be part of North Korea's export offer to China, as demonstrated by its polyethylene exports to Heilongjiang. In fact, the resource-based manufactures may well become more important in exports to China: primary goods at low stages of processing may be competitive in international markets, and be earmarked for cash trade with developed market economies. In contrast, experience in meeting specifications for trade in manufactures may be easier to develop under barter trade arrangements with the two northern neighbours.

In addition to border and barter trade, there is increasing trade on the part of private individuals. While only 150 people crossed the border in the city of Tumen into North Korea and Russia between 1986 and 1990, there were 50,000 visits by Chinese to North Korea in 1991. At the border station in Tumen, most of these visitors take along large quantities of goods, primarily food items and electronic consumer goods (TVs, radios, etc.). It is estimated that the average earnings from individual trade per visit is about 1000 yuan. Assuming a margin of 100 per cent (which does not seem unrealistic), this would add another unrecorded 50 million yuan

(US$10 million) FOB to Chinese exports in this prefecture alone. The number of North Korean citizens visiting China was estimated at just 5,000, reportedly because of difficulties in North Korea in obtaining a visa.

Observers familiar with the situation estimate that border trade with North Korea and Russia could amount to as much as US$20 million per annum in Yanbian prefecture. One indicator for the order of magnitude of funds generated by informal border trade are the growing US dollar holdings by individuals in Yanbian banks. These were estimated at US$17 million in 1992, in addition to yuan holdings of about 3 billion.

This clearly shows the dynamic development of individual trade. It is possible that it may increase, from the present 10 per cent or so, to a share of 30 per cent and more in the future. Several measures are being introduced to further facilitate this flourishing border trade. Upper limits on the value of goods exported by individuals to North Korea have been significantly increased and are, in addition, leniently enforced. In theory, goods imported from North Korea under border trade are subject to 50 per cent of the normal duty. In practice, these duties are reportedly not collected on individual imports and exports.

The Yanbian authorities, in collaboration with their North Korean counterparts, plan to set up a border market in Tumen, in which individuals from both sides could sell their goods.

The advantage of individual trade is that large numbers of people in continental north-east Asia are unable to assess demand and supply conditions, and hence the resulting business opportunities in the region. Individual trade is an important step towards developing border trade. The growth of this type of informal trade is bound to have a positive effect on formal trade. It exposes enterprises in continental north-east Asia to import competition and thus forces them to concentrate on areas in which they have a comparative advantage. Moreover, this type of trade encourages the diffusion of production technology and marketing know-how.

North Korean-Russian trade

Among the bilateral trade flows in north-east Asia, least is known about North Korean-Russian trade, although its volume is far from negligible. North Korea will continue to be interested in Russian raw materials – i.e. crude oil, coal and metals, transport equipment and machinery – and Russian buyers have expressed interest in

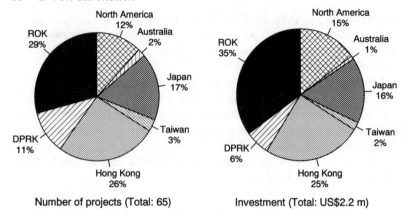

Number of projects (Total: 65)   Investment (Total: US$2.2 m)

Source: Yanbian Prefecture

Figure 2.3 FDI into Yanbian Prefecture, Jilin, by country of origin: Jan 1991–June 1992

fruits and vegetables, food products such as soy sauce, and cosmetics, but voiced concern about the difficulties of finding suitable products in North Korea. At present, North-Korean-Russian trade is in fact plummeting, and it would be unsurprising to see this trend continue. New trade promotion initiatives are likely to be successful only after the present, difficult transition from politically-determined to market-oriented trade is completed.

Trade with South Korea

South Korea's trade with the countries under review has been rising rapidly, with considerable diversity of product composition, direction and form.

South Korea's imports from China represent the largest bilateral trade flow among the countries under review, with US$3.4 billion in 1991, up 52 per cent on 1990 levels. Indicators for 1992 suggest that this growth will continue unabated. Sino-South Korean trade flows are accompanied by rapidly increasing direct investment in China, estimated at US$64 million in 1992.[2] South Korea has become the largest investor in Yanbian Autonomous Prefecture in Jilin, in which the Tumen River delta is located, and in which around 40 per cent of the two million inhabitants are ethnic Koreans (see Figure 2.3).

South Korea's cereal imports from China alone accounted for US$0.5 billion and have good prospects. Imports of raw materials

and intermediate inputs for South Korea's textile and garment industry have been expanding very rapidly and reached more than US$0.8
billion in 1991. Similarly, imports of mineral fuels, cement and steel
products have each reached in the order of several hundreds of
millions of US dollars, and have still further potential.

In the industrial sector, intra-industrial trade is developing very
dynamically between the two countries. This applies in particular to
the textile, chemical, steel and electronics sectors. Judging by the
proximity of the two economies, the complementarity of their comparative advantages, their rapid economic growth rates and the fact
that trade between them is still very young, we can expect that the
rapid development of trade over the past few years will continue in
the future.

Similarly, observers believe that trade and cooperation potential
between South Korea and Russia is far from being fully tapped.
The diversified structure of South Korea's industrial exports to the
CIS is obvious. Imports of primary goods such as fish, fuels, iron
and steel, copper and nickel, fully correspond to the complementarities of the two economies and are expected by many to increase
rapidly in the future.

Problem areas

Lack of mutual confidence

The elimination of the distrust inherited from the days of the Cold
War, and due to economic isolation, is far from complete. Several
north-east Asian enterprises or government institutions feel that
they have been taken advantage of by business partners in neighbouring countries. Two foreign trade companies in Yanbian Autonomous Prefecture, in Jilin, have reportedly accumulated claims *vis-à-
vis* Russian partners of US$19 and 16 million respectively. This
exceeded the Prefecture's annual import value from Russia.

Closer mutual cooperation requires a higher degree of predictability in economic behaviour, and compliance with rules and regulations which have been agreed upon. Institutions in the government
and business sectors have to realize that non-compliance with obli-
gations in any particular case is likely to have negative repercussions
on the climate for economic cooperation in general. Confidence is
a public asset that must be developed and protected by all parties
concerned.

Ineffective barter trade

Barter deals are the most common form of trade in continental north-east Asia, South Korean trade apart. The principal advantage of barter deals is that they do not require any foreign exchange, which is scarce in the region. On the other hand, barter trade is complicated by several factors:

First, bilateral trade must be balanced yet north-east China runs a trade surplus with the Russian Far East and North Korea, as China does with nearly all its other neighbouring countries, i.e. Afghanistan, Pakistan, Nepal, Bhutan, Myanmar, Laos, Mongolia, Kazakhstan and Tadzikistan.

Second, transaction costs are high, as it is difficult to find a partner interested in the two sides of the transaction. This holds true particularly if the enterprises authorized to do foreign trade can sell only their own products or the products of their associated companies, and buy only for their own requirements. Trilateral deals are even more difficult to put together, although there appears to be a large potential for such deals (e.g. Russian exports of raw materials to Japan, Japanese exports of machinery to Jilin, Jilin exports of consumer goods to Russia).

Third, transactions are sometimes crude as it is often difficult to set prices and quantities correctly. For example, a truck full of potatoes might drive from Jilin to Primorski, returning with a load of fertilizer.

Fourth, experience shows that firms in Primorski and in North Korea find it difficult to deliver, either because goods contracted are not available on the local market, or because export licences cannot be obtained. The availability of goods is perhaps the most important bottleneck factor in Primorski and North Korea for expanding trade with China.

Finally, product specifications in barter deals do not always seem to be sufficiently clear, which has led to disagreements. Moreover, barter contracts with North Korea reportedly do not include arbitration clauses.

For all these reasons, the implementation of barter contracts remains low. In Heilongjiang, only 25 per cent of contract volume is actually implemented. In Mudangjiang Prefecture it is thought to be even lower. As one trader pointed out succinctly, barter trade is simple to conclude and difficult to transact, whereas cash trade is difficult to conclude and easy to transact.

Low level of direct investment flows

Direct investment is a powerful tool for promoting economic cooperation, and probably indispensable for promoting real integration.
This is particularly true if goods can cross borders less easily than
capital or labour, due to border measures such as high tariffs and
quotas, transport problems, and difficulties in currency exchange.

There is increasing investment among the three riparian countries
of the Tumen River (including North Korean outward and inward
direct investment). The order of magnitude of these investments,
however, remains small, and many joint ventures have gone into
the service sector. An example is shown in Figure 2.3. Inflows of
foreign investment into Yanbian Prefecture in Jilin have rapidly
increased over the past three years. Investors from South Korea
accounted for the largest share, and there were several projects from
North Korea. In contrast, there was not one single investment
from Europe.

For China and Russia, cross-border investment would be essential
in order to prevent them from being left out of the present investment spree on the part of Western companies and firms from Japan
and the Asian NIEs. It is, however, quite unlikely that such investment will be forthcoming: Russia is far away from providing FDI.
China has become a major source of FDI in recent years, with over
500 projects with total investment of US$1.9 million back in 1988.
However, only a negligible share of these investments have gone to
Russia (Ye Gang 1992).

SUMMARY AND IMPLICATIONS

Normalization is driven by economic factors

Economic normalization in north-east Asia began only after the end
of the Cold War. Now, however, the process of economic normalization is fuelled by profits and pressures at the micro-economic level,
as elsewhere in Asia. Economic normalization has clearly taken the
lead over political relations.

Throughout continental north-east Asia the enterprise sector and
individual businessmen have taken the initiative towards intensifying
economic relations. The role of individual private businessmen is
the most dynamic element in regional economics. Provincial and
small companies have proved to be very flexible, benefiting from
border trade and other forms of collaboration. In contrast, the large
state-owned enterprises based in Beijing and Moscow have taken

less interest, and central governments have achieved little progress in providing the required physical and trade service infrastructure (i.e. transport, customs facilities, communications, etc.).

The same argument has applied up to now to Japanese relations with the Russian Far East and North Korea. Most activities have been initiated by second- and third-tier Japanese firms. The major exception to this trend has been South Korean and Japanese trade with, and investment in, China and, although to a lesser extent, the activities of South Korean firms in Russia.

Economic normalization is low profile and – in view of the many remaining political and administrative obstacles – happens in spite of official policies, rather than because of them.

Intra-regional trade in continental north-east Asia will benefit from buoyant economic growth and infrastructure bottlenecks in China

Economic forecasts are unanimous in their bullish assessment of growth prospects, and of growing openness and trade orientation in China.[3] North-east China is no exception to this trend. However, logistical problems in moving goods out of north-east China to overseas markets, or to the southern part of the country, will make Russia and North Korea preferential partners. Congestion on China's inadequate road and rail networks, and in her ports, is likely to increase along with the rapid economic growth, notwithstanding the efforts in the Eighth Five-Year plan to address this issue.

The importance of trade with neighbouring countries for China's border provinces is by no means limited to Manchuria. As Table 2.4 shows, it applies to most other border provinces, as well. Trade with neighbouring countries accounted for about half of total trade in most of the border provinces. The presence of Chinese goods is increasingly felt in Mongolia, Myanmar and Vietnam. Closer ties with neighbouring countries could help to mitigate the uneven patterns of regional development in China at the economic level, but might also reinforce centrifugal political forces.

Trade between China, Russia and North Korea will continue to grow, but at below-average rates

The untapped potential of business opportunities between China, Russia and North Korea is considerable. There are, however, several major impediments that are likely to reduce the pace of trade expansion below the average of total Chinese trade:

Table 2.4 Importance of trade with neighbouring countries for Chinese border provinces: 1988/90

Chinese province	Neighbouring country	Value of exports (US$ million) 1989	Value of imports (US$ million) 1989	% share in total provincial Exports	Imports	Value of exports (US$ million) 1990	Value of imports (US$ million) 1990	% share in total provincial Exports	Imports
Heilongjiang	Soviet Union	365	147	36	56	359	283	33	70
	DPRK	56	n.a.	5	n.a.	76	n.a.	7	n.a.
Jilin	Soviet Union	158	9	24	4	161	32	21	16
	DPRK	35	32	5	12	19	13	2	7
Inner Mongolia	Soviet Union	107	52	32	54	99	85	30	61
	Mongolia	6	6	2	6	9	8	3	5
Yunnan	Myanmar	161	87	30	33	124	72	22	38
	Laos	4	3	1	1	4	3	1	1
Tibet	Nepal	7	4	43	29	n.a.	n.a.	n.a.	n.a.
Xinjiang	Soviet Union	73	47	22	63	68	51	19	41
Subtotal		972	387	33	40	919	547	30	52
Guangdong	Hong Kong	6,366	n.a.	78	n.a.	8,543	n.a.	81	n.a.
	Macau	148	n.a.	2	n.a.	166	n.a.	2	n.a.
Guangxi	Hong Kong & Macau	302	62	52	36	382	65	52	47
Total		7,788	449	67	39	10,010	612	70	51

Note: Values refer to exports and imports by the border provinces, excluding transit trade
Source: Almanac of China's Foreign Economic Relations and Trade 1991 & 1992

First, barter trade represents, in general, a second-best solution. In view of the scarcity of foreign exchange, producers and exporters will eventually shift to cash trade and hard currencies. This preference will put potential buyers in China, North Korea and Russia at a disadvantage. The collapse of intra-regional trade in central and eastern Europe in 1989 should be a warning in this context. Unless the dynamic development of individuals, cooperatives and private firms in intra-regional trade can be sustained, a similar contraction of the trade volume may be in store.

Second, complementarity is, after all, limited between China, North Korea and the Russian Far East. There is a considerable shortage of investment capital in all three countries. Intra-regional investment flows are likely to remain at the present low level.

Third, complementarities in technology exist between China and Russia, but collaboration will be difficult to put into practice due to financial and bureaucratic obstacles. Opportunities exist in energy (including Russian nuclear power plant technology) and Chinese capital goods for light industries, only to the extent to which they can be financed on the Russian side.

Finally, the export of hundreds of thousands of labourers (rather than goods or capital) from north-east China and North Korea to Russia has yielded mixed results. The privatization of farming and the high and rising level of unemployment will discourage the expansion and possibly the continuation of this form of collaboration.

Trade and investment flows between South Korea and China will be the most dynamic element in economic relations in continental north-east Asia

China has rapidly moved up in the ranking of South Korea's major trading partners. In 1991, China had reached fourth position after Japan, the USA and Germany as a source of Korean imports, and it is likely to have moved up to third place in 1992. On the export side, China was South Korea's sixth most important market. Bilateral trade flows were the largest in continental north-east Asia, with US$5.8 billion in 1991, and the underlying factors of this trend continue to apply. In fact, one may expect a shift of interest on the part of Korean firms, from south-east Asia to north-east Asia.

Japan continues to be the economic centre of north-east Asia.

Normalization and cooperation in continental north-east Asia evolves in the shadow of the Japanese economy. As was shown in Table 2.1, Japanese GNP is eight times larger than the combined GNP of continental north-east Asia. Japan remains the leading supplier of imports to South Korea and China (if Hong Kong is disregarded). Yet it would be wrong to assume that economic development in continental north-east Asia is entirely dependent on Japan: for the countries and provinces under review in this chapter, the closer Chinese and Korean economies are by and large in the same league as that of Japan. This applies certainly to the Russian border provinces and North Korea.

A tissue of closer economic relations is emerging in continental north-east Asia

In summary, the development of economic relations in continental north-east Asia has come a long way over the past five years. Growth and economic rapprochement has been more consistent than for central and eastern Europe, although it started, of course, from a much lower base. The prospects for continuation of this trend are good.

Implications for international business

The recent changes in continental north-east Asia have certainly put this region on the map for large international companies.

To date, European companies are very unevenly represented in the region: overall, their share in trade and investment flows is small as compared with that of Japan, the rest of Asia, and North America (Figure 2.3). Yet there are a number of striking exceptions to the overall limited representation of European firms: Volkswagen in Changchung, the capital of Jilin province in China, accounts for 55 per cent of total passenger car production in China (Deutsches Institut für Wirtschaftsforschung 1992). Nestlé has established one of its first factories in China, in Heilongjiang province near Harbin, and has ambitious expansion plans. In fact, Europe's share in Chinese imports – 13 per cent in 1991–was on a par with imports from the USA or Japan. Daimler Benz is a major supplier of passenger cars to North Korea, and, more generally, several European firms are presently looking into new business opportunities in North Korea.

Continental north-east Asia was, in the past, attractive solely to leading European multinationals and a few individual and adventurous entrepreneurs. In the future, however, the region is likely to appeal to a somewhat broader spectrum of companies. In spite of progress in the normalization of economic relations within the region, firms will have to continue to pursue business strategies tailored to provincial and national conditions, rather than to regional potential. Opportunities for truly regional operations, however, may well arise in the not too distant future, and companies already present in the region will be the first to benefit.

For the time being, one of the major difficulties for international firms in the region is to cope with the coexistence of different segments in the economies of China, Russia and North Korea. Governments and enterprises are likely to give preference to world market integration. Effective opening-up to international competition and cooperation, however, will be limited to a small number of leading firms in the region. A second tier of local companies will find regional trade and cooperation under the shielded conditions of barter trade a more manageable option. The great majority of firms will struggle to survive on domestic markets. Only those foreign firms able to blend into this heterogeneous structure will be able to benefit fully from the region's potential.

Notes

1 The Chinese province Jilin has access to the Sea of Japan via the Tumen River.
2 In comparison to total foreign investment in China of over US$30 billion, and around US$5 billion from Taiwan, this is of course very low.
3 See, for instance, the autumn 1992 forecast of UNDIESA, which projects an annual GNP growth of 9.6 per cent in constant 1988 US dollars for the period of time 1991 to 1996, and an increase of the foreign trade ratio (exports plus imports divided by national income) from 31 per cent in 1990 to 46 per cent in 1996.

Bibliography

Deutsches Institut für Wissenschaft im Wandel (1992) 'Chinas Aussenwirtschaft im Wandel', *Wochenbericht* 51, Berlin.
Far Eastern Economic Review (1992) 'Hinterland of Hope', 16 January.
Jones, R., King, R. and Klein, M. (1992) 'The Chinese Economic Area: Economic Integration without a Free Trade Agreement', OECD Economics Department Working Paper 124, Paris.
Miller, M. Holm, and Kelleher (1991) 'Tumen River Area Development', UNDP mission report, Pyongyang, October.
Papers presented at the 1st International Conference on Economic Development in the Area of North-east Asia, Changchun, China, July 1990.
von Kirchbach, F. (1992) 'Subregional Trade Expansion in North-east Asia in the Context of the Tumen River Area Development Programme', International Trade Centre, UNCTAD/GATT, Geneva, 4 September.
—— (1993) 'Trade Promotion in Continental North-East Asia: Product Patterns and Issues for Trade Promotion', International Trade Centre, UNCTAD/GATT, Research Paper 3, Geneva.
von Rabenau, B. (1992) 'Regional Development in the Tumen River Area, TRADP Justification and Alternative Development Scenarios', UNDP report, Columbus, Ohio, 8 September.
Wang Guiland (1992) 'Prospects of economic cooperation in Northeast Asia', *Intertrade*, September.
Won Bae Kim and Campbell, B.O. (eds) (1991) *Proceedings of the Conference 'Economic Development in the Coastal Area of Northeast Asia'* (organized by the East-West Centre and the Sasakawa Peace Foundation).
Ye Gang (1992) 'Chinese Transnational Corporations', *Transnational Corporations* 1, 2: 125–33, New York: UNCTC.

3 The Asian trading bloc

Evelyne Dourille-Feer

INTRODUCTION

In the 1991 *Asian Outlook*, published by the Asian Development Bank, the section dealing with trade and foreign investment ends thus:

> The Asian countries' hope for relief from the discriminatory trade policies of the United States and Europe was the promise of renewed strength in, and an expanded role for, the GATT system from the Uruguay Round of trade negotiations. However if the Uruguay Round fails, it is more likely that the international trading system will slide further toward the establishment of regional trading groups.
>
> Asian Development Outlook, 1991, ADB, April 1991, Manila, page 49.

This was quite a far-sighted point of view! Although the Uruguay Round has not, at the time of writing, failed completely, it was unable to reach a conclusion before the end of 1992. During that very year, the signing of two free trade agreements – namely NAFTA (the North American Free Trade Agreement, including the United States, Canada and Mexico), and AFTA (the Asian Free Trade Agreement) heralded the formation of two regional trade blocs. AFTA was signed by ASEAN countries, in order to minimize the potential risks of Fortress north America and Fortress Europe, and to secure itself a stronger position in world trade negotiations.

Most of the world's governments are officially advocating free trade, and asking for more multilateralism in negotiations, but by far the strongest defenders of free trade are Asian countries. This is because exports have been the engine of their economic growth. With the world economic slump, the threat of protectionism is growing, and this raises at least three sets of questions concerning Asia's economic future.

The first set of questions concerns the validity of the Japanese model for other Asian countries. The second deals with the emergence of a united Asian bloc, and the last set refers to the future economic development of Asia as a whole.

FLYING GEESE FOR EVER?

The economies of Asian countries have taken off in turn throughout the 1970s and the 1980s, adopting (in the eyes of the commentators, at least) the oft-cited 'V-formation' of flying geese, with Japan leading the flight, followed by the four NIEs (Taiwan, South Korea, Hong Kong, Singapore), who are in turn followed by the south-east Asian nations. The economies of Indochina countries (Vietnam, Laos and Cambodia) hope to be carried along by ASEAN's dynamism, and China is now trying to join the formation, too.

This classic pattern of Asian development, with each country gradually upgrading its production, technology and standard of living, has relied heavily upon Japanese leadership. And so it is necessary briefly to examine the Japanese model, if we are to assess whether, despite the current crisis, it will be strong enough to generate the vital momentum that will enable most Asian countries to join the club of developed nations.

The ageing Japanese model

Japanese economic development started during the latter half of the nineteenth century. At that time, Japan was the only industrializing Asian country, with much of the rest of the region coping with overwhelming demographic problems (Fouquin *et al* 1991).

After the Second World War, the Japanese economy resumed its expansion, with three distinct periods of growth. From 1955 to 1973, Japanese GDP registered roughly 10 per cent growth, twice that of the American economy. Growth was centred on domestic demand, especially household consumption and fixed capital investment. Between the first oil shock and 1984, exports were strongly emphasized, leading to unsustainable trade surpluses with Japan's major trading partners (the merchandise trade balance with the United States jumped from US$459 million in 1975 to US$18.2 billion in 1983; from US$2.3 billion to US$10.4 billion with the EEC; and

Table 3.1 Demand contributions to Japanese economic growth (percentage)

	Domestic demand	External demand	GNP
1970–3	7.4	−0.7	6.7
1973/80	2.8	1.1	3.9
1980–3	2.0	1.3	3.3
1983	2.2	1.5	3.7
1984	3.8	1.3	5.1
1985	3.7	0.8	4.5
1986	4.1	−1.4	2.7
1987	6.2	−1.0	5.2
1988	6.7	−1.6	5.1
1989**	4.8	−0.8	5.6
1990**	5.7	0	5.7
1991**	2.4	1.1	3.5
1992***	1.3	0.7	2.0

**Constant 1985 prices as of 1989 ***NRI forecasts.
Source: EPA, based on financial years and Nomura Research Institute

from US$2 billion to US$6.6 billions with south-east Asia). From 1974–83, exports have been the engine of Japanese economic growth.

Since 1984, Japanese domestic demand has gradually recovered its leading role in economic growth. External demand even had a negative impact on the increase of GDP from 1986 to 1991 (Table 3.1).

Nevertheless, the domestic market was heavily depressed during the fiscal year 1992–3, with exports gaining strong momentum, while imports stood still. A trade surplus of at least US$116 billion seems likely for the year.

Japan has, then, traditionally been capable of adapting to shifts in external and domestic demand, as needs dictated. The economic success and dynamism now seen throughout Asia could be said to have originated from this flexibility.

Japan relies upon a very powerful and healthy production system. In 1990, manufacturing still accounted for 28 per cent of GNP, compared to 21.8 per cent in America, and 25 per cent in France.[1] After the Second World War, Japan's strong political will spurred on the rebuilding of its industrial sector. Priority sectors were carefully selected as scarce savings were properly channelled into industry. High levels of education, high household saving rates, along with a flexible wage system (high bonuses and extra working time

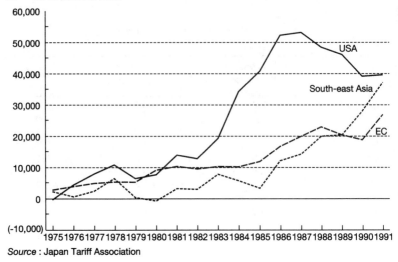

Source : Japan Tariff Association

Figure 3.1 Japanese bilateral trade balance with the United States, EEC and south-east Asia

allowances), and a system of stable employment (including life-long training) also explains why Japan has become such a strong industrial and financial power, generating huge flows of goods and capital to irrigate its Asian neighbourhood. The trouble is that the Japanese model worked perfectly when the world economy was growing far faster than now, and when there was still much room to penetrate other markets, specifically the highly developed American market (Figure 3.1).

Owing to a series of protection measures, encompassing its financial system (strict exchange controls and regulations), and its domestic industries (cocooning infant industries, quotas for sociologically sensitive sectors, non-tariff barriers as in the *keiretsu* system, and an archaic distribution network), Japan has been able to exert control on its monetary instruments, on its stock exchange, and on its industrial restructuring.

This control allowed Japan to monitor its employment situation better than did the United States or Europe. But now, as Japan deregulates its financial system under American and Western pressure, it has less scope to manipulate monetary policy, and its banks are reducing their international activities (Aglietta 1992). The *keiretsu* system is under attack, and so is the distribution system. So the Japanese model is losing some of its traditional characteristics. That

Table 3.2 Japanese ODA: 1989/90

	$ million		Share (%)	
	1989	*1990*	*1989*	*1990*
Asia	4,240	4,117	62.5	59.3
North-east	919	835	13.6	12.0
South-east	2,226	2,379	32.8	34.3
(ASEAN)	(2,132)	(2,299)	(31.5)	(33.1)
South-east	1,091	898	16.1	12.9
Others	3	4	0.0	0.0
Middle East	368	705	5.4	10.2
Africa	1,040	792	15.3	11.4
Central and Latin America	563	561	8.3	8.1
Oceania	98	114	1.4	1.6
Europe	11	158	0.2	2.3
Non-paid ODA	458	494	6.8	7.1
Total	6,779	6,940	100.0	100.0

Note: net payments
Source: Ministry of Foreign Affairs

which the rest of Asia is trying to imitate is perhaps already outmoded.

Nevertheless, even if the Japanese model cannot be entirely recreated under today's circumstances, it has generated tremendous wealth which has been partly recycled through aid to Asia (Table 3.2). It has also generated trade and capital synergy among Asian countries. The present slow-down of the Japanese economy is not a prelude to its decline. Its industrial production system has never performed better, after the double-digit fixed capital investment growth registered between 1987 and 1991. Its 121 million consumers have amongst the highest standards of living in the world. So Japan still has the strength required to play a central role in Asia. Its Asian imitators have often adopted their own development strategies, based on their different historical backgrounds and resource endowments.

Strategies adopted by Japan's Asian followers

Although the Asian NIEs have been registering high economic growth for more than three decades (Table 3.4), their trade performance only became really striking during the 1980s. The American market has been their top priority for exports (38 per cent of total exports in 1985). They even gained market shares in electronic

Table 3.3 Japanese economic outlook for 1992* (percentage)

Read GNP	1.6
Consumer spending	1.5
Residential investment	2.5
Non-residential investment	−3.8
Contribution of domestic demand	0.7
Contribution of external demand	0.8
Nominal GNP	3.0
Wholesale prices	−1.3
Retail prices	1.8
Current account surplus (billion dollars)	116.5
Trade surplus (billion dollars)	136.0

*Outlook revised last December
Source: EPA

products at the expense of their Japanese competitors at the beginning of the so-called *endaka* period, when the yen surged in value. Later, they started breaking down the barriers protecting the Japanese market (the NIEs' exports to Japan jumped from US$11.3 billion in 1985 to US$27.4 billion in 1991).

As the NIE currencies abruptly appreciated against the dollar in 1987,[2] South Korean and Taiwanese exports fell. National production was absorbed by booming domestic demand, and external demand started having a negative impact on growth in 1988, for Taiwan and 1989 for South Korea. Both countries also delocalized low value-added activities in south-east Asia because of the increase in production costs.

South-east Asian nations such as Thailand, Malaysia and Indonesia have also implemented similar strategies, such as export-led growth, upgrading industrial production and investments in third countries.

Most Asian countries do seem to be adopting development schemes along Japanese lines. But closer examination of each country's particular circumstances shows that the development patterns are, in fact, quite different.

Unlike the big industrial groups that dominate Japan and South Korea, business in the Chinese world (Taiwan, Hong Kong, etc.) is the preserve of smaller, more flexible, often family-run enterprises (Fouquin *et al* 1991). Market size has also given Japan the opportunity to build a broad-based production system far less specialized than those of the NIEs, which have had to adapt quickly to external market demands. This explains why Japan could afford such a low

Table 3.4 GDP growth rate in Asian NIEs and ASEAN countries
(percentage)

	1960–70	1970–80	1980–90	1990	1991	1992
South Korea	8.4	7.7	9.6	9.2	8.4	6.0
Taiwan	9.0	9.7	8.3	4.9	7.2	6.4
Hong Kong	9.7	9.4	6.6	3.2	4.2	5.3
Singapore	9.2	9.0	7.1	8.3	6.7	5.5
Thailand	8.3	6.8	7.4	11.5	7.9	7.5
Malaysia	—	8.0	5.9	9.7	8.7	8.3
Indonesia	4.5	7.3	5.5	7.5	7.1	6.6
Philippines	5.2	6.3	1.8	2.5	−1.0	0.5

Note: 1992 data are forecasts.
Source: Nomura Research Institute and the Institute of Developing Economies (1990 to 1992)

volume of manufacturing imports until very recently (US$88 billion in imports in 1988 versus US$261 billion of manufacturing exports).[3]

For other ASEAN countries, richly endowed with natural resources, attempts to attract manufacturing investment at any price, and excessive reliance on cheap manpower, could prove costly in the long run. It might prove wise to attract investment in natural resource development, and to try to test other economic development patterns. The alternative is to risk running into a dead end if markets in the developed world stop absorbing their exports. At present, the flock of Asian geese is still flying together, but the formation may split if the 'glue' becomes insufficiently binding.

THE EMERGENCE OF AN ASIAN ECONOMIC BLOC

When trans-Pacific trade overtook trans-Atlantic trade in 1983, most specialists thought that America's ties with Asia would quickly strengthen. Very few forecast that intra-Asian economic linkages would grow even faster.

Asia first

In 1970, intra-Asian trade flows were still negligible compared to those registered between north America and Asia. After the yen rise against the dollar in 1985, intra-Asian trade expanded sharply (23 per cent between 1986 and 1989). In 1989, intra-Asian exports reached US$270 billion, with Asian exports to North America amounting to US$206 and US$182 billion for Europe. Asian trade

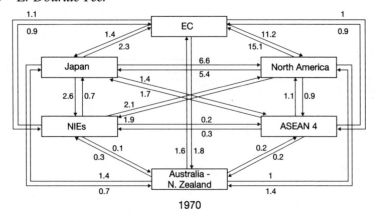

1970

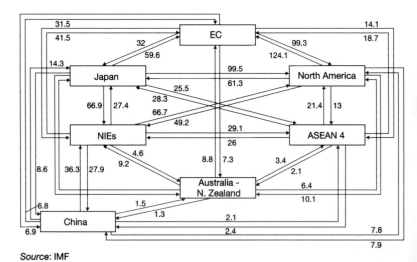

Source: IMF

Figure 3.2 Asian trade flows: 1970 and 1991

flows are far greater now than in 1970 (Figure 3.2). Nevertheless, intra-Asian exports account for roughly only one-third of total Asian exports; so Western markets are still vital for the economic prosperity of the region.

The pulling factor of Japanese trade

Until the mid-1980s, Japan was selling the bulk of its products to America (40 per cent of total exports). Since 1986, the Asian coun-

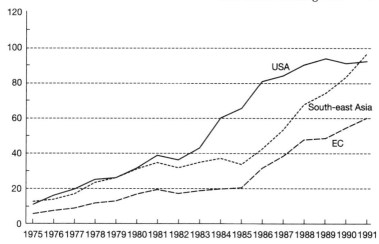

Source: Japan Tariff Association

Figure 3.3 Evolution of Japanese exports by region

tries' share of Japanese exports has quickly widened to almost equal the United States share in 1990 (31 per cent versus 34 per cent) (Figure 3.3). According to preliminary 1991 statistics, the Asian market has become the first outlet for Japanese exports with US$96.2 billion versus US$91.5 billion for the United States. Although Japanese imports from the NIEs progressed swiftly from 1985–90 (US$11.3 billion in 1985 and US$27.4 billion in 1991),[4] those from south-east Asia were less dynamic (and even shrank in value terms).

The ASEAN area, which used to register a trade surplus with Japan owing to its raw materials exports, has recorded a deficit since 1989. It reached US$5.9 billion in 1991.[5] This mainly resulted from the large flows of Japanese machinery and equipment exports to Singapore, Thailand and Malaysia (Figure 3.4).

The Asian NIEs also have a negative trade balance with their Japanese partners as they rely more heavily on Japanese machines and components for their most sophisticated products. Nevertheless, these imbalances reflect the NIEs' fast development which has played a major role in south-east Asia.

The importance of the NIEs

Between 1970 and 1991 the NIEs exploded into economic activity. Together with Japan, they accounted for nearly 70 per cent of Asian trade in this period (Figure 3.2).

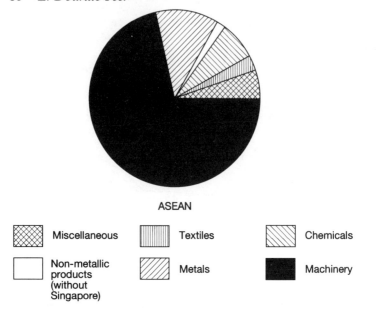

ASEAN

Miscellaneous	Textiles	Chemicals
Non-metallic products (without Singapore)	Metals	Machinery

Source: Custom and Tariff Bureau

Figure 3.4 Japanese exports to ASEAN by sectors: 1991

Their influence has been particularly strong in the ASEAN countries: they absorbed 16.2 per cent of these countries' exports in 1984, and 18.3 per cent in 1990 (versus 19.8 per cent in the case of both Japan and the United States). They have also traded very actively together. The intra-NIEs trade increased 42 per cent in 1988.[6] South Korea and Taiwan's dynamism is directed towards both ASEAN and the NIEs. The NIEs are also very active in China owing to the Chinese diaspora: the momentum of the Hong Kong economy in 1992 relied mostly upon growth in southern China (Goldstein 1992).

Until the end of the Cold War, ASEAN remained primarily a political association. Economic flows in the region had not developed much. Intra-ASEAN trade (excluding Singapore) amounted to 3.9 per cent of total trade in the area in 1970, and 4.1 per cent in 1989.[7] By signing the ASEAN Free Trade Agreement on 29 January 1993, these countries have shown a new will to strengthen their economic links in the face of NAFTA and the European economic bloc. Within 15 years (2008), the customs duties of AFTA members will be curbed for a wide range of manufactured and agricultural products, and will have a new ceiling of 5 per cent.

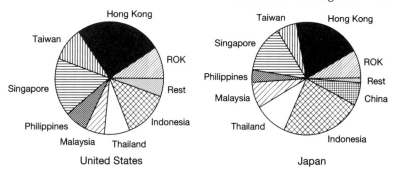

Source: *Survey of Current Business*, Ministry of Finance

Figure 3.5 American and Japanese investment in Asia: 1991 stock

Since intra-ASEAN trade flows are very small compared with regional trade flows, and as China embarks on her economic expansion, Japan and the NIEs find themselves playing a central role as Asia's main trade dynamos. Nevertheless, ASEAN is also playing an increasing role, with several initiatives in Indochina already taking effect. Apart from trade, direct investment flows have been a determinant for regional growth.

The challenged supremacy of Japanese investors

America's dominant position as the world's leading investor has considerably weakened during the past two decades (39 per cent of total world direct investment stock in 1973, 25 per cent in 1989) while Japan's share has quickly progressed (from 3.5 per cent to 16.5 per cent during the same period)[8]

In 1980, the direct investment stock of American industrial companies in Asia amounted to US$2.3 billion, while that of Japanese companies was already equal to US$4.6 billion. This showed the prime importance of Asia for Japanese investors, whereas the Americans has been concentrating on Europe and Canada. Eleven years later, the gap is even wider (US$8.7 billion for the United States, and US$21.6 billion for Japan in 1991).[9]

Aggregated data show a very heavy concentration of American investments in the NIEs. Nevertheless, when looking at detailed data, the weight of Hong Kong and Singapore is overwhelming (Figure 3.5).

Even if the Japanese industrial presence in Asia has more or less supplanted the American one, it is not linked to a special focus by Japanese investors on Asia during the 1980s. On the contrary,

Table 3.5 Japanese direct investments: first half fiscal 1992/first half 1991 (percentage)

North America	−8.3
Europe	−25.4
Asia	+5.5
World	−12.0
($ billion)	(17.3)

Source: Ministry of Finance

Table 3.6 FDI approvals in south-east Asia: 1986–9 (US$ million)

From \ To	Indonesia 1986–8*	Indonesia 1989	Malaysia 1986–8*	Malaysia 1989	Philippines 1986–8*	Philippines 1989	Thailand 1986–8*	Thailand 1989
Japan	369	769	265	993	49	158	1,522	3,524
NIEs	663	1,197	315	1,335	63	323	815	2,012
Hong Kong	157	407	57	130	21	133	211	562
Korea	78	466	7	70	1	17	41	171
Singapore	116	166	112	338	1	24	157	411
Taipei, China	312	158	139	797	40	149	406	868
Asia	1,032	1,966	580	2,328	112	481	2,337	5,536
WORLD	2,231	4,719	1,112	3,194	239	804	3,279	7,996

*Annual average
Source: Asian Development Bank

Japanese investments have been flooding into the United States since 1986, and into Europe since 1987 (Dourille-Feer 1992), with a brief upsurge in manufacturing investment flows to Taiwan and South Korea between the beginning of the *endaka* period and the rise of the won and the Taiwanese dollar (1985–7). The relatively quick increase of total Japanese investment in Asia is related to its tremendous global investment effort during the latter part of the 1980s. Since 1990, the yearly amount of Japanese direct investment world-wide has been decreasing. Preliminary results for the fiscal year 1992–3 tend to show that Asia is the only region to register no decline (Table 3.5).

These strong capital flows have been very important and some-times determinant for the development of countries with scarce savings. Nevertheless, Japanese investors have been overtaken in countries such as Malaysia and Indonesia. The challengers are South Korea, Taiwan, Singapore and Hong Kong (Table 3.6).

As with trade, Japan has initiated direct investment flows through-out the region. It has been followed by the NIEs and, now, by the ASEAN countries. Trade of both goods and capital flows is gradually shaping a potential Asian bloc, based on strengthening mutual interests.

ASIA: THE WORLD'S ECONOMIC GROWTH CENTRE?

Europe is losing steam, burdened by the cost of German reunification and the austere economic policies applied by numerous countries in order to meet the necessary requirements for a unified European currency. The United States is, it would seem, only just emerging from recession. Asian countries, however, have continued to achieve brilliant results, and a new middle class is now emerging in even the poorest ASEAN country, namely Indonesia. But the future of this region is still uncertain. Is the current growth rate sustainable, despite the gloomy outlook in Europe, and the uncertainties of American recovery? What are the prospects for China, and is there any hint that the other neighbouring giant, India, will integrate with the Asian trading bloc?

Firm growth forecasts

Preliminary data for 1992 paint a bright picture for east and southeast Asia, even if the NIEs are registering a slight decline in their growth rates compared to those of 1991 (an average reduction of 1.3 per cent). The four ASEAN countries (Thailand, Malaysia, Indonesia and the Philippines) are following a stable course, and China is particularly dynamic (Table 3.7).

The growth forecasts of the Institute of Developing Economies for the Asian NIEs and ASEAN countries in 1993 are again very optimistic, predicating an acceleration of activity. The Institute assumes that the American economy will recover, along with Japan, during the second part of the year. European economies should also improve. According to the majority of regional analysts, a 6–7 per cent growth rate seems most likely for the year to come if the United States registers a 2 per cent increase in GNP, and if Japan recovers from its slump in order to absorb Asian products (Suzuki 1992).

It is interesting to note the convergence of growth rates for the NIEs and ASEAN countries. As a result of the latter, the NIEs remain ahead of ASEAN, and are able to have a dynamic impact on the less developed countries of the region. Nevertheless, two events could have a very strong impact on Asian growth. One is a change in trade policy in Washington. The other is a weaker than expected economic recovery in Japan.

Table 3.7 GDP growth rate for Pacific countries

	1992[1]	1993[1]	1990–2000[2]
South Korea	6.0	7.3	7.8
	(6.2)	(5.3)	
Taiwan	6.4	7.0	6.7
	(3.5)	(3.8)	
Hong Kong	5.3	6.1	6.0
	(10.2)	(9.2)	
Singapore	5.3	6.5	7.0
	(2.3)	(2.5)	
Thailand	7.5	8.5	8.1
	(5.8)	(4.7)	
Malaysia	8.5	8.7	7.2
	(4.2)	(4.5)	
Indonesia	6.3	6.5	6.8
	(7.1)	(8.0)	
Philippines	1.0	2.0	5.0
	(9.5)	(11.0)	
Japan	1.6	3.3	4.0
		(2.1)	
United States	3.0	3.5	2.4

(. . .): inflation rate.
Sources:
1: NIEs: IDE forecasts, ASEAN: Agence Financière pour l'ASEAN, Japan: EPA,
   United States: Federal Reserve Bank estimates
2: Nomura Research Institute. NRI *Quarterly Economic Review*, May 1991

Strong pressure from the Clinton administration to open up Asia's markets, and a decision not to extend China's Most Favoured Nation trading status, would constitute a heavy blow to Asian trade. Taiwanese, Hong Kong and Macao companies, which have invested massively in southern China, would be especially hurt; the investment plans of South Korean companies would be ruined, and economic growth in east Asian economies would slow to around 5 per cent.

The other scenario is based on a 10 per cent growth rate for the Asian countries. This could take place within the context of a continued slump in Japan, resulting in stronger demand for medium-range quality products from the NIEs by Japanese consumers. Japanese money could also move to Asian stock markets, as confidence in the Kabutocho wanes. Growth in ASEAN could resume, with recent infrastructure improvements. Nevertheless, this scenario would seem to have little chance of becoming a reality.

Whatever happens, growth forecasts for the region are not lower than 5 per cent, which is still pretty high by Western standards. Asia's

Table 3.8 Chinese economic indicators (percentage)

	1991	1992	1990–2000
GDP	+7.0	+12.0	7.1
Industrial production	+14.2	+19.3[1]	ND
Retail prices	+2.9	+4.8[1]	ND
M2	+26.4	+27[2]	ND
		+30[3]	

1 9 months 1992
2 1st quarter 1992
3 1st quarter 1992
Source: 1991 and 1992 Statistical Bureau; 1990–2000 NRI

Table 3.9 Major FDI in China: first half 1992

	Million dollars
Hong Kong	2,100
Taiwan	377
Japan	247
United States	210
World total	3,300

Source: FEER

dynamism should continue for a while yet. None of the economic indicators (inflation, debt, budget deficit) has reached alarming levels, a situation which seems likely to obtain for the rest of the decade according to NRI forecasts, barring an abrupt change in the world economic environment. Asia will, it seems, continue to follow Japan's lead for some time to come (Japan Economic Planning Agency 1992).

Japan's central role is not contested, then, in the different scenarios, and neither is the increasing importance of China.

The Chinese potential

From the introduction of market forces in 1979, the Chinese economy has experienced alternate periods of rapid growth and stagnation. The 1990s have started with moderate growth (5 per cent), and should reach 12 per cent in 1992, according to official sources (Agence Financière pour l'Asie 1992) (Table 3.8).

Although 1993 is clouded by uncertainties, owing to bottle-necks in China's energy and communications infrastructure, rising inflation, and increases in the monetary supply volume (all 'orange' signals

of economic overheating), high growth levels could still be maintained, since foreign investors remain enthusiastic about setting up
there. If preliminary estimations are confirmed, foreign investments
will have reached US$9 billion in 1992, equivalent to 28 per cent of
the total Chinese stock of direct investments. During the first half
of the year, Hong Kong was particularly active (Table 3.9).

Chinese exports to Asia are also growing quickly, and as economic
liberalization progresses, China is able to play a more influential
role in Asia. Nevertheless, rivalry with neighbours (such as the
Pratleys Island dispute), and domestic political tensions could undermine its integration in Asia from the start.

The isolation of India

Since 1970, India has maintained its strong trade links with the EC. Its
presence on the American market has expanded much faster than in
Japan (Figure 3.6). India has also failed to attract more Asian investment. Japan, for example, invested US$18 million in 1989, US$30 in
1990, and US$14 in 1991. The total Japanese direct investment stock
in India amounts to a mere US$210 million, less than the sums
invested during the first half of 1992 in China. Even stock investors
trust the embryonic Canton stock exchange more than its Indian
counterpart (Sesit and Steiner 1993). India is thus not benefiting from
the dynamics of the east and south-east Asian region.

Renewed ties between Japan and Indochina

Last November, Japan announced its decision to resume official aid
to Vietnam, which was interrupted in 1979 after the invasion of
Cambodia. The decision could give a very strong economic impetus
to Vietnam, amounting to US$270 million, compared with a total
of just US$100 million in aid received by Vietnam from the other
industrial nations in 1990.

Japan is Vietnam's chief trading partner, accounting for 14 per
cent of Vietnamese exports in 1991, and 28 per cent in 1992. Hong
Kong ranked second, and Singapore third. Singapore is the chief
exporter to Vietnam, followed by the CIS, with Japan only fourth.
One reason for this is that Japan has made very few direct investments in Vietnam, compared to investments made by other Asian
countries. By the end of June 1992, the Vietnamese authorities had
approved 384 foreign investment projects amounting to US$2.97
billion, of which just 24 were Japanese, worth US$159.4 million.

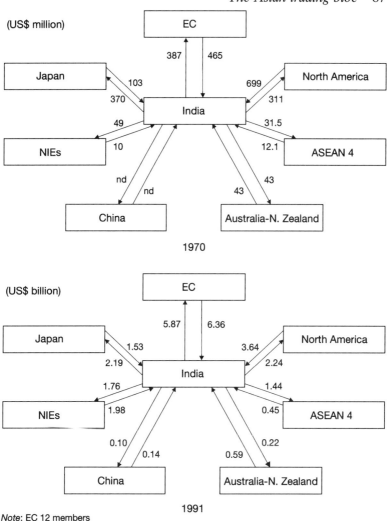

Figure 3.6 Trade links between India and Asia: 1970 and 1991

Japan's weak presence stems from the Vietnamese government's investment policy, granting incentives mostly to development projects in natural resources (*Journal of Japanese Trade and Industry* No. 6, December 1992–January 1993, pages 21–23.) Taiwan and Hong Kong are the biggest investors, and Japan ranks lower than both France and the Netherlands.

The aid funded by Japan should boost infrastructure projects, enhancing Vietnam's manufacturing sector. The United States should also resume trade and investment in Vietnam, in the near future, helping Japan's position without hurting the other Asian economies. Laos' economy is also gaining momentum, and Indochina in general is soon expected to match the dynamism of other south-east Asian nations.

South-east and east Asian countries are engaged in a rapid development process, relying more and more heavily upon Japan, but also upon other Asian countries. The Asian trade bloc already exists commercially, even if it still has no formal political base. The increasing importance of China and Chinese communities throughout Asia might provide Japan with the back-up necessary to allow it to develop a role as regional leader in a political and diplomatic, rather than purely economic, sense. If Asia's dynamism persists for the rest of the decade, we should see a prominent economic bloc forming by the year 2000 (Lafay 1992). The development of Asia's biggest companies should boost the region's globalization efforts – i.e. the settlement of subsidiaries in other markets such as Europe and the United States – and prevent the Asian bloc from becoming a fortress.

Notes

1 These figures are published by the Keizai Koho Center, Japan, 1993. Manufacturing also includes mining, electricity, gas and water supply.
2 The appreciation of Asian currencies against the dollar in 1987 was 8.7 per cent for the Korean won (15.8 per cent in 1988), and 19.5 per cent for the Taiwanese dollar.
3 OECD, Statistics of Foreign Trade, exports FOB, imports CIF.
4 If the 1985 dollar value is deflated with 1990 deflator, the Japanese imports amount to US$1.9 billion as against US$30.4 billion in 1990. Source: CHELEM.
5 Source: Ministry of Finance, Japan Tariff Association.
6 Source: Asian Development Bank statistics.
7 Including Singapore the figures are respectively 19.8 per cent in 1970 and 18.0 per cent in 1989.
8 Calculation by D. de Laubier, based on the last available year's figures at the time of writing.
9 Sources: Survey of Current Business, and Ministry of Finance.

Bibliography

Agence Financière pour l'Asie (1992) 'Situation Economique et Financière de la Chine', *Etude* 320, December.

Aglietta, M. (1992), 'Les Dérapages de la Finance Japonaise', *EPI*, 3e trimestre.

Asian Development Bank (1992) *Asian Outlook*.

Asian Development Outlook 1991, Manila.

Besson, D. (1992) 'A L'Ombre du Soleil Levant', *Courrier Economique Financier, Agence Financière pour l'ANSEA* 75, March.

—— (1993) 'Les Pays de l'ANSEA en 1993: Le Rebond', *Agence Financière pour l'ANSEA*, January.

Bank of Tokyo (1991) 'Japan's Role in Changing World', *Tokyo Financial Review* 16, 11. November 1991.

—— (1992) 'The 1992 Economic Outlook for the Developing Nations of Asia', *Tokyo Financial Review*, 17. 2.

Dourille-Feer, E. (1991) 'L'Asie Fait Bloc', *Epargne et Finance*, 4.

—— (1992) 'L'Europe sur l'Echiqiuer Productif du Japon: Le Cas des Industries Électroniqies et Automobiles', *EPI*, 49, 1st quarter.

Fouquin, M., Dourille-Feer, E. and Oliveira-Martins, J. (1991) 'Pacifique, le Recentrage Asiatique', *Economica*.

Goldstein, C. (1992) 'Numbers Game', *Far Eastern Economic Review*, 24 December.

Grimm, M. (1992) 'Japan and ASEAN: Aspects of a New Independence', *Japan Economic Institute*, 12A, March.

Hirata, A. (1992) 'Economic Interdependence in Asia and the Pacific', *Journal of Japanese Trade and Industry*, 2.

Institute of Developing Economies (1992) '1993 Economic Outlook for Asian NIEs and ASEAN Countries', December 10.

Japan Economic Planning Agency (1992) Report of the year 2010 Committee.

Lafay, G. (1992) 'L'industrie Mondiale: Trois Scenarios pour l'an 2000', *Economie et Statistique*, July-August.

Lanteri, M. (1992a) 'Afta 1–EAEC 0', *Courrier Economique et Financier, Agence Financière pour l'ANSEA*, 73, January.

—— (1992b) 'Les Investissements Étrangers dans l'ANSEA: Un Ralentissement Durable?', *Courrier Economique et Financier, Agence Finacière pour l'ANSEA*, 78, June.

Nomura Research Institute (1991) 'Medium-term Economic Outlook for Japan and the World', *Nomura Quarterly*, May.

Office Franco-Japonais (1992) 'Aide au Développement', *Japan Economie et Société*, July.

Okita, S. (1991) 'Japan's Role in Asia Pacific Cooperation', *The Annals of the American Academy*, January.

Okumura, K. (1991) 'La Nouvelle Division Régionale du Travail entre le Japon et l'Asie du Sud-Est', *Hosei Daigaku Keizai Ronshu*, 2, 9.

Schwab, L. Servoise, R. and Watanabe, T. (1991) 'Dossier sur le Pacifique Ouest', *Futuribles*, January.

Sesist, M. R. and Steiner, R. (1993) 'Asian Investing', *Wall Street Journal*, 13 January.

Suzuki, S. (1992) 'Analysts mixed on Asian growth' *Nikkei Journal*, 14 December.

Taylor, R. (1985) *The Sino-Japanese Axis, a New Force in Asia?* The Athlone Press.

4 Recent changes in Korea and their possible economic implications

Didier Cazal

INTRODUCTION

South Korea provides a vivid example of the interweaving of economic, political and cultural issues. In 1992, significant changes occurred here in the political field – with the first civilian-only presidential elections, the candidacy of the founder and former president of Hyundai, the acceleration of normalization with North Korea, and the development of relations with former eastern bloc countries in Europe – and in the economic field, which saw the signing of a bilateral trade accord with the US concerning the protection of intellectual property, the streamlining of investment rules, the improvement of standards, testing regulations and custom-clearance procedures, the decreasing importance of the US as a trade partner and external market, the lowest growth rate during ten years, and growing export competition with lower wage countries.

The various aspects of each of these changes are obviously interrelated. This chapter will, with some reluctance, exclude changes directly related to EC countries and companies, to concentrate on changes within South Korea and in the Far East – in particular the election of the new president, North-South Korean relations, and relations with China and the CIS.

The main purpose of this chapter is to underline some of the more significant changes (in my opinion) and their possible implications for European companies, i.e. the threats and opportunities they might offer.

MANAGING CONTINUITY AND CHANGE IN THE DOMESTIC POLITICAL ARENA

The political context and the possible implications of the elections on 18 December 1992 should be stressed in the context of the political background and culture that have long been decisive factors in South Korea's economy. The various candidates' economic proposals, and the new president's programme, indicate some possible economic developments in the near future. The policies proposed or already adopted constitute both threats and opportunities for European companies in their economic relations with Korea.

Portrait of a campaign

The most remarkable aspect of the 1992 campaign was that it was the first since 1960 to include no former generals. The elected president, whoever won, would inevitably be a civilian. This point has deep significance as a new step towards democracy.

The campaign itself could be said to have heralded a new political era. The three major candidates presented highly contrasting profiles. Kim Young-Sam is a professional politician, a relatively moderate former government opponent, who surprisingly joined the ruling party two years ago. In the 1987 elections, he failed to form an alliance with the other opposition candidate, Kim Dae-Jung, so that the polls were almost equally shared between them, letting in Roh Tae Woh, the ruling party candidate and designated successor of Chun Doo-Hwan, by a relatively narrow majority. Young-Sam had long dreamed of becoming president, and this may explain the turnabout in his political orientation.

Kim Dae-Jung has long been at the forefront of political opposition in South Korea. As such, he has been sentenced to death, placed under house arrest many times, and tortured and kidnapped by the South Korean CIA. He is seen as a political martyr, advocating democracy, a role to which he brings considerable charisma. Kim Dae-Jung hails from Cholla, the south-western region which has traditionally (for at least ten centuries) been opposed to Korea's central powers, and which has thus come to be regarded by the latter as seditious. More seriously, his past and present radicalism have led him to be suspected of North Korean sympathies, a mortal sin in South Korea.

The third candidate in 1992, Chung Ju-Yung, appears to be an outsider. He is sometimes described as the Korean Ross Perot. A billionaire, he is the founder and former president of Hyundai, a leading South Korean conglomerate. In his opinion, economic management and policy are too important to be left to politicians. With South Korea recently experiencing economic setbacks, and the *chaebols* as a major pillar of Korean competitiveness, Chung Ju-

Yung was able to present himself as the saviour of the South Korean economy. Of course, he enjoyed the support of his company and some other conglomerates, but this ultimately smacked of coercion, with allegations of illegal funding and staffing for his campaign from Hyundai Corp., which were probably harmful to him and to his chances of being elected.

Faced with the essentially conservative candidacies of Chung Ju-Yung and Kim Young-Sam, Kim Dae-Jung's only hope of election was to play the same 'divide and rule' game as Roh Tae-Woo had played in 1987. Unfortunately, Chung Ju-Yung appeared weakened in the last weeks before the election and was not able to win enough support away from Kim Young-Sam to split the conservative vote, thus allowing Kim Dae-Jung to establish himself as the winner.

Political analysts found few significant differences in economic policy between the candidates (*Les Echos* 22 October 1992). Given South Korea's worrying economic troubles, their respective economic messages were considered more critical to the poll than their democratic credentials. All three attacked President Roh's economic legacy and called for economic reforms, each 'outbidding' the other. The economic debate also allowed each candidate to assert himself as a credible successor, rather than as a loyal heir (in the case of Kim Young-Sam), a realistic opponent (in the case of Kim Dae-Jung), or an economic saviour (in the case of Chung Ju-Yung).

On domestic economic policy (*Far Eastern Economic Review* 10 December 1992), there was little to choose between the candidates' respective positions, with debate focusing merely on the pace of broadly similar reforms, and their alleged consequences. All agreed on the necessity for domestic financial reform, the liberalization of interest rates and 'real name' financial transactions, although Kim Young-Sam proposed gradual reforms under Ministry of Finance control, while the others recommended that they be immediate, with a strong central bank. All agreed on a tight budget and support for small businesses (Kim Dae-Jung placed particular emphasis on this), and Kim Young-Sam advocated government support.

The dominant issues in economic deregulation were its pace, and attitudes towards big business: Kim Young-Sam proposed gradual reform with controls on big business, while the others proposed speedier measures, including the breaking-up of big business conglomerates, and tight, if somewhat non-specific, controls on the expansion of the *chaebols*, from Chung Ju-Yung.

More generally, all three candidates strove to present themselves as squeaky clean, and best able to fight the crippling 'Korean disease' of anarchy and endemic corruption, at all levels of society.

The 1992 poll inaugurated a new democracy and a new, highly theatrical, political atmosphere (Edelman 1988). The election campaign was relatively peaceful, with no demonstrations or violence. Of course, some malpractice did occur, but this was not serious enough to threaten democracy. In many respects, the campaign resembled a typical election battle in the West.

Symbolically, Kim Dae-Jung, a major tragic hero of South Korea's former political dramas, left the arena after his defeat and even resigned his National Assembly seat. Indeed, his character does not fit well into the new political scene, all the more because his failure represents a serious loss of face.

A page of South Korea's political history does seem to have been turned, and all eyes are now on the future. South Korea's diplomatic affairs have always strongly conditioned her foreign economic relations, as with the recent negotiations on nuclear and other power plants, subway construction in Seoul and Pusan, and high-speed train construction for which French, German and Japanese companies competed. Diplomatic relations are expected to undergo change, because of their economic implications, and, as we will see further on, relations with North Korea, China and the CIS will play an increasingly important role.

Economic prospects after the election

According to political analysts, South Korea's new president was elected because he presented the ideal compromise between change and continuity (*Newsweek* 4 January 1993). Despite some clear weaknesses in his economic programme (chiefly his lack of credibility in the field) (*FEER* 10 December 1992), Kim Young-Sam's advocacy of gradual reform and smooth transition was probably decisive.

But the major challenge facing him remains whether, despite his good will, he will be strong enough to counter conservative forces, such as the *chaebols*, and an entrenched bureaucracy (*FEER* 13 August 1992; 7 January 1993) both of which helped him to succeed, and which are still the twin pillars of South Korea's economy and politics.

Kim Young-Sam will have to tread a cautious path between his political legitimacy (mostly founded upon a gradual transition towards achieved democracy and normalization with North Korea) and his economic efficiency policy in restoring growth or building a new growth pattern relying more on free market forces, GATT procedures and deregulation.

The thorny issue of business-government relations

Kim Young-Sam's position on the *chaebols* will doubtless become a major issue. Once heralded by the government as the major engine of South Korean growth, their practices are facing increasing criticism. Their efforts in R&D are considered to be insufficient, family control and ownership is seen as contrary to the modernization of management and strategy, and their overwhelming economic weight is said to be responsible for South Korea's insufficiently developed small- and medium-sized industries, the latter often unable to obtain government support and credits, or to overcome red tape.

Even now, and despite the hostile rhetoric of the new president, the *chaebols* are still the economy's main vehicle for recovery and growth. Observers consider that eventually the government's relations with them are likely to be conciliatory rather than confrontational (*FEER* 7 January 1993).

According to the leader of the DLP's economic policy caucus, and former vice-president of the Korea Development Institute, 'like Japan, there needs to be a consensus between government and business'. The current resistance from the *chaebols* is due to a lack of government consultation on economic issues which is in itself harmful to industrial competitiveness (*FEER* 10 December 1992).

The government has influenced the decisions of large South Korean companies to an extraordinary extent, having recourse to various policy instruments, but most importantly their control over credit allocation. Some authors describe South Korean government and business as a single, closed organization, defined as a 'hierarchical organization which handles transactions, that might otherwise be carried out in the market place, with administrative processes' (Lee 1992). According to Lee, this relationship stems from a nexus of implicit contracts so that, for instance, preferential loans favour those companies working in line with government economic policy targets, focusing on exports.

As Jones and Sakong (1980) mentioned, this relationship is a partnership with government as the senior partner and private enterprises the junior partners. Such channels as 'deliberation councils' and 'discussion groups' create a more direct and easy exchange of information, so that the government's control is far from being exclusively legal and administrative.

The trouble is that red tape seems now to be increasingly hindering modernization, even if it can be bypassed through string-pulling or thanks to the administration's acknowledged favouritism towards the *chaebol*, in other words by nepotism or corruption. If the 'Korean disease' mentioned earlier is, above all, societal, its main effects are nonetheless economic. Nepotism, corruption and the absence of authority are still endemic to South Korean public life, and the new president will have to show a sharp sense of authority and political astuteness to overcome them.

In fact, trying to cure the 'Korean disease' implies de-stabilizing the country's former structures, a risky business even if they had begun to falter anyway, and alienating the support of its two prime economic movers, while providing nothing strong enough to replace them, such as markets or small- and medium-sized industries. Kim Young-Sam therefore intends to direct more credit resources to small business (*FEER* 7 January 1993).

The main, and probably most arduous, task of the new government will be to set up a new business and administrative hierarchy with somewhat less inequality, more real consultation, and less control. Small- and medium-sized industries should be to some extent included in this new structure, and market forces should infiltrate it more significantly.

The issue of succession in the *chaebol*, i.e. the progressive replacement of family control and ownership by more widespread share holding and professional management, which seems necessary if not inescapable, will no doubt facilitate this transition. Significantly, though never publicly stated, Kim Young-Sam wants to reduce the power of the *chaebols* by separating ownership and management, and compelling them to go public (*FEER* 7 January 1993).

Unfortunately, many observers doubt that Kim Young-Sam can actually reform the *chaebols*, 'because he was supported by big business' according to Lim Hyun-Chin, Chairman of the Sociology Department of Seoul National University (*Newsweek* 4 January 1993).

The failure of Chung Ju-Yung's bid for election is significant in that the electorate were unconvinced both by his business credentials, and by the implicit notion that the close relationship between government and the *chaebols* means that managing a *chaebol* qualifies one to manage the economy. His failure can be compared to that of Ross Perot in the US.

Steps to a new industrial policy

Most commentators, economists and economic policy-makers call for a new industrial policy in South Korea. The industries that long sustained growth are no longer viable, since wages are still growing, and are increasingly challenged by competition from south-east Asian countries with lower wages, and by 'transplant' factories in, for example, China.

Faced with growing protectionism and prospective price wars, the government considers a move towards more up-market production as essential. In order to ease this shift, it is taking encouraging measures to maximize the performance of high-tech investments and pool resources in high-tech projects, and is spending 1 trillion won on the promotion of science and technology (*FEER* 13 August 1992).

During the election campaign, even Kim Dae-Jung was in favour of this necessary shift, and advocated an industrial structural adjustment policy under which 'the large conglomerates concentrate on capital and high-tech intensive investment and leave the rest to small and medium-sized industry' (*FEER* 10 December 1992).

The success of this shift is heavily dependent on financial reform, due to South Korean firms' high debt-servicing costs, and the lack of reasonably priced local financing (*FEER* 13 August 1992). Nevertheless, the *chaebol* are blamed for their short-term sales- and profit-oriented outlook, and their reluctance to make long-term investments in R&D.

South Korea now badly needs foreign investment in the high-tech sector. Plans to adopt the intellectual property rights enforcement Act, together with the streamlining of FDI guidelines will no doubt facilitate this (*FEER* 13 August and 3 December 1992).

In 1992, South Korea signed an accord with Japan aimed at jointly funding technology-sharing institutes in Seoul and Tokyo at a cost of around US$8 million (*FEER* 13 August 1992). On 2 October, Roh Tae-Woo and George Bush signed a new trade deal obliging South Korea to dismantle non-tariff barriers facing US exports, and enact legislation to protect the intellectual property rights of US companies, in exchange for which the US would foster technology-sharing between the two countries. These conditions are tough on South Korea, since the US cannot in fact guarantee actual technology transfers and investments from US companies (*FEER* 22 October 1992).

Negotiations are also underway between Seoul and Brussels to improve high-tech transfers between small- and medium-sized EC and South Korean companies.

Diplomacy and politics are likely to play an increasing role in dealing with these issues. South Korea represents a real opportunity for European companies, since EC relations with South Korea are historically less emotionally charged than those with Japan, and less acrimonious and stick-brandishing than those with the US.

THE TWO KOREAS: COOPERATION AND INTENDED REUNIFICATION

The division of Korea into two parts after the Second World War has always been seen as a painful and unfair result of the Cold War. Comparisons with Germany have long been made, but there are significant differences. The first important distinction is that Korea was the victim of Japanese military expansion, and was not herself an aggressor. Second, a terrible civil war occurred, and Korea became the theatre of a deadly fight between the great world powers. As a result, both North and South Korea developed strong-arm regimes and authoritarian styles of leadership.

Even now, after the collapse of the eastern European Communist bloc, Germany is still regarded by Korea with a degree of aspirational longing. However, the recent setbacks linked to German reunification have given pause for thought. Clearly, the process of reunification will have to be cautiously managed; the Korean economy is not as strong, stable and prosperous as that of former West Germany, and has shown some signs of particular fragility in recent times.

Moreover, the political and economic divisions between the two Koreas have greatly widened since the 1970s, as described by several commentators, along with the gulf between their respective external trade and per capita GNP figures. The ideological bias of this stark image of two diametrically opposed Koreas should, however, be considered (Foster-Carter 1987). Indeed, the most likely scenario at present would seem to be that of a relatively quicker and easier reunification.

Reunification is an absolute prerequisite of any political programme in South Korea, most of whose governments have had a specific Ministry of Unification. Nonetheless, public and political debate on the issue has invariably been conducted in highly emotional rather than realistic or pragmatic terms.

Normalization or reunification ?

In the late 1980s, the South Korean government made significant, if perhaps symbolic, advances towards the normalization of relations with North Korea. Lessons were clearly drawn from the German experience by Korean economists, so that even if normalization seems to be making great progress, reunification still cannot be reasonably forecast in the near future.

Although interwoven, the political and economic dimensions may be usefully distinguished (Foster-Carter 1987). Normalization does involve diplomatic talks to some extent, but is mainly concerned with economic relations. According to a recent KDI study (*FEER* 26 March 1992), the path to economic integration is in three stages. First, indirect trade (mostly through China) should be replaced by direct trade. Second, joint cooperation would be instigated on infrastructural and industrial projects in north-eastern China and the Russian Far East. In the third stage, direct investment would begin in light manufacturing ventures in North Korea.

It should be stressed that this 'economic integration' is in effect an attempt to establish normal economic relations between two separate countries. Economic integration is an essential step towards actual reunification, but it does not necessarily imply that reunification will inevitably follow. In other words, while the benefits of economic integration are unquestionable, those of political integration remain in doubt.

The political context

The jointly ratified non-aggression pact of December 1991 was the first piece of legislation addressing the development of political and economic exchanges between North and South Korea. The integrated and balanced development of both economies, through trade, the joint development of resources, and cooperation in science and technology, were its most significant aspects. The pact was politically significant, but seems to have been more symbolic than effective in economic terms, since apart from trade, no actual cooperation beyond talks and further statements has, as yet, occurred.

At the beginning of 1992, Pyongyang agreed, significantly, to allow visits by inspectors from the International Atomic Energy Agency. However, Seoul (as well as Tokyo) wanted the North Korean leader Kim Il Sung to agree to the mutual inspection of nuclear facilities. The North's failure to implement this drove Roh's government to suspend all talks on potential investments (*FEER* 26 March 1992). Nevertheless, Pyongyang's Premier claimed during a press conference that pilot investment projects would begin soon, and asserted that economic cooperation was not linked to the nuclear issue, in blatant contradiction to Roh (*FEER* 26 August 1992).

According to observers, the framework for rapprochement that has been so patiently built could become invalid, setting relations with North Korea back to square one, unless Pyongyang abandons its nuclear plans, a move which could be forced by economic difficulties or the hypothetical collapse of Kim Il Sung's regime.

Another precondition for reunification should not be forgotten. The recognition of the South Korean government by Pyongyang, even implicitly by permitting direct trade, is considered imperative (*FEER* 26 March 1992). South Korea's insistence on this can be partially accounted for as a 'face' issue.

Why is the South Korean government dragging its feet in this way? North Korea has for many years been the 'bogey man' of South Korea, the perpetrator of civil war atrocities, and the den of a much-dreaded hard-line Communist regime. It was also seen as an important competitor, since the economic and diplomatic race with the North was a source of motivation to the working population in the South. It lent a kind of legitimacy to certain authoritarian practices in the South, both political and in labour relations, since these were styled as a protection against Communism. It allowed the army to remain powerful and to keep elements of the country's political and social life under control. It enabled South Korean bureaucracy to entrench firmly its partly invisible power, and, to some extent, it even allowed protectionism, unfair practices, economic state interventionism and favouritism towards the *chaebol* to flourish.

If the benefits of reunification are unclear, the drawbacks are unavoidable. The dynamic structures that underpinned South Korean growth would cease to function, and new models would have to be found – a high-risk process given the country's present difficulties. The issue of reunification remains a buoyant element of political rhetoric due to its highly emotional impact, but its realization is still tangled in the intricate web of contradictory interests at stake.

New economic relations

North-South trade between the two Koreas is mainly in the form of barter or indirect trade, but it has nonetheless risen from virtually zero in 1988 to US$192 million in 1991, so that South Korea is now North Korea's fourth economic partner after Japan, China and the former Soviet Union. Since 1988, shipments from the North have been regarded as internal trade, i.e. with no import duties. Chinese traders take unfair advantage of this system by falsely labelling their goods as made in North Korea. Of course, the first step towards economic integration (and direct trade) would be to eliminate this kind of fraud (*FEER* 26 March 1992).

Trade with the North is now financed by a North-South cooperation fund which gives compensation for 90–100 per cent of losses arising from deals with the North. Twenty-five billion won were budgeted by the government in 1991, and 40 billion won were expected in 1992 (*FEER* 26 March 1992).

Chaebol leaders have visited North Korea. Chung Ju-Yung, founder of Hyundai and unlucky election candidate, made a private visit in January 1989. However, several agreed development projects came to naught. Daewoo Chairman Kim Woo-Chung was the first *chaebol* leader to be officially invited to North Korea. He agreed to establish eight light industry plants in North Korea (an investment worth US$10–20 million) (*FEER* 20 February 1992). Some observers even considered this as the sign of a bold new strategy to overcome Daewoo's current financial and operational problems, and the weakening and vulnerability of the company's competitive position (*FEER* 20 February 1992). But due to the nuclear issue, Daewoo's plans remain pending (*FEER* 26 March 1992).

When the North Korean Deputy Premier Kim Dal-Hyon visited South Korea last July for an industry tour and a meeting with President Roh, he clearly had a second agenda: 'to persuade South Korean businesses to proceed with investments in the North' (*FEER* 30 July 1992). It has even been said that he intended to convince southern businessmen to lobby Roh's administration for increased economic ties (*FEER* 30 July 1992).

Clearly, South Korean businesses are the driving force for normalization. Almost all suffered a fall in profits, and all are being encouraged to invest by Pyongyang's premier, the so-called 'North Korean Deng Xiaoping' (*FEER* 26 August 1992).

Southern businessmen are expecting three main benefits from economic normalization with North Korea. First is the opening of open new markets. For example, Posco, the world's third largest steel producer, could supply steel-making equipment and know-how to the North. According to an observer, 'North Korea is making . . . cement producers "salivate" ' (*FEER* 26 March 1992) – so much so that the latter are extending their capacity in order to export to the North. One top producer is building special port facilities on the east coast in order to ship cement to the North. Due to substantial excess refining capacity, South Korean petrochemical industries also see North Korea as a potential new market, provided the North can pay. North Korea's natural resources are also of great interest to southern companies, signalling a potential end to their current dependence on non-Korean countries.

Second, South Korean companies are very interested in sources of cheap, well-disciplined labour. Wages in South Korea are about eleven times those in the North. North Korean workers, used to long hours and low wages, are often scornfully referred to as 'slave labour' by southerners (*FEER* 26 March 1992). Obviously, the gap in wages and conditions would close in the event of reunification.

Third, since high wages have already made many southern companies uncompetitive, a move north of the border would save the companies themselves, and the hundreds of millions of dollars of capital equipment invested.

If economic cooperation is conditioned by political prerequisites, it would seem that further advances in political integration would probably adversely affect the former.

Geopolitical aspects of North-South relations

Finally, it should be stressed that North-South relations in Korea are not an exclusively Korean issue. Of course, since the Second World War, the Korean peninsula has had strategic importance in world affairs for the major powers, whose interests (despite the protests of independence from both North and South) nevertheless underpin the stability of the peninsula.

An interesting paradox is that although South Korea seems to have all the advantages, it still behaves 'as a supplicant' in its relations with North Korea (*FEER* 26 March 1992).

Normalization is, of course, the process of establishing normal economic and diplomatic relations between two states. The fact that Seoul has now established various economic and even diplomatic relations with most former eastern Bloc countries obviously pleads all the more in favour of normalization with the North, particularly with the support of China, which has for some years been a moderator between the two.

According to a North Korean diplomat now in Seoul, the North Korean deputy premier's trip to the South last July was 'a matter of geopolitics' in which Japan featured largely. In fact, Seoul has been increasingly fearing Japan's 'competition' in the North (*FEER* 6 August 1992). Pressure from southern businessmen might have led their government to soften its stance on bilateral nuclear inspection.

And North Korea, despite its alleged economic difficulties, has progressed from being politically isolated to being economically courted. Deep-seated Korean resentment at Japan's past colonization and present economic supremacy makes economic rivalry with Japan a matter of national pride, urging Seoul to develop cooperation with Pyongyang. If South Korea were to take second place to Japan as a trading partner with the North, the result would be shame and a loss of face: 'the South will not take kindly to being usurped in what it regards as its backyard' (*FEER* 6 August 1992).

Of course, Kim Il Sung must be given credit for his great political astuteness in playing off South Korea and Japan against each other, just as he did previously with the USSR and China.

Russia is, it seems, a major ally of Seoul on the issue of normalization. Projects such as the planned pipeline running through North Korea, from Russian oil fields in Yakustk to South Korea, are entirely dependent on good relations between all three nations (*FEER* 6 August 1992).

The Tumen River Area Development Plan, including delegations from the two Koreas, Japan, China, Russia and Mongolia, seems a highly ambitious project. It would provide South Korea with the economic hinterland her companies are so eagerly seeking. A popular argument in favour of the project is that, due to historical population displacements, people of Korean origin now inhabit the Tumen area.

Such a project raises numerous diplomatic difficulties, which, according to UNDP consultants are being overcome through engineering solutions (*FEER* 16 January 1992). That such a project be sponsored by the United Nations Development Programme is a major indicator of its geopolitical significance.

According to Japanese observers, however, Japan's involvement has been cautious and discreet because of the project's 'sensitive historical background' and because of the suspicion aroused 'by the heavy involvement of "US proxies" such as the UN, the East West Centre and the Seoul regime' (*FEER* 16 January 1992).

Perspectives for European companies

What role could European companies play in possible economic cooperation, and what threats and opportunities can be identified?

Some degree of cooperation with North Korea has already occurred, especially since the enactment of a joint venture law in 1984. Of course, the Soviets provided assistance for approximately 50 power plants and factories and the pro-North Korean community in Japan has funded about 100 joint ventures. Germany, and to a lesser extent Denmark, Sweden and Switzerland, have helped in building plants (said to be among the best in the country) in various fields: cement, confectionery, electronic components, aluminium and non-ferrous metal (*FEER* 26 March 1992).

In February 1992, the North Korean deputy premier visited Germany with the purpose of 'shopping for infrastructure' and, most notably, discussed the possibility of Siemens building a power plant (*FEER*, 26 March 1992). At the end of 1992, two Nestlé executives visited North Korea in order to evaluate the possibility of setting up a factory – the first putative investment here by a Western food company (*FEER* 17 December 1992).

Economic interests can fashion geopolitics. For instance, in January 1992 Chinese Premier Li Peng urged European countries to provide aid for North Korea. It is increasingly clear that north-east Asian countries are hand in glove with one another. Their joint development requires adequate partnership, and European countries are probably the most suitable partners. The main reason for this (and one which might seem cynical) is that they are less involved geopolitically in Pacific Rim issues than are the US and Japan.

THE DREAM OF AN ECONOMIC HINTERLAND

Some attention will now be paid to changes that have recently occurred in relations between South Korea and continental east Asian countries. Facing increasing international competition and especially fearing 'fortress Europe' and NAFTA, economic cooperation with Russia and China would provide the Korean economy with a potentially more secure, less saturated and more promising base.

The political stakes should not be forgotten: Korea desires revenge against former Communist regimes, and is seeking to achieve a degree of supremacy in the area. Japan certainly harbours the same ambitions; but may not be in a position to fulfil them in view of its past military expansionism, its colonial exactions and its current claim to regional domination. Finally, South Korea would be able to surpass North Korea as a trade partner with China and the former Soviet Union – a kind of victory in itself, and another means of pressurizing the North on normalization, or even reunification, thanks to the South's strong negotiating position.

Economically, South Korea and north-east Asian countries are complementary – the main weaknesses (labour, energy, raw materials) and strengths (capital, technology, management, industry) of the former balancing those of the latter.

Relations with Russia have simplified since the collapse of the Soviet Union, while relations with China have become increasingly complex. China is North Korea's only remaining ally, but it should not be forgotten, that since the 1980s, China has played a moderating role, sometimes applying strong pressure with regard to North Korea. It should also be remembered that in the course of her on-going economic reforms, China is seeking economic partners.

The economic and geopolitical stakes are of the utmost importance since they are related to the rise of a new regional and national economic power among the Pacific Rim countries, independent of both the US and Japan. The current world-wide tendency towards the formation of regional blocs, such as the EC and NAFTA, threatens South Korea's competitive edge, and may weaken its economy. This, and Japan's drive to become the leading economic and political power in north-east Asia, make Korea all the more eager to establish an economic hinterland. Of course, the other Pacific Rim nations are generally on more of a par economically with each other than they are with Japan, and their relations with one another are less tainted with historical resentment, although South Korea does seem to suffer from a degree of selective amnesia with regard to the leading role played by China during the Korean war.

Politically, South Korea has demonstrated a sophisticated ideological flexibility. Until 1988, most South Korean businessmen and scholars usually declared that Communism was an evil to be fought and challenged both politically and economically. One year later, their position had changed significantly: 'business is business, politics is politics' was the new refrain, implying that if diplomatic normalization was now in progress, especially with China, economic cooperation was thus conceivable, i.e. legitimate, although China remains a Communist country.

Relations with Russia

The collapse of the Soviet Union obviously simplified South Korea's relations with Russia. Since Russia is now seeking economic help, it has to show its good will. For instance, during his visit to Seoul in November 1992, Boris Yeltsin unexpectedly offered the two black boxes of the KAL flight 007, shot down by a Soviet missile in 1983, as a sign of 'our new friendship as well as our apology'. Such a gesture of reconciliation was all the more attractive and easy for Yeltsin in that it discredited Gorbachev and denied any kind of legacy from him. Yeltsin handled former South Korean President Roh with considerable sensitivity, in order to serve his economic interests.

Similarly, Yeltsin promised to do everything possible to make Pyongyang accept bilateral nuclear inspection, and pledged to stop supplying arms and MIG29 technology to North Korea. This was another highly valued testimony of good will, although it is clear that he is less likely to be heard and followed by Pyongyang than was the former Communist regime.

Bilateral trade and Korean investment in Russia are expected to increase. Korean companies are interested in new markets as well as in energy sourcing, and most of the leading *chaebols* are excited at the opportunities Russia affords.

Arguably the most interesting prospect is that of redirecting the Russian defence industry to peaceful purposes, as stated in the formal agreement signed on 1 September 1992. This industry was the most advanced and efficient economic sector in the former Soviet Union, accounting for more than one-third of economic output, and employing the country's top scientists and most educated workers (*FEER* 17 September 1992). Economic considerations apart, the symbolic aspects of such an agreement are not to be underestimated.

South Korea's cooperation with Russia is all the more interesting from a geopolitical perspective.Thanks to Japan's strained diplomatic relations with Russia over its claim to the Kurile Islands, South Korea seems well-placed to challenge Japan and to become one of Russia's major economic partners. Such a symbolic victory over Japan would flatter Korean national pride, and be used to motivate South Korea's workforce.

Economic cooperation may nevertheless become overshadowed by Russia's economic and political uncertainties in Russia, her former payment defaults and questionable ability to pay her bills in the future, not to mention the cumbersome Russian bureaucracy, and poor-quality labour, which is not compensated by its cheapness.

Quite how increased cooperation between Russia and Korea would benefit European companies is not clear. Russia could perhaps become a new export base for Korean companies, enabling them to regain their competitive advantage for labour-intensive industries, to decrease their energy dependency thanks to preferential access to Russian energy sources, and to access new markets. Increased cooperation would also help South Korea to implement its new domestic industrial policy, focusing on high-tech products. Korea will thus be increasingly in search of vital high technologies and related foreign investments.

Relations with China

China is seen as Korea's major potential market. It offers various advantages to South Korea: proximity, labour discipline and high productivity, and 'the availability of a large number of ethnic Koreans, mostly in the north-eastern region of China, providing a backup supply of mid-level managerial manpower' (*FEER* 13 August 1992). Because of its sources of raw materials, China could be a major host for investment by Korean companies, and a prime location for transfer plants in labour-intensive industries such as the footwear and garment sectors.

If the economic prospects here seem more interesting and less risky than those with Russia, their realization is nonetheless closely dependent on more complex political issues.

First, the normalization of Sino-Korean relations opened a breach in the unity of the east Asian NICs, and especially with Taiwan, which considered the agreement signed with China in August 1992 as 'betrayal and deceit' (*FEER* 3 September 1992). While the benefits of this move for Korea have yet to materialize, the losses for Taiwan are already being felt, in tourism, air transport and bilateral trade. Second, as described above, the constitution of a new zone of economic integration led by South Korea could counterbalance Japan's ambitions for regional domination. The main actors of such integration are generally thought to be South Korea, because of its economic potential, North Korea, because of its natural resources and strategic position for the establishment of railway links and pipelines from the continent to South Korea, and China, because of its potential market and its labour.

According to local analysts, China, and especially its northern and north-eastern regions, are likely to attract the lion's share of South Korean investment (*FEER* 16 January 1992).

The UN-sponsored effort to develop the Tumen River Basin may provide European companies with several interesting opportunities. An executive of Nestlé recently declared, for example, that the firm was considering the possibility of investing in the Tumen Delta. This last project would depend to a great extent on the opening of Japanese and South Korean markets (*FEER* 17 December 1992).

Private industrialists, especially in the construction, telecommunications and shipping sectors, are also expected to fund the Tumen project, if only for fear of being left out of the action (*FEER* 16 January 1992).

CONCLUSION

Several issues, such as Korea's labour relations, its relations with Japan, or its fervent export policy, have of necessity been left out of this discussion, or been only briefly dealt with.

European companies can learn some lessons from South Korea's internal business and government structures. Several projects involving French cooperation in Korea failed, for example, either because of insufficient back-up, follow-up or support from diplomatic services or, on the contrary, because companies failed to take advantage of diplomatic openings.

This chapter has attempted to illustrate the degree to which political and economic issues are interrelated in Korea, and to demonstrate how even Korea's most domestic issues have some geopolitical implications. The east Asian economic world is highly complex, and complicated by many political factors, often highly charged with emotional, symbolic and historical overtones.

These characteristics should all be taken into account when we consider, for example, the ideological flexibility of South Korea, its propensity to turnabout, or its political sensitivity. Of course, South Korea and China's shared Confucian culture undoubtedly favours increased economic cooperation, as does the existence of Chinese-Korean ethnicity.

Some changes in the region have been hailed as surprising and unpredictable, such as the normalization of bilateral ties with Beijing. These should be viewed in the context of the establishment of a new regional economic prosperity and the creation of stability in east Asia. Even the current acceleration of North-South normalization, though hoped for by many countries, and central to many issues, was difficult to foresee.

As one French ambassador to Seoul has said, the Koreans are facing a new and vital challenge: 'it remains to be seen if their pragmatism will be an asset in their attempt to achieve the cultural change necessary to fulfil their highly ambitious objectives, for which they are seeking European cooperation' (*Les Echos* 22 October 1992).

Any study of South Korea inevitably demands a multidimensional approach, and the capacity to detect even the smallest clues to a potential change, or a complete turnaround, in her political or economic stance.

Bibliography

Chaponnière, J. R. (1988) 'L'Etat Manipule le Marché. Le Cas de la République de Corée', *Cahiers IREP/Développement*, 13: 25–47.

Edelman, M. (1988) *Constructing the Political Spectacle*, Chicago: University of Chicago Press.

Evans, P. (1987) 'Dependency and the State in Recent Korean Development: Some Comparisons with Latin American NICs', in Kim, K. D. (ed.) *Dependency Issues in Korean Development*, Seoul: Seoul National University Press.

Foster-Carter, A. G. (1987) 'Standing up: The Two Korean States and the Dependency Debate – A Bipartisan Approach', in Kim, K.D. (ed.) *Dependency Issues in Korean Development*, Seoul: Seoul National University Press.

Han, S. J. (1987) 'Bureaucratic Authoritarianism and Economic Development in Korea during the Yushin Period: A reexamination', in Kim, K. D. (ed.) *Dependency Issues in Korean Development*, Seoul: Seoul National University Press.

Jones, L. P. and Sakong, I. (1980) *Government, Business and Entrepreneuship in Economic Development: the Korean Case*, Cambridge, Mass.: Harvard University Press.

Judet, P. (1988) 'Rôle de l'Etat dans le Développement Economique en Asie: Approches', *Cahiers IREP/Développement*, 13: 1–10.

Kim, B. W. and Bell, D. S. Jr (1985) 'Bureaucratic Elitism and Democratic Development in Korea?', in Kim, B. W., Bell, D. S. Jr and Lee, C. B. (eds) *Administrative Dynamics and Development: The Korean Experience*, Seoul: Kyobo.

Kim, K. D.(1985) *Man and Society in Korea's Economic Growth*, Seoul: Seoul National University Press.

Lee, C. H. (1992) 'The Government, Financial System, and Large Private Enterprises in the Economic Development of South Korea', *World Development* 20, 2: 187–97.

Lim, H. C. and Yang, J. (1987) 'The State, Local Capitalists, and Multinationals: The Changing Nature of a Triple Alliance in Korea', in Kim, K. D. (ed.) *Dependency Issues in Korean Development*, Seoul: Seoul National University Press.

Steers, R. M., Shin, Y. K. and Ungson, G. R. (1989) *The Chaebol*, New York: Harper Collins.

Vandermeersch, L. (1986) *Le nouveau monde sinisé*, Paris: PUF.

5 Korea and north-east Asian economic cooperation

The Tumen River 'golden delta' project

Jin Park

THE TUMEN RIVER AREA: ASIA'S NEW ECONOMIC FRONTIER

The end of the Cold War in Europe and the collapse of the Soviet Union in the 1990s have generated a significant momentum for change towards the reduction of tension and the forging of new economic partnerships in Pacific north-east Asia. In the Korean peninsula alone, the process of detente is clearly becoming increasingly entrenched. Post-Communist Russia has become a major diplomatic partner of South Korea and is now aiming to expand mutual cooperation in business and even military technology.[1] China has already become an important trading partner for South Korea and is expected to enter into official diplomacy with the latter shortly. Japan, meanwhile, has been negotiating with North Korea since January 1992 on rapprochement and possible economic cooperation, thus moving explicitly towards 'cross-recognition'. Finally, the two Koreas themselves have entered the UN separately to become full members of the international community, and have made an agreement on reconciliation and non-aggression as a means of building mutual confidence and ensuring peaceful coexistence in that divided country. Although the reunification of Korea may not necessarily transpire in the short term (despite the impact of German reunion), the country has certainly stepped boldly into the newly unfolding post-Cold War arena of north-east Asia.

In a wider perspective, the trends of vigorous economic integration in north-east Asia – against the background of the demise of the Cold War in Europe and the collapse of the 'Iron Curtain' in the former Soviet Union – indicate that the ideological, geographical and psychological barriers existing between Europe and the Asia-Pacific region will be progressively weakened or removed. Conse-

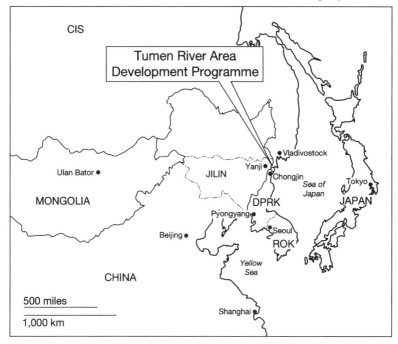

Figure 5.1 The location of the TRADP
Source: Financial Times 8 July 1992

quently the economic links between the European Community and north-east Asia, including China, Russia, Japan, the two Koreas, Taiwan and landlocked Mongolia, will be strengthened through increasing dependence on quicker land transportation crossing the Eurasian continent, and more efficient modern telecommunications (Figure 5.1). The new economic frontier in north-east Asia currently being seriously considered in the context of these expanding Euro-Asian economic links is the Tumen River delta area located at the meeting-point of the Russian, Chinese and North Korean borders and facing the 'Sea of Japan' or East Sea.

In north-east Asia, the reasons for the growing interest in the development of the strategic Tumen River delta area seem evident. (Figure 5.2). Of the three adjacent countries, Russia wants to estab-lish solid links between its Far East maritime region and the dynamic Asia-Pacific economy (particularly South Korea and Japan), for capi-tal and technology transfer, which may require an industrial forward base with ice-free ports to the south of Vladivostok and Nakhodka. The Tumen River area is a logical choice for that purpose. In its

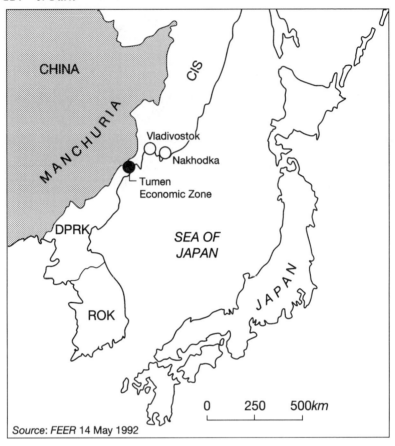

CHINA

CIS

MANCHURIA

Vladivostok

Nakhodka

Tumen
Economic Zone

DPRK

SEA OF
JAPAN

JAPAN

ROK

0   250   500*km*

Source: *FEER* 14 May 1992

Figure 5.2 The Tumen zone

turn China strongly feels the need to harness the economic potential
of its Manchurian hinterland in the north-east, especially Jilin and
Heilongjiang provinces, to add vitality to its economic reform policy.
The Tumen River provides the most convenient natural outlet to
the Sea of Japan for China. As for North Korea, the search for a
way out of its diplomatic isolation and economic crisis in terms of
food, energy and hard currency shortages dictates the creation
of new economic opportunities to induce foreign capital investment
which would provide both hard currencies and effective stimulation
to the country's stagnant economy. For this purpose, the region of
northern Hamkyong province, relatively contained and sharing the

border with China and, partly, Russia along the 516-km Tumen River flow, is perhaps the ideal choice as seen for North Korea.

In terms of natural resources, the Tumen River delta area offers the cheap and abundant water and land necessary for the building of a large-scale industrial infrastructure. The area is at present mostly marshland and rice fields, but it could easily benefit from the surrounding forestry and mineral resources, including a gold mine and coal reserves near the Hunchun area in Jilin province to the northwest, and other key minerals such as ferrous metals, lead, zinc and tungsten in the maritime region of Primorsky in Russia to the northeast (see, *Beijing Review*, 20–6 April 1992: p 6; and *Sisa Journal*, 16 January 1992: p 35). As for railroad transportation, three lines currently reach the Tumen estuary: one coming from the north-east through Kabarovsk in Russia, another other coming from the northwest through Harbin in China, and finally one coming from the south-west through Chongjin in North Korea. The rail infrastructure is therefore relatively favourable, although the existing lines need to be repaired and expanded and new lines need to be built to cover the whole area effectively. If the sea transportation route connecting with the south-east, for example Niigata in Japan, is added to the picture, then the Tumen River delta area can indeed be seen to lie at the geo-economic centre of the new Russian, Chinese, Korean and Japanese industrial network currently developing in north-east Asia around the Sea of Japan. The Tumen delta area, as a potential entrepôt of the so-called 'Sea of Japan Economic circle' to the east of Korean peninsula, and including north-east China and maritime Russia, could be expected to complement or even outweigh the importance of the existing 'Yellow Sea Economic Circle' to the west of Korea and facing the coastal provinces of eastern China.

THE TUMEN RIVER DELTA PROJECT: AN EMERGING CONCEPT

Based on this potential convergence of interests by the three border-sharing countries in north-east Asia, the first serious international discussion of the development of the Tumen River basin was held in the Chinese city of Changchun in Jilin province in July 1990. Supported by the East-West Centre in Hawaii and the State Science and Technology Commission, the conference highlighted the need for joint development and usage of the 'golden delta' of the Tumen estuary through the creation of special economic zones. For this, the

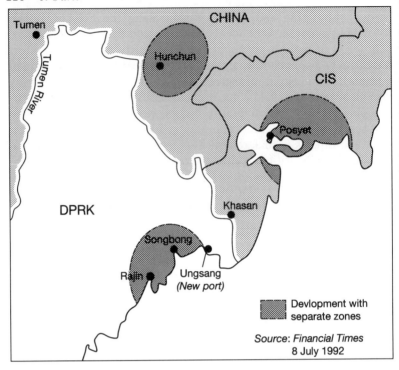

Figure 5.3 The site of Hunchun

Chinese side specifically called for the construction of a port in the city of Hunchun located about 15 km north of the trilateral border junction, which is about the same distance from the river's sea entrance (Figure 5.3) The idea was to use the new port facilities to be built in Hunchun (or alternatively in Fangchuan located further downstream) as the 'front gate' for the industrial development of its provincial hinterland, which would in turn be helped by China's revived access to the Sea of Japan.[2] The Chinese participants also called for financial assistance by Japan and South Korea (Valencia 1991: 265).

The seminal discussions at the first Changchun Forum for North-east Asian Economic Development were developed further at the Ulan Bator conference in July 1991 which was organized by the United Nations Development Program (UNDP) with participation from the four governments of China, Mongolia and the two Koreas, all of them UNDP aid-recipient countries. As the priority agenda of UNDP's north-east Asia sub-regional programme, the proposed

Tumen River Area Development Programme (TRADP) was examined by the four countries in an attempt to assess each other's
basic position regarding the idea.[3] There was, however, a delicate
difference of approach between China and North Korea. While
China, and to some extent Mongolia, advocated the idea of developing major port facilities in Hunchun as the eastern terminus of a
10,000-km Euro-east Asian land bridge, North Korea showed more
interest in developing its own north-eastern ports close to the Tumen
River area such as Chongjin, the capital city of northern Hamkyong
province, and, even closer, Rajin and Sonbong. The South Korean
position was relatively neutral, given its growing economic links
with China and sensitive political relations with North Korea. Also
in the meeting, the UNDP was asked to contact the governments
of Japan and the Russian Federation so that they could participate
in the process as observers, thus establishing the framework of 'four
plus two'.

The overall direction of the Tumen development was again discussed in the second Changchun forum in August 1991, which
decided to launch the new annual 'North-east Asian Economic
Forum' (NAEF) with its first meeting in Vladivostok in August 1992.
But it was at the second UNDP-supported conference in Pyongyang
in October 1992, held immediately after the entry of the two Koreas
to the UN, that a more concrete plan for the Tumen project was
produced. Agreeing on a strategy of cooperation, the four participating countries adopted an 'Action Plan' that envisaged an initial
investment phase of 18 months, beginning in January 1992, to undertake feasibility studies of the TRADP.[4] More importantly, the Pyongyang conference made a decision to set up a Programme
Management Committee (PMC) for coordination, together with
three supporting working groups in the areas of legal affairs, economic feasibility and physical planning.

At the Pyongyang meeting, North Korea (where the UNDP has
been operating since 1979) displayed serious interest in the proposed
Tumen River development project, arguing for the 'early realization'
of the grandiose scheme.[5] One of the reasons was perhaps the slow
progress of the Japan-North Korea rapprochement talks, caused by
North Korea's suspected nuclear project in Yongbyon, with the
resulting difficulty of securing substantial investment from Japan in
the short term. The cash-strapped Kim Il-Sung regime may have
thought that the UN-initiated project near its northern border region
would attract the Japanese business community or even the United
States (Kobayashi 1992: 27). But, more fundamentally, the dilemma

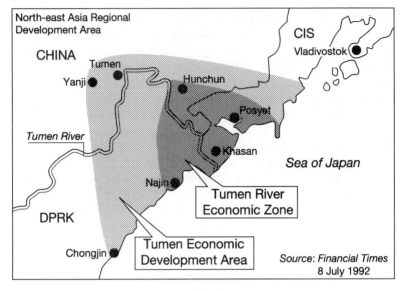

Figure 5.4 The three categories of the TRADP

of *'juche'*, or self-reliance ideology, in the face of the worsening energy and food situation, and the increasing shortage of hard currency to pay for Russian oil imports and other strategic goods, made North Korea finally agree to endorse a limited 'door-opening' for foreign capital inducement. The best example of this cautious economic pragmatism developing in North Korea was the designation of Chongjin as a 'free trade port' in December 1991, two months after Kim Il-Sung's visit to China, and the Rajin-Sonbong area as a 'free economy and trade zone'.[6] With preferential tax and investment laws, the Rajin-Sonbong area – 621 sq. km on the country's northernmost coastline – therefore marked the first special economic zone (SEZ) in North Korea, apparently based on the Chinese model, thus implying a partial deviation from the revolutionary line of the autarchic economy.

Reflecting such visible North Korean enthusiasm, the Seoul conference on the Tumen delta project organized by the UNDP in February 1993 adopted a more refined planning strategy. In particular, the first PMC meeting and the working group sessions dealt with not only the technical issues related to the feasibility of the TRADP but also the crucial issue of the financing of the plan as a whole. First of all, the target areas of the TRADP were divided into three categories. (Figure 5.4) The core area within the small triangle

Table 5.1 Tumen outlays (US$ billion)

Ports and terminals	4
Inland port	1
Airport	2
Railroads	2
Roads	2
Community development	8
Power plants	2
Telecoms	1
Potable water	1
Waste disposal	1
Education	1
Contingencies	5
Total	30

Sources: UNDP estimates and *FEER* 16 January 1992

of 1,000 sq. km linking Rajin, Hunchun, and Posyet was named the Tumen River Economic Zone (TREZ), while the larger outer triangle of 10,000 sq. km linking Chongjin, Yanji and Vladivostok was defined as the Tumen Economic Development Area (TEDA). Finally, the surrounding economic sphere beyond the larger triangle, in the hinterland of the three bordering countries, was called the North-East Asia Regional Development Area (NEARDA). Through this differentiated development approach, the planners aimed to accommodate the diversified interests of the participating countries while providing the basic perimeters of the multinational project.

With regard to the financing of the project, the UNDP's estimates of US$30 billion to be spent over the next 15–20 years for the construction of industrial infrastructure and community development was largely accepted (Table 5.1). But on the question of how to raise the necessary funds, concrete answers were reserved. The reason can be found first in the sheer magnitude of the amount required, and second in the uncertainty of the reactions of the prospective sponsors (Table 5.2). Among the six countries involved, only Japan and South Korea possess relative strength in capital and technology, compared to labour and raw materials which can be provided by China, North Korea, and partly by Mongolia and Russia. Despite such complementarity, the South Korean economy is not yet so strong as to underwrite the major cost of the project, and Japan is reluctant to take the burden alone for both economic and political reasons. Russia, and especially North Korea, do not enjoy high credit ratings in the investment markets, and Japan's

Table 5.2 Economic complementarities

	Capital	Tech-nology	Mana-gement	Labour	Energy	Raw mater-ials	Agri-culture	Live-stock	Indus-try
China (north-east)	•	•	•	★	★	★	★	–	–
Japan	★	★	★	•	•	•	•	•	★
North Korea	•	•	–	★	–	★	•	•	–
South Korea	★	★	★	•	•	•	–	–	★
Mongolia	•	•	–	–	–	★	•	★	–
Russia (Far East)	•	–	•	•	★	★	•	–	•

★ Strengths
• Weaknesses
– Not applicable
Sources: Geographical Institute, Northeast Normal University, Changchun and *FEER* 16 January 1992

pending problems with both countries, i.e. the Northern Territories dispute and the nuclear inspection issue, severely constrain the economic partnership. Considering these predicaments, the Seoul conference confirmed a multilateral approach for fund-raising open to outside countries, such as the United States, and international organizations for financial participation. Most notably, the Asian Development Bank (ADB) was represented as an observer in the Seoul meeting and the World Bank is soon to be invited for participation.

PERCEIVED BENEFITS AND POTENTIAL PROBLEMS

There seems to be no question that the proposed Tumen River delta project will, if successfully implemented, bring substantial economic benefits to the countries involved, and also facilitate the economic partnership between east Asia and Europe. This ambitious multi-national venture is already being described as having the capacity to establish a second Hong Kong or Rotterdam in north-east Asia (Kaye 1992b: 16). Given the steady growth of both intra-Pacific and Euro-Asian trade volumes, such optimism may not necessarily be regarded as overly unrealistic.

Of the six countries involved or interested, North Korea is most notably enthusiastic about the project. As Kim Sang-Gi, the North Korean chief representative at the Changchun conference, has mentioned, the proposed joint development and usage of the Tumen River delta, and the building of cross-Korean railways, will undoubtedly add importance to the North Korean border region in terms of stimulating north-east Asian economic integration and facilitating access to resource-rich Siberia (Kobayashi 1992). For this reason, the North Korean leadership has been showing interest in the cautious replication of special economic zones on the pattern of southern China, particularly the Shenzen SEZ in Guangdong province across the northern border of Hong Kong's New Territories. The Shenzen area, which is depicted as the 'socialist Hong Kong' (and which hosted a visit by Kim Il-Sung for the first time in October 1991), has made impressive strides under Deng Xiaoping's reformist economic policy during the past decade, with average annual export growth of 75 per cent, and annual GDP growth of 50 per cent, thus reaching roughly 9 per cent (i.e. US$3.16 billion) of Hong Kong's 1991 GDP (Cheng and Mosher 1992: 24). Encouraged by this performance, and apparently expecting quick returns on investment, the North Korean government decided to introduce a similar version of the SEZ in the Rajin-Sonbong area with trade privileges including the full retention of foreign exchange earnings and other advantages in the specified zone. According to Kim Jong Woo of North Korea's Ministry of External Economic Affairs, and Chairman of the External Economic Cooperation Promotion Committee (which has been closely dealing with the Tumen River delta project), the designated 'free economy and trade zone' in the ports of Rajin and Sonbong will hopefully attract both heavy industry such as shipbuilding, and light industry such as garment manufacturing based on the relatively cheap rates for the use of ports and factory sites, as well as lower tax rates for the corporate incomes and profit remittances (Kobayashi 1992).

This new foreign-capital-dependent approach, although limited to a specific case and locality, is in direct contradiction to the obsessively autarchic and xenophobic approach based on the centralist Stalinist economy which the North Korean leadership has repeatedly claimed works so efficiently for the welfare of its people. This incongruence reflects the essential dilemma of the Kim Il-Sung regime, which now has to face the unexpected end results of its revolutionary political economic strategy – most notably international isolation and economic stagnation. In this context, Kin Tal-Hyon, North Korea's vice-premier in charge of external economic affairs (including the Tumen River development project), was surprisingly unreserved when he indicated to the foreign delegations visiting Pyongyang and the three 'free trade' ports in the north-east in late April and early May 1992 that the 'loss' of the socialist markets and the difficulty of oil imports in the aftermath of the collapse of eastern European and Soviet Communism created an 'economic predicament' for North Korea. One of the solutions he proposed was to seek a new economic partnership with the West (Kang 1992: 88–9). Although the vice-premier went on to argue that it was a 'wise and realistic reponse, to the challenge of changing external circumstances', it was clear that North Korea was trying to send a different signal to the outside world in order to attract foreign capital.

On the occasion of the Pyongyang international conference in May,[7] Kim Tal-Hyon also revealed that a total of US$4.2 billion would be needed to create an infrastructural base for the development of the Rajin-Sonbong 'free economy and trade zone'. He also proposed that if the Rajin-Sonbong experience proved successful, then the North Korean government would be willing to open another special zone for tourism in the coastal areas of Nampo and Wonsan (Ike 1992). Given North Korea's estimated US$ 6 billion foreign debts, including those owed to eastern Europe and the former Soviet Union, it is difficult to see how Pyongyang could finance the expensive Rajin-Sonbong project without appealing to international lending authorities, foreign governments or private investors. This is perhaps the reason why North Korea has disclosed its intention to join the Asian Development Bank while urging Japan for an early rapprochement and inviting leading South Korean businessmen (as well as the Reverend Sun-Myung Moon, the leader of the Unification Church, with various business affiliates), to Pyongyang to discuss potential investment proposals. For the financially defaulted Kim Il-Sung regime, which is burdened by the leadership succession problem, the best option for the time being will be to offer the potential benefits of the proposed special economic zone as the strategic 'window of limited experimental reform and foreign capital inducement while at the same time maintaining a tight control of North Korean society lest possible undesirable capitalist influences' should penetrate it.

As for South Korea, the perceived benefits of joining in the multinational development of the Tumen River basin are both economic and political. On the one hand, the establishment of a major industrial foothold in the new geo-economic centre of north-east Asia means the upgrading of the country's position in the important 'northern markets' of Russia and China, not to mention North Korea, in terms of manufacturing and exports. The European market will also come within easier reach if the land route is used through Russia; this would also greatly facilitate access to the natural resources of north-east China and Siberia. On the other hand, the expansion of pragmatic economic ties with less-developed North Korea could increase the latter's dependence on the dynamic South Korean capitalist economy whose GNP (US$240 billion as of 1990) is now at least ten times larger than that of the North.[8] Consequently, South Korea might be able to exercise its political influence based on increased economic leverage to encourage the closed and regimented society of North Korea to move more visibly towards liberal domestic reforms, and to reduced hostility *vis à vis* the South. According to the mainstream South Korean view, this will certainly help to create a situation of peaceful coexistence between the two Koreas with growing dominance of the South eventually achieving the non-violent 'absorption' of North Korea.[9] In other words, the South Korean government seems poised to apply an economic solution to its political problems with the North by pushing the latter gently towards becoming a 'silent dependent' on the thriving southern economy, as was the case with the two Germanies before their dramatic reunification.

Because of these implications of the unification policy, as well as its perceived economic benefits, South Korea's approach to the proposed Tumen River project has been basically positive, if not as urgent as that of North Korea. Kim In-Ho, the former assistant minister of the Economic Planning Board (EPB), who led the South Korean delegation to the UNDP-sponsored Pyongyang conference in October 1991, confirmed that South Korea would be willing and eager to help the North for both economic and political reasons (Clifford *et al.* 1992: 18–19). This positive attitude towards economic cooperation with North Korea was echoed again this year when the 18-member South Korean delegation visited Pyongyang and the three 'free trade' ports. For example, Yoo Jang-Hee, the leader of the delegation and the president of the Korean Institute for International Economic Policy (KIEP), emphasized the need to create a new multinational 'centre' for information exchange and technological cooperation for the Tumen project, and favoured the expansion of existing port facilities in Chongjin, Rajin and Sonbong instead of opening a new one in China (Kang 1992: 89). In a similar vein, Kim Duk-Choong, another member of the delegation and an economics professor at Sogang University in South Korea, stressed the economic complementarity of the two Koreas by pointing out that the small and medium-sized companies of South Korea could effectively benefit from the cheap labour costs and the quality of the workforce of the North, thereby contributing to the promotion of the light industry and exports capability of the latter (Kang 1992).

South Korea's perception of the merits of joining the Tumen delta project has also been favourably influenced by the prospects of national economic reunion with the sizeable Korean community in China's north-eastern region, particularly the Yanbian Autonomous Prefecture across the North Korean border. Yanbian, or 'Yobyon' in Korean, covers the eastern sector of Jilin Province including the cities of Yanji (the capital of Yanbian), Tumen, Longjing, Dunhua and Hunchun. In terms of population, the ethnic Koreans, called 'chaoxianzu' in Chinese, almost one million and largely concentrated along the Tumen River area, account for more than two-fifths of the population of the whole prefecture and about three-fifths in the above cities.[10] The Autonomous Prefecture, or 'zizhizhou', with an area of 42,700 sq. km (roughly the size of Denmark or nearly half – i.e. about 43 per cent – of the size of South Korea), has been the political, educational and cultural centre of the Korean minority in China since 1952 when autonomous status was given to the region. The area has not only key natural resources, such as coal, oil, minerals and forestry, but also an educated industrial labour force which is attractive to foreign investors.[11] For South Korean and Japanese companies, which are being pressed by rising inflation and industrial wages, the cheap labour costs of US$150–200 per month for a worker in the region offer great advantages. The prefecture also has a mixture of various light and heavy industries including machine manufacturing, petrochemical engineering, metallurgy, paper and textile production, pharmaceutical technology, and basic audio-visual electronics.

What is more important, however, from the unification-oriented viewpoint of South Korea, is the fact that Korean nationalism and a sense of identity remain strong in the Yanbian chaoxianzu community, which still retains traditional Korean customs and culture.[12] Among the 55 minority nationalities or shaoshu minzu of China, the ethnic Koreans, who form the eleventh largest national group, have indeed developed an exemplary model for minority self-rule in Yanbian. But the relationship between the Han Chinese and the ethnic Koreans, and for that matter between the central and provincial governments in Beijing and Changchun and the local government in Yanbian, still poses sensitive political, cultural and emotional issues in the Korean comunity, which has long been subject to the fluctuating domestic politics of China.[13] So far the idea of an ancestral 'fatherland' for the Yanbian Koreans educated under Chinese socialism has been linked to North Korea for both ideological and geographical reasons (Chae-Jin 1986: 2–12 and 99–110). After the Seoul Olympics in 1988 and the rapid improvement of Chinese-South Korean relations in the early 1990s, however, the pro-Pyongyang sentiment in Yanbian has been gradually weakened by a growing interest in South Korea as the second largest capitalist economic power-house in north-east Asia after Japan. As a result of the economic reform policy, the need for capital, management, and technology is relatively high in Yanbian. The Tumen River project therefore provides an excellent opportunity for South Korea to expand its economic, cultural and political influence in Yanbian, thereby achieving a partial *de facto* national reunion outside the divided Korea as the first stage of the reunification. Elements of nostalgia and nationalism certainly underlie the South Korean image of the 'blue water of the Tumen River' or the 'national spirit of Mt Paiktu', the main part of the Changbaishan mountain chain touching the borders of Yanbian, North Korea and Jilin Province. South Korea's nationalistic perception of the Tumen project also stems from the fact that the Yanbian territory was the site of the old Korean kingdom of 'Haedong Songkuk' or Palhae.

At present the leading South Korean companies such as Daewoo, Samsung, Goldstar, Hyundai and Ssangyong are undertaking individual feasibility studies for investment in the area. Kim Woo-Choong, the Chairman of the Daewoo group, who has recently concluded a major Siberian and cross-Korean gas pipeline construction projcct[14] with Russia and North Korea, had already visited Yabian in the mid-1980s to explore business opportunities. Samsung has made a US$20–million investment for the manufacture of colour television sets in Yanbian, and Goldstar is expected to set up its factories soon. With the opening of the three 'free trade' ports in North Korea, the Yanbian area now has potentially closer links with South Korean and Japanese markets, in terms of securing the supply of parts and exporting the finished products. In this context, the two Koreas and Yanbian are moving in the direction of creating a 'greater Korean economic Community' in north-east Asia.

By contrast, Japan, like Russia, has so far stayed behind the front line of the Tumen River project as an 'observer'. But there is no doubt that Japan's financial and technological contribution is crucial for the pursuit of the project, given Japan's dominant influence in the ADB, and that both the Japanese government and the business community share a perceived long-term interest in the project. In

Japan, the Tumen River delta project is conceived as a vital aspect of the evolution of the 'Sea of Japan Economic Circle' or Nihonkai Keizaiken, comprising Japan, the two Koreas, China and Russia.[15] According to Touma Takeo, the coordinating director of the Economic Research Institute for the Japan Sea Rim, which is based in Niigata, the key reasons for Japan's interest in the realization of the project are first, the need to restore a balance between the less-developed '*lira Nihon*' or inner Japan facing the Asian continent and the '*tomote Nihon*' or outer Japan facing the Pacific Ocean, and second, the need to 'return to Asia' for the sake of Asian solidarity and prosperity after more than a century of post-Meiji Japan's conscious 'escape from Asia' (Touma 1991).

More practically, Japan's interest in the Tumen River project is clearly focused on its perceived economic benefits. The industrialization of the Tumen delta area implies that Japan can integrate itself more closely with the continental Asian economy and also reach out for the Siberian natural resources and the European market more easily (Figure 5.5). As for the first aspect of northeast Asian economic integration, the basic idea is to conceive a circular 'bullet route' around the Japan Sea Rim linking the cities of Sapporo, Niigata and Fukuoka along the coastal area of inner Japan, and Pusan, Seoul, Chongjin, Changchun, Sanjiang Plain in Heilongjiang Province, maritime Russia, and Sakhalin on the Asian continent. The Tumen River industrial complex, when completed, is expected to provide a convenient central gateway to the continental economy for Japan. For one thing, the distance of direct maritime transportation between Niigata and Hunchun is less than 850 km, whereas the current indirect route via Dalian port in Liaoning Province towards the Yellow Sea by rail and sea is about 2,000 km (Figure 5.6). As for the second factor, namely access to Siberia and Europe, the advantages for Japan are unmistakeable. At present, maritime transportation between Niigata and Hamburg through the Singapore straits and the Suez Canal takes a full month. But a sea and land route through the Tumen River area and via the trans-Siberian railway would shorten the journey to less than two weeks. The idea of using the Eurasian land bridge to reach the European market seems to have become a more realistic possibility from the Japanese viewpoint (Watanabe 1992).

Japan's perception of such wider economic benefits, based on the country's new active international strategy, was aptly summarized by Kanamori Hisao, the Chairman of the Japan Economic Research Centre, in his speech for the Pyongyang international conference on

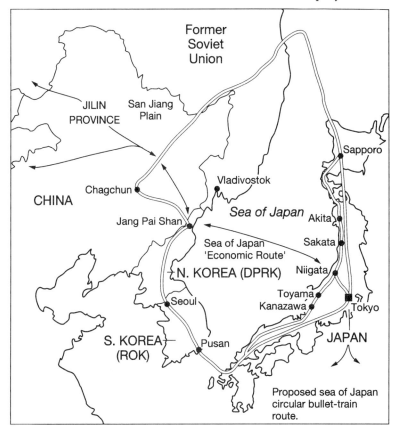

Source: Nikkaiken Document

Figure 5.5 How the Tumen River project will benefit Japan

the Tumen River project in early May (Kanamori 1992a: 14–15). While pointing out the long-term economic benefits of the project, he emphasized Japan's growth as a 'globally-oriented country' as one of the main reasons for the increasing attention given to the importance of the 'Sea of Japan Economic Circle'. Kanamori, however, also indicated potential problems such as the uncertain political relations between Japan, Russia and North Korea, the lack of a 'grand design' for the project, the conflict of interests between China and North Korea, an inadequate infrastructure, and insufficient economic information on the region (Kanamori 1992:15). The Japanese side therefore seems to be taking a pragmatic and incremental approach to the project at present, favouring the option of develop-

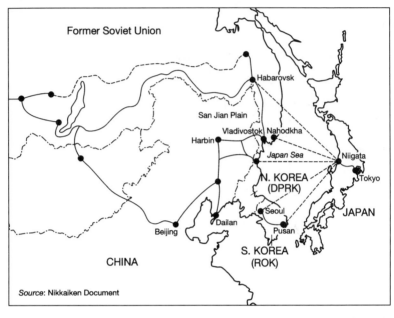

Figure 5.6 The Tumen River as Japan's central gateway to the continental economy

ing the existing Choncgjin and Rajin ports in North Korea which were built by Japan during the colonial period of the 1930s (Kanamori 1992b: 15). In fact Japan sent a specialist team to carry out a preliminary survey of the three North Korean ports in March this year, and confirmed the advantages of such an option, particularly noting the future potential of the port at Rajin within the TREZ.[16]

Compared to Japan, the Chinese government has shown more active interest in its approach to the Tumen River project. China has already set up its own Asia Pacific Institute (API) for the Tumen delta development, ahead of any other countries involved, and the Jilin provincial government, at its API branch and the State Science and Technology Commission, have launched a feasibility study on the comprehensive development of the Yanbian prefecture and the Tumen River area (*Nihonkai Newsletter* 71: 7–9). The Chinese position is focused on the securing of guaranteed access to the Sea of Japan through the Tumen River. To secure this access, China has been arguing for the need to create a port in Fanqchuan, China's easternmost point along the Tumen River. The UNDP, however, is reluctant to support the idea because of the financial implications of the massive dredging required. Instead the UNDP consultant, Aage Holm, has proposed building an 'inland port' at Hunchun for the trans-shipping of rail and track cargo moving to and from the Russian and North Korean harbours in the region (Clifford 1992: 18). This broader regional approach adopted by the UNDP for its shared benefits does not necessarily satisfy the Chinese strategic interest, oriented towards the sea. In order to strengthen its own position, China has recently designated Hunchun as a new SEZ similar to the five others on the country's southern coast. Unlike North Korea, which prefers the individual approach, China is relatively in favour of the idea of joint supranational management within the TREZ area. But the relationship between the new Hunchun SEZ and the TREZ has yet to be clarified (Kaye 1992c: 32). Domestically, the potential conflict of interests between the central government in Beijing and the local authorities in Jilin and Yanbian, over the determining of economic priorities, will continue.

Russia, on the other hand, is more interested in further developing the Vladivostok area into a thriving 'free economic zone', rather than tackling the TREZ or TEDA as a whole.[17] This reserved attitude towards the collective long-term Tumen project is explained by the practical need of Russia to develop its Far Eastern maritime area as quickly as possible, for more economic integration with the neighbouring capitalist countries, and also Russia's underlying concern about the possibility of losing its existing advantage as the potential location for major industrial port facilities to North Korea or China.

The fact that both Vladivostok and Nakhodka ports are frozen for several months during the winter season seems to undermine the Russian position and to favour the option of developing the North Korean ports. Russia therefore seems willing to forge ahead regardless of the Tumen River project, and to establish a solid position in the region whatever the outcome of the current multilateral discussions. There is another Russian concern involved. As Arcady Alekseev, Chief Deputy Director of the Pacific Oceanology Institute in Vladivostok, has pointed out, the Russian side has repeatedly emphasized its concern about the possible disruption of the regional ecological balance that might result from large construction works needed for the Tumen project (*Nihonkai Newsletter* 71: 11–12). Khasan, which is the closest Russian city to the Tumen River estuary, located in the 'small delta' of TREZ, is particularly opposed to the idea of dredging the river basin because of its negative effect on ecology and tourism. Also, the major cities of Vladivostok and

Nakhodka, respectively within and close to the 'larger delta' of TEDA, apparently cannot agree on how to deal with the Tumen project (Kazuhiko 1992: 30).

The 'North-east Asian Economic Forum' conference, hosted by the Russian maritime regional authorities in Vladivostok in late August 1992, looked set to provide an important and timely occasion for discussing the potential links between the Russian regional development initiative and the progress of the Tumen River project.

Finally, the landlocked country of Mongolia, which is undergoing conversion from a Stalinist economy to a free market system, perceives the clear advantage of linking itself to the dynamic Japanese and South Korean economies through the Tumen River outlet to the sea. The basic aim of Mongolia is to play the role of an important transport corridor for the growing Euro-Asian links rather than continuing to rely on the port of Dalian for the Yellow Sea route. As the country with a territory eleven times greater than that of the whole of Korea, but with a population of only two million, which is less than one-fifth that of Seoul, Mongolia strongly needs an injection of capital and technology from the advanced Asian economies as well as from Western capitalist countries. Seen in this context, the Tumen delta project provides a timely opportunity for Mongolia to strengthen its efforts to return to Asia, based on the country's restored veneration for the legacy of Ghenghis Khan.

PROSPECTS FOR THE FUTURE

Despite the divergence of interest among the countries involved and the uncertainty of the financial support to be given to the project, the momentum for the Tumen River delta development as the central focus of new economic integration in north-east Asia has been clearly set in motion. Potentially it is a key 'peace dividend' in a region where the post-Cold War order, now beginning to be felt in Europe, has yet to have its impact. The two Koreas still have to develop a mutual confidence in peaceful coexistence before reunification. The political, as well as the economic, situation in the three countries sharing the border along the Tumen River estuary is not stable. But the economic 'miracle' of a new metropolis of half a million people in the remote area of the Tumen delta, ready for the challenges of the twenty-first century, can be materialized if the participating countries and related international organizations can agree to find a better framework for adjusting their interests in the major shared benefits.

   Currently three scenarios for implementation of the project can be envisaged.[18] The first one is to 'do it together' by building a centrally planned, multinational industrial complex in the larger delta area along the lines of the TEDA. This broadly collective approach would seem to be the best possible option, but in practice national interests will easily prevail, at least during the initial stage. The second option is to 'keep it small' by concentrating the development in the specified core area, possibly within the TREZ. This narrow approach is more realistic than the first one and would be more efficient, but still the coordination of conflicting national interests will pose potential problems. The third option is to 'go it alone', and to develop the delta region according to the individual demands and decisions of the countries involved. China's focus on Hunchun and Fangchuan, in order to secure access to the sea; North Korea's focus on Chongjin, Rajin and Sonbong, in order to attract foreign capital; and Russia's focus on Vladivostok and Nakhodka, in order to maintain its advantage, are clear examples. This individual approach is perhaps the most probable course of action during the next two or three years pending the agreement on the general blueprint of the project. But gradually, a limited collective approach will have to emerge due to financial and technological reasons, and will develop concurrently with the individual approach.
   The hybrid multitargeted individual and collective approach to the Tumen delta project will therefore set the pace of the discussions during the pre-investment stage until a more concrete and realistic blueprint of the project begins to surface. The countries involved will need to compare and evaluate their various options and scenarios need to compare and evaluate their various options and scenarios carefully so that they can reach a workable consensus. At the moment, as Mr Jacob Gujit, resident representative of the UNDP office in Seoul, points out, the 'national teams' have become the main actors, while the UNDP is playing more of a supporting role.[19] Once the 'political decision' of the countries involved is achieved, however (and this could come about as early as July 1993 if things progress as scheduled), it will become necessary to provide central institutional support for the administration and management of the project, along with the efforts of the national teams, to minimize the multilateral conflict of political, economic and legal interests, not to mention the differences of language. The UNDP's idea – creating a central multinational administrative entity such as the Tumen River Area Management Company (TRAMCO) for efficient financing of the project, coordination of national interests, regulation

of the currency regime, and the making of legal adjustments – will certainly be relevant for that purpose. In this sense, the Tumen River delta project serves as a touchstone for the widening and deepening of north-east Asian economic cooperation in the future. It also signals the dawning of a real post-Cold War era in north-east Asia.

Notes

1 In his meeting with South Korean Foreign Minister Lee Sang-Ock on 30 June 1992 in Moscow, the Russian President Boris Yeltsin declared an end to 'ideological bonds' between Russia and North Korea, and expressed hope for active business investment in South Korean companies. The two countries were scheduled to sign the 'Treaty of Basic Relations' in September 1992, when Yeltsin visited Seoul (*The Korea Times* 1992).
2 China's navigation rights to the Sea of Japan along the Turaen River were maintained even after China was forced to cede the entire Siberian coast area to Russia in 1858. The use of the last 15 km of the Tumen River, however, was blocked for China when Japan lost a battle to the Soviet Union in 1938.
    It was only in May 1991, after more than half a decade, that China could finally restore its maritime access to the sea as a result of Sino-Soviet rapprochement (Kaye 1992: 19–20). For the main points of the Changchum conference, see Valencia, no. 3, 1991, p. 265.
3 The other north-east Asian sub-regional programmes undertaken by UNDP were new and renewable energy, coal utilization and air pollution, as well as temperate-zone food crop production.
4 UNDP assigned US$825,000 for the feasibility studies of the TRADP at the end of 1991.
5 The author's interview with Jacob Gujit, President Representative of the UNDP office in Seoul, in December 1991. For his written interview regarding North Korea's active approach to the Tumen River project, see *Sisa Journal*, 1992: 38.
6 A 'free economy and trade zone' offers preferential treatment to foreign investors in most industrial sectors, unlike a 'free trade port'.
7 The Pyongyang conference invited a total of 122 foreign participants representing South Korea, Japan, China, Russia, the US, Mongolia, Hungary and the UNDP, together with 85 delegates from North Korea.
8 The per capita GNP of South Korea (US$5,569 as of 1990) is about five times larger than that of the North.
9 This view of South Korea's eventual economic 'absorption' of the North possibly after the year 2000, is shared by the Korea Development Institute, a think tank associated with the Economic Planning Board. According to the KDI estimates, North Korean GDP would be less than

8 per cent, or even 6 per cent of that of the South by the beginning of the twenty-first century (US$498.8 billion by 2000), thus creating an extreme imbalance between the two economies. For this and more explicitly 'absorption-oriented' views, see *The Economist Intelligence Unit* 1992: 96–101.

10 Considering the fact that the total population of ethnic Koreans in China is less than 0.2 per cent of China's population as a whole, Yanbian indeed presents a very special case. According to the data available for 1991, some 815,000 ethnic Koreans were living in Yanbian prefecture – 40 per cent of the area's 2 million or so residents. The Han Chinese, however, were still the largest ethnic group within the prefecture, forming 56.65 per cent of the population (Kim *et al.* 1991: 21–2.

11 Nearly 80 per cent of the Yanbian area is covered with forest, and accounts for 53 per cent of wood resources for Jilin province as a whole. The area also contains estimated reserves of 1 billion tons of coal and 100 million tons of oil. It also contains other important minerals such as gold, lead, zinc and manganese (Kim *et al.* 1991: 13–14).

12 Such nationalistic consciousness has been nurtured by the ethnically-based education system. For example, at Yonbyon Dachak (Yanbian University) – the highest academic institution in Yanbian prefecture, and the centre of Korean studies in north-east China – as many as 77 per cent of the faculty and staff members, and 65 per cent of the students, were ethnic Koreans as of 1991. The Korean community also circulates its own Korean- and Chinese-language newspaper, the *Yonbyon Ibo* ('Yanbian Daily'), and publishes the *Yonbyon Kyoyuk* ('Yanbian Education'), a Korean-language educational journal that was forbidden by the Chinese authorities during the Cultural Revolution. There are local Korean radio and television broadcasting services as well (Kim *et al.* 1991: 71–3 and 105–12).

13 For the political implications of ethnic Korean education, and the underlying nationalism in Yanbian, see Chae-Jin 1986: 2–12 and 99–110.

14 The project, which envisages the building of a 2,000–km pipeline linking the gas deposits in the Yakutsk area and the two Koreas was finally agreed upon between Kim Woo-Choong and Boris Yeltsin in Moscow in early July 1992 (*The Korea Times* 1992).

15 The idea of promoting the Nihonkai Keizaiken around the Sea of Japan, for the expansion of mutual economic benefits in north-east Asia has been enthusiastically proposed by the Niigata-based Nikkaiken organization. Officially launched in 1985, the Nikkainken has hosted numerous public forums to publicize the 'Nihonkai Undo', or 'Sea of Japan Movement', both within and outside Japan, and has actively participated in the major international conferences and meetings regarding the Tumen River project. Also, the organization regularly publishes its own Nihonkai Newsletter, providing the most up-to-date information on the Nihonkai 'economic circle'.

16 The Japanese specialist team checked the specific aspects of the cargo capacity, maritime traffic and railway services of the three ports. In terms of cargo capacity, the team found that both the Chongjin and Rajin ports were using less than half of their 8 million- and 3 million-

ton full capacities respectively. For the report of the team, see Wada 1992: 16–18.
17 On 1 January 1992, Vladivostok was designated as an 'open city' by the Russian government, for extensive development of the area, and the inducement of substantial foreign investment. The idea of creating a greater Vladivostok Free Economic Zone was based on the ambitious three-stage and 20–year regional development plan recommended by the UNIDO office in Vienna on 30 October 1991. The plan envisages first the construction of an industrial infrastructure and the promotion of resource development (1991–5); second, the reduction of economic dependence on the European side of Russia and the manufacturing of diversified products (1996–2000) and last, a gradual shift to high-tech industries (2001–10). See Niigata Nippon 1991.
18 This discussion is largely based on the author's interview with Kwak Young-Hoon in July 1992. As the president of the Hwangkyung ('Environment') Group in Seoul, Mr Kwak has been closely monitoring the development of the Tumen River project.
19 The author's written interview with Jacob Gujit, 4 August 1992.

6 Investment strategies of European companies for east and south-east Asia

Aiming at the centre or the periphery?

Wolfgang Klenner

INTRODUCTION

Several European companies have taken up the challenge of east and south-east Asia's fast-growing markets, attempting to reap the benefits of increased trade with the regions. Rather fewer European firms, however, are investing in the region. Investment is undeniably the tougher option, although it is becoming increasingly essential in order to exploit Asia fully both as a market and as a production base.

Extending a company's manufacturing base and sales reach into Asia is difficult, because Asia, in spite of the progress made towards the creation of 'open regions' will, for the foreseeable future, remain fragmented, with a multitude of quite different economic structures, cultures, politics, languages and history. However, this very diversity, if properly dealt with, provides enormous opportunities, as well.

This chapter will focus on the various investment strategies open to those European companies prepared to take account of Asia's rich diversity, by studying the approaches of their successful Asian competitors. The first section presents a global view of trends towards regionalization and internationalization in east and south-east Asia, as compared with North America and western Europe. The second section will focus on selected patterns within east and south-east Asia that might affect foreign investment strategies. Against this background, the last section discusses questions concerning the choice of location for operations within the region.

TRENDS TOWARDS INTRA-REGIONAL AND EXTRA-REGIONAL ECONOMIC RELATIONS

As far as trends in foreign economic relations are concerned, east and south-east Asia display particular features that are distinct from those of the 'old' industrial areas of North America and western Europe.

North America

In North America, where regional co-operation between the United States, Canada and Mexico is based on the North American Free Trade Agreement, a dramatic rise in intra-regional trade is being forecast. The growth of overseas economic activity might be negatively affected by this development, but North America's traditional 'open regionalism' will surely not give way to a protected trade bloc. However, low labour costs in Mexico might induce American firms to invest less overseas, and eventually to import less, while investing more within NAFT, and importing more from the region. Moreover, should United States companies lose their international competitiveness, calls for a national industrial policy, and for more bilateral trade agreements, might become more strident, resulting finally in increased inward trade flows.

Western Europe

Within the European common market, regionalism has a slightly different basis. Germany, for instance, is promoting regional economic integration in view of growing uncertainties around Western Europe. It is pointed out that political and economic difficulties in central and eastern Europe, deficits in foreign trade and budgets across the Atlantic, and political and military uncertainties in the Far East make it advisable to clear up one's own European house and press on with the creation of the single market.

This 'cautious regionalism', guarding against adverse developments in world economics, is reinforced by rising capital flows attracted by low wages, low costs and EC subsidies for investment by northern European countries in Spain, Portugal and, to a lesser extent, southern Italy and Greece.

However, Europe's south is not comparable to Mexico. Inflows of capital here have already led to considerable rises in factor-prices. Moreover, there is, unlike in Mexico, strong political pressure for 'social harmonization', with the probable result that north south differences in labour costs will be further levelled out in the foreseeable future. Thus, it is easy to predict that investment in labour-intensive production will no longer be channelled towards Europe's south but shifted to low-wage countries outside the Common

Market. Portugal, for instance, already has a significantly smaller number of foreign investors, in spite of the fact that it expects more than DM40 billion from EC coffers between now and the turn of the century.

We should not overstate the regionalizing tendencies of the 'old' industrial world, however. North America and western Europe, in the past, advanced international trade and production and established rules for international business strategies and operations. There is no reason to assume that past attitudes towards the international division of labour should change. Moreover, a great many enterprises have a long tradition of international operations. These are not only well-known multinational firms, but also smaller, highly specialized enterprises who have for generations exported a substantial share of their products overseas. It seems safe to assume that such firms will continue to give the highest priority to world markets.

East and south-east Asia

Trends in east and south-east Asia do not follow the patterns outlined above. Foreign economic relations, after the Second World War, began mostly with bilateral trade. Japan, in its post-war period, exported and imported mainly to and from the United States, as did South Korea, Taiwan and other countries in the region. Only later did foreign trade with other non-Asian regions, especially western Europe, begin to grow, reaching today's considerable proportions.

Factors motivating intra-regional trade

Trade within the Asian region developed only gradually in terms of the volume and structure of traded commodities. Japan, primarily an importer of raw materials and an exporter of finished products, has long been accused of 'colonial trade patterns' with its Asian neighbours. Trade patterns within the region were only recently 'normalized', and are still not comparable to foreign trade structures, such as those existing, for instance, between France and the Netherlands.

Intra-regional trade is spurred by a classic, textbook series of factors, usually cited as causing international transactions. There are tremendous differences in factor-endowment between, for instance, Japan, Singapore and Hong Kong – providing highly sophisticated technologies and capital – and China or Indonesia, offering an abundance of natural resources and cheap labour.

There are differences in the structure of demand due to the enormous disparities in per capita income within the region. Japan's per capita income is roughly 60 times that of China, and disparities in per capita income among even well-established industrial Asian countries such as Japan, South Korea and Taiwan are just as great as those between the more and less advanced member states of the EC.

Foreign trade and direct investment are based further on causes described in the product cycle model, where production location migrates from advanced economies to less advanced countries with low wages. East and south-east Asia, with production moving down from Japan, first to South Korea and Taiwan, then to countries such as Thailand and finally to Indonesia, China and Vietnam, could be said to exemplify this model in practice. In this connection, increasing returns to scale that render large firms more competitive than smaller companies provide an additional driving force.

There are no signs that Asian intra-regional trade will lose its dynamics. Differentials between factor prices, increasingly eliminated in the EC, still prevail in Asia. Of course, labour and property in Seoul or Taipei has become much more expensive than five years ago, but entrepreneurs can shift to Thailand or Malaysia and from there, should wages increase, to China, Indonesia or Vietnam. It will probably take a very long time before workers in Sechuan or Indonesia's provinces enjoy the same benefits as their colleagues in Japan.

Development patterns of intra-regional trade

Trade and economic co-operation within the region developed along two lines. First, political borders between Asia's market economies have become less and less restrictive to commodity and capital flows, although they are still operating, almost as rigidly as before, as far as manpower flows are concerned. It seems there will be no drastic change on this matter in the near future – the easing of restrictions on labour movements within the region is not being currently discussed.

Second, most of Asia's socialist countries have gradually opened their borders to international trade and capital flows on the basis of comparative advantage, with the consequence that international economic relations were no longer limited to transactions aiming at easing or eliminating the bottle-necks of planned economies.

The result of these two developments is the emergence of completely new zones of cross-border economic dynamism which, because of the spill-over effect, are becoming hubs for the economic development of vast areas within the region. These include, for instance, 'Greater South China' (Hong Kong, Macao and Guangdong), 'Greater South-east China' (Fujiian and Taiwan), north-east Asia (China's north-east, South Korea, eastern Russian and Japan) and a northern zone (China's Heilongjiang province, east Russia and Korea). These areas add to the 'old' zones of intense economic transaction stretching from South Korea and Japan southwards towards Singapore and Indonesia.

It is interesting to note that a substantial proportion of economic activity in the region has been initiated not by politicians but by businessmen. Their operations often lack political 'ointment' and have even sometimes, in their initial phase, been banned. But while not necessarily appealing to all politicians, such enterprises would no doubt receive the plaudits of the economists, based as they were on pure comparative advantage, and not distorted by political infringements. In this climate, economically absurd transactions such as Brazil's purchases of heavily-subsidized beef from the EC, rather than from the cattle farmers of neighbouring Uruguay could not take place (to the fury of the free traders).

Outward orientation

As for Asia's future external trade, there is, unlike in North America and the EC, almost no sign of this giving way to intra-regional economic transactions. On the contrary, everything points to further increases, provided this is not limited by countermeasures taken by Asia's overseas partners. Asia has huge production capacity for sophisticated, high-quality commodities that suit markets in North America and western Europe. Moreover, the stated aim of many Asian firms is to become world, rather than merely regional, market leaders. By increasing cooperation at enterprise level in Asia, and exploiting Asia as a production base, they aim to realize their strategic goal of conquering world markets.

PATTERNS WITHIN EAST AND SOUTH-EAST ASIA AFFECTING INVESTMENT STRATEGIES

The question of whether east and south-east Asia's intra-regional or extra-regional trade segment will grow fastest is of little significance for European entrepreneurs deciding where to establish operational bases within the region. The large size of the market, the expected high growth rates of per capita income, and easy access to the latest technology, qualified and cheap labour, and abundant natural resources are reasons enough.

But strategic decisions on matters such as scope, location, duration and timing of engagements within the region will be affected by its prevailing trade tendencies, i.e. intra- or extra-regional. It is self-evident that Asian governments were actively supporting an international free trading system (which could be taken as a decisive indicator of increasing outward orientation), while governments in North America and western Europe became paralyzed by internal squabbles; so any strategic decisions taken would be quite different to those based on the assumption that east and south-east Asia would remain segmented and politically unstable.

ASIA'S SCANT CONTRIBUTIONS TO A LIBERAL INTERNATIONAL ORDER

What are Asian governments currently contributing to a functioning economic world order? First, let us examine the kind of contributions it is possible to make: for example, spurring the growth of the world economy, co-ordinating actions in order to level off business cycles, strengthening and spreading market elements, providing an international currency for transactions and reserve requirements.

It seems that only in the first field can we identify contributions from most of the countries in the region; the extraordinary economic dynamism of east and south-east Asian countries is indeed promoting world-wide economic growth by producing ever greater quantities of commodities, and by forcing Western enterprises (through aggressive exports) to cut costs and raise the quality of their products.

However, quite a few economists and politicians in Western countries point out that Asian markets are still not as open for Western products as Western markets are for Asian commodities, thereby restricting a more advanced international division of labour, keeping growth well below the rate that could be achieved with free exchange of commodities.

In the other areas, east and south-east Asian nations, expect perhaps Japan, hardly feel obliged to make any contributions. Even Japan is often accused of not seriously co-operating in the fight against world economic slow-down, and is sometimes even accused of taking advantage of this cyclical weakness in its world trading partners. Moreover, it is said that Japan is not doing enough to promote liberal market principles, within its own economy or world-wide, having refused help, for example, to former socialist countries seeking to establish a market economy, and failing to accept the yen's role as an international currency in trade and reserves.

Of course, similar criticisms could be levelled against the other members of the Group of Seven. It seems that all the G7 member states have focussed on domestic political issues. The group has rarely proved capable of co-ordinating policies whenever contentious domestic issues were involved; successful co-operation has only ever come about as a result of the occasional, accidental coincidence of the member nation's individual economic priorities. Thus far, Japan's policies, and its scant regard for world economics, might not arouse any more criticism than its partners. It does, for instance, make sense to criticize policy-makers in the US (the now undisputed super-power when it comes to ideas and actions for which others have to pay), since a decade of deficit spending has now placed serious constraints on its policies.

But we are not here concerned with whether and how Japan outperforms its Western partners. Suffice to say that Japan, together with Asian economies, has taken the lead in economic growth, but not in promoting an adequate international world order. Japan is the only Asian country involved in attempts to stabilize the international economic system, while most of its regional neighbours continue to freeload, often with no vision of what should be done in order to support and promote an appropriate economic world order.

Weak foundations

European entrepreneurs faced with the bureaucratic constraints of the Common Market should not base their investment strategies on the expectation that east Asia will become the world's hub of free trade. Moreover, the principles of free trade and liberalism within east and south-east Asia are not necessarily always very firmly or deeply entrenched. One of the most unpredictable countries in this respect is China.

There can be no doubt that China's performance, since it started its economic transformation, has been excellent, unlike most of Europe's ex-socialist countries where reform was invariably followed by catastrophic recession, industry in China showed up to 10 per cent growth. At present, China can be said to be fuelling world economic growth.

However, China's economic policy is essentially 'stop-go', due to the country's contradictory system combining state planning and market mechanisms. This is harmful to its own economy and for its trading partners. Another shortcoming is that China, thirteenth among world trading nations, does not have an internationally accepted currency. The renminbi is not even accepted at the offices of the Bank of China (China's central bank) in Hong Kong.

These shortcomings are extremely significant, since if China continues to be economically successful in the coming decades, it will rank second in the world, in absolute terms of its social product, after the US. China, unlike Japan, is displaying all the potential characteristics of what is commonly known as an economic superpower. It will thus become a real economic and political giant, capable of causing enormous problems if unable and unwilling to co-operate in world economic matters.

It should also be stressed that drastic political changes within China still cannot be ruled out, although following recent domestic developments they are admittedly a little less probable. It is interesting that China's neighbours seem less confident than their Western partners in this regard.

Added to this are China's territorial claims, disputed by Japan, Vietnam and other countries in the region. These might explain why a few Asian countries have been buying weapons in tremendous quantities – there are fears that the dynamism and energy that up to now have promoted economic growth might one day be channelled into less peaceful undertakings should serious economic or other problems arise.

Businessmen certainly should not expect worst-case scenarios to happen – and should things go wrong, they usually know how to make the best of it. But European companies investigating setting up operations in east and south-east Asia would be well advised to take account of the potential economic and political risks. Asian companies invariably consider all kinds of risks very carefully when taking decisions on the volume and type of investment, and when operating within the area.

CHOICE OF LOCATION

Decisions on where to operate and invest in east and south-east Asia will, of course, depend on the business, product, size and other features of the investing firms. Banks, large chemical firms or medium-sized consumer goods companies will all need to establish individual strategies. However, I will attempt to make a few general remarks on the crucial matter of location.

It is important to distinguish between central and peripheral locations. Industrial hubs with world-wide communications and transportation networks will be defined as central, while less-developed regions will be termed peripheral. We will assess the costs and benefits of both locations.

Costs and benefits of central locations

Investing and operating in Asia's central locations can be very costly, even more so than in Europe. Property prices are extremely high, not only in Tokyo and Seoul, but also in Hanoi or Saigon. Wages in Asia's industrialized countries are equally high. Moreover, in countries such as Japan, it can be extremely difficult for foreign companies to hire qualified local personnel and to build up loyalty among local employees.

There are, however, considerable benefits to weigh against the costs. Central locations provide the best communication and transportation networks; they allow insights into the present state and future trends of the most dynamic markets, with discriminating customers; and they are usually the centre of operations for the most important Asian competitors, and subsidiaries of Western competitors. Thus, a central location provides access to the latest intelligence when planning future decisions on products, research, production technology, organization, marketing, world market strategies, etc.

The proximity to influential state organs, industrial organizations and research institutions is also invaluable. As in Japan, within the framework of industrial policy, these often have an important voice in determining future trends of technological research, norms and standards, sectoral and regional development priorities, and so on.

The availability of top-quality local personnel from first-rate schools and universities is another asset, enabling firms to utilize the most modern technologies and advanced organizational schemes; similarly, central locations are usually more attractive for expatriate personnel wishing to relocate with their families.

However, two important points should be made. Many of the above advantages can only pre-suppose an excellent local and expatriate staff, willing and able to analyse the market, collect information on competitors, and establish connections with ministries and other organizations. Since not all central locations in east and south-east Asia provide equal advantages, operations at two or more complementary centres might be advisable.

Costs and benefits of peripheral locations

The setting up of operations in a peripheral location entails a completely different set of considerations, including what we might call 'opportunity costs'.

Peripheral locations do not usually provide the company with sophisticated inputs in the widest sense. Everything, apart from labour, property and natural resources, has to be provided by the company itself. Technical and organizational know-how, market knowledge and sometimes even electricity generators have to be brought in by the foreign investor. There is no easy access to or dialogue with influential state organizations, competitors or research institutes, and simply being present in Asia does not, under these conditions, necessarily guarantee first-hand insights into Asian market developments.

The two striking advantages of peripheral locations, however, are the low cost of property and labour – provided that cost advantages are not offset by low factor-quality – and, frequently, the possibility of easy access to natural resources.

Another important consideration is that by virtue of their very isolation, companies setting up in peripheral locations often enjoy preferential relations with local administrations, and closer interpersonal relations among their staff. Similarly, the presence of an expatriate population is often much appreciated in such locations, bringing with it spending power and international connections.

The dual approach of Asian competitors

What is the best way in which to combine the advantages of central and peripheral locations, while at the same time minimize their disadvantages? It is often helpful to study the corresponding approaches of Asian competitors.

When looking at Japanese, South Korean, Taiwanese and other companies it becomes evident that many of them have quite complex networks of production facilities and operation centres spread all over east and south-east Asia.[1] Even small Asian companies with only a few hundred employees sometimes have a dozen and more subsidiaries.[2] There is usually one or more head office and/or factory in a central location, applying capital-intensive technologies, plus a wide range of operation bases in the Asian periphery, taking advantage of low factor costs and, in some cases, natural resources.

The individual operation bases are inter-connected through

sophisticated networks which provide information on products, inputs, prices, etc. Moreover, they are able to liaise in the selection of additional operation bases offering cheaper labour than that available at existing production locations.

The strategies of Asian firms become clearer if we study how various companies' networks of subsidiaries in central and peripheral locations have developed over the last two or three decades. A few general trends can be observed:

- There seems to be a preference for a larger number of small projects within different areas of the region, and not for just one or a few large-scale projects.
- Many of the larger projects seem to be the result of consolidation and expansion of smaller investments.
- Companies do not hesitate to set up a new base, as soon as a new market, or an even cheaper source of labour has been identified. The result of this strategy is often a 'downward' shift of operations from one location to another.

Asian firms have adapted this kind of investment pattern with considerable success. A recent study by the Nomura and Mitsubishi research institutes, for example, shows that 80 per cent of Japan's direct investment in Asia in the late 1980s began yielding profits within two years. Let us take one example. A Japanese company with subsidiaries in low-cost countries, and a European company producing in Europe, are competing on the Chinese market. Both, during the first round of negotiations, offer best quality for a high price. The Chinese partner, however, requests a reduction of 40 per cent. On top of this, since imports have to be brought in line with China's tight planning process, an early decision and delivery of commodities is required.

The European company is not usually able to lower its prices substantially, even if it were prepared to sell without profits in order to gain a foothold in the Chinese market. Moreover, due to European holiday-terms and other social regulations, it is difficult or even impossible to agree on early delivery as stipulated by China's planning schedules.

The Japanese company, with its network of Asian subsidiaries, is in a completely different position as far as costs and time schedules are concerned. If the requested price for top-notch quality is not accepted, a comparable but much cheaper product, with the same brand name but with components made by low-cost subsidiaries, could be offered. Moreover, with subsidiaries located in Thailand or Indonesia, the Japanese firm is not subject to the same social regulations as is EC competitors, and can easily comply with short-term delivery requirements.

Asian firms thus demonstrate how to cope efficiently with differences and changes in the economic, cultural and political sphere of east and south-east Asian countries. The key word in this context is flexibility.

Problems of emulating 'Asian' strategies

European companies would do well to emulate 'Asian' strategies in order to exploit low costs, quickly penetrate new markets and gain in flexibility.

However, they should not expect, simply by following these investment patterns, always to become as successful as Asian competitors within the region. Even if expected gross margins are good, net margins often turn out to be much lower. An awareness of the most important reasons for this (outlined below) might help to overcome comparative shortcomings.

Asian companies are usually already well established in a central location within the region, and are thus able to build up their network of subsidiaries abroad. European companies (alone or pooling their efforts) often have to 'buy in' to a central location, a process which, by now, is extremely costly.

Western companies usually appear 'later' on peripheral Asian markets than their Asian rivals. Asian competitors might be yielding profits already, and may even, because of rising factor costs, be considering shifting operations to cheaper locations. They are inevitably one step ahead of European corporations in the region. Consequently, the latter have to pay higher prices for property and labour. A recent example is Vietnam, where property prices in Hanoi and Saigon are now as expensive as those in Singapore or Sydney. Many European corporations looking to break into this market therefore face less favourable cost-structures than did Asian competitors in the initial phase of operations.

Western companies are often not as practical as, for instance, firms run by Japanese or Overseas Chinese, when it comes to adapting to the difficult political, legal and personal environment in which any investment in Asia has to operate.[3] They have problems in extending personal networks in order to gather information, to stabilize sources of supply and markets and to cement certain key relationships in their organization in order to control uncertainty. They are generally unable to build relationships based on regional or family ties. Moreover, they have difficulty adjusting to Asian practices, such as the preference for taking a small share in a variety of projects, thus fostering a network of local business partnerships.[4]

The cost to Westerners of doing business in east and south-east Asia is usually high because their organization tends to be more complicated and more heavily staffed with highly-paid expatriates than that of their Asian rivals. And even if European subsidiaries are not headed by European expatriates, many European managers find it difficult to compete with the 'workaholism' of their more driven Asian counterparts.

The specific comparative disadvantages for European corporations investing and competing in Asia are clear, but should not discourage Western investment, since any corporation failing to invest here will find itself in a weaker position globally. Moreover, these disadvantages are not insurmountable. Much can be done in order to improve the situation by carefully selecting local personnel, improving flexibility, and taking other measures aimed at adjusting better to local conditions. Western firms aiming at Asian markets must be prepared to take these specific strategic considerations on board, while at the same time retaining those features and elements that are an essential part of the firm's global identity.

Notes

1 The strategies of Japanese companies are analysed in various issues of *Nihon yushutsuniuu ginkoo kaigai tooshi Kenyuujo: Kaigai tooshi kenkyu-uio hoo.*
2 This, however, is not the case as far as South Korean companies are concerned, since the South Korean government has fostered the *chaebols* at the expense of smaller companies that have not yet been able to invest abroad.
3 Differences in Chinese and Western organizational methods are described in S. Gordon Redding (1990) *The Spirit of Chinese Capitalism*, New York.
4 However, it would be wrong to conclude that co-operation between Asian firms is necessarily trouble-free. Intra-regional differences in culture and behaviour often make for rather difficult inter-personal relations. In Indonesia, for example, cool and precise Japanese managers, or Korean expatriates favouring a rough and aggressive factory culture, will quickly encounter problems when dealing with local staff.

7 Post Soviet east Asia

European responses and strategies

Gordon Daniels

INTRODUCTION

Although the final disintegration of the Soviet Union brought major changes to east Asia, the region's transformation was already well advanced. The late 1980s saw the weakening of aggressive ideology in the Soviet Union, China and Vietnam. Military tensions were eased, and the mythical glamour of guerrilla warfare was long forgotten. Almost everywhere the supremacy of economic objectives and successes was acknowledged, and the emptiness of utopian rhetoric admitted. Consequently, new prestige accrued to Japan, South Korea, Taiwan and Singapore, while Moscow and Beijing searched for new equations of Marxism and the market that might harness economic growth to a form of Communist-led society.

Yet relics of the Cold War still concealed the scale of this transformation. Military tension still plagued the Korean peninsula; American and Soviet forces continued to shadow each other in the skies and seas of north-east Asia, and the Tienanmen Square massacre recalled European events of 1956 and 1968, as well as the despotism of an earlier age. In these years the very survival of Deng Xiao Ping and Kim Il Sung was a reality that no observer could easily ignore. Conversely, the resignation in December 1990 of Sheverdnadze, the leader of the new Soviet diplomacy, suggested that the Soviet future remained deeply uncertain. Yet amid these doubts the subordination of military to economic calculation in the shaping of Soviet policy was a reality, as was the collapse of Soviet investment, trade, production and the value of the rouble. Indeed, these desired and undesired changes were so dramatic that Soviet policies towards Asian friends and foes underwent rapid and drastic reconstruction.

Nowhere was this transformation more radical than in Moscow's policies towards the Korean peninsula. Since the 1940s the Soviet Union had supported and supplied its fraternal comrades in Pyongyang; but between 1988 and 1991 Gorbachev turned to South Korea for investment and trade, and sought to promote peace along the 38th parallel.

In 1988 Moscow sent athletes to the Seoul Olympics. A year later semi-official trade offices were established in Moscow and Seoul, and in June 1990 President Roh met Gorbachev for the first time in San Francisco. In September 1990, the opening of formal diplomatic relations was announced, and mutual trade quadrupled within two years. At the same time Moscow threatened to cut off aid to Pyongyang and to demand hard currency for future exports. Equally significant were articles in the Soviet press praising South Korean achievements and ridiculing the lies and postures of Kim Il Sung's propagandists.

In its diplomacy Moscow also sought to cooperate with Beijing in leaning hard on North Korean policies. This new commitment to the capitalist South reached a new climax when Gorbachev met President Roh on Cheju island in April 1991, after his abortive visit to Tokyo and western Japan. During these talks the Soviet leader promised to support South Korea's entry to the United Nations. In return President Roh confirmed that his government would provide US$3 billion in loans to aid the Soviet economy. In contrast to many of Gorbachev's radical policies, his overture to Seoul had a clear constituency of support. Many economists welcomed South Korean goods and investment, and ethnic Koreans in republics such as Kazakhstan were keen to cooperate with their cousins from South Korea. Moscow's reformist ideology increasingly diverged away from the Stalinesque conservatism of Kim Il Sung's circle, and the abortive Moscow coup in August 1991 elicited contrasting responses from Pyongyang and Seoul. In Pyongyang the coup was warmly welcomed. In Seoul, pleasure was expressed at its demise. In the midst of the August turmoil, South Korean companies halted major projects in the Soviet Union. Hyundai, Lucky Goldstar, Daewoo and Samsung all froze development plans or were rumoured to be likely to do so. But within weeks, Yeltsin's victory gave a new impetus to South Korean activity.

Nowhere was this more evident than in the Soviet Far East, where branch offices of South Korean companies were opened to compete for new development contracts. Samsung planned an outpost in Khabarovsk, and Hyundai one in Vladivostock, while Lucky Goldstar showed a lively interest in Uzbekistan, Kazakhstan and the

Ukraine. In part, these activities were a quick response to the activities of Japanese trading companies in Soviet Asia. Not only was Soviet-South Korean barter trade growing, but it represented Seoul's obvious technical superiority, since South Korean consumer goods were traded for Russian raw materials.

The attractiveness of South Korea's goods, investments and services was also reflected in increasing commercial links with her Chinese neighbour. By the end of 1991 China had agreed to give 'most favoured' status to South Korean goods and to reduce existing tariffs on South Korean products. Trade offices were opened in both capitals and these began limited consular duties. Although scheduled air services were still some way off, Korean Air set up a symbolic office in Beijing and charter flights began operation. Although the trade balance remained in China's favour, South Korea had by now invested US$40 million in plants to manufacture textiles and shoes in the People's Republic.

While China cooperated with Seoul, her attitude towards North Korea was increasingly detached and uncooperative. When Pyongyang hoped for help in developing nuclear technology, Beijing rejected this notion and urged the creation of a nuclear-free Korean peninsula. Indeed, in adopting this stance China was demonstrating the extent of its non-ideological diplomacy, for it shared the views of Washington, Tokyo and Moscow in regarding North Korean nuclear research as a serious threat to the stability of north-east Asia.

By this time, military links and exchanges had become a further symbol of the importance of Marxist ideologies. In October 1991 South Korea and the Soviet Union began to explore military exchanges, and the commander of the Far Eastern Military Region visited Seoul to participate in an academic seminar. Perhaps more significant was the Soviet Union's acquiescence in Seoul's request to reduce supplies of arms to Pyongyang.

However, Seoul's policy towards the North was not one of crude hostility, or one designed to precipitate the immediate collapse of its Communist neighbour. Either course might have precipitated a violent reaction from Pyongyang and South Korea, in comparison with West Germany, had few resources to finance the social and economic revival of her Communist neighbour. In these months, high-level meetings between North and South continued, and Seoul took economic and diplomatic steps to alleviate Pyongyang's economic difficulties and international isolation. In November 1991 a million-dollar barter deal enabled Lucky Goldstar to supply colour televisions, sugar and films to North Korea, in exchange for coal.

Soon after, Samsung and Daewoo representatives visited Pyongyang to discuss the establishment of local offices. Samsung also sought to participate in the US$30 billion development of a special economic zone in the Tumen River delta, which included part of North Korean territory. New talks were held on the sale of textiles and the purchase of coal, and Daewoo was said to be interested in highway construction, tourist developments and the creation of a car component factory.

Equally dramatic was a mutual agreement that both Korean republics would join the United Nations simultaneously. This marked the abandonment of Pyongyang's claim to represent the entire Korean peninsula. Seoul also lent its support to North Korea's policy of building links with the Asian Development Bank and other Western-oriented international organizations.

By the end of 1991 this semi-convergence of diplomatic paths led to agreement on a non-aggression treaty between North and South, and a South Korean warning to Tokyo and Washington to exercise care and discretion in attempts to press Pyongyang into adopting new policies. Even more striking was a South Korean (not American) statement that United States forces had no nuclear weapons in South Korean bases. This was clearly designed to promote Northern acceptance of a nuclear-free Korean peninsula.

Although 1992 saw the continuation of constructive patterns in Russian-Korean relations, some new elements suggested even closer relations between Seoul and Moscow. Even before the fall of the USSR, Korean ministers had regarded Russia as a likely source of cheap, advanced technology, but it was not until April 1992 that this proposal was reciprocated by influential Russians. On a visit to Seoul, the President of the Russian Nuclear Society offered to sell technology, or to engage in joint research with South Korea, at a time when South Korean leaders were becoming concerned at their low level of R&D, and the need to move to compete with the cheap labour forces of south and south-east Asia. It was against this background that South Korea decided to use Russian-enriched uranium as fuel for its nuclear plants.

Nevertheless, Russo-Korean cooperation was not without its difficulties. By now South Korea had cut off economic assistance to Russia, as Moscow had reneged on interest payments on loans. It was not until November 1992 that South Korea responded to Russian assurances by resuming aid. There were further signs that South Korea's economic rule in Russia might be waning. Whereas 1990 had seen South Korean investment of US$16.45 million, the first ten months of 1992 saw just US$7.3 million invested, spread over 12 new projects. Not surprisingly, Boris Yeltsin's visit to Seoul provided an opportunity to reassure South Korean traders and investors. In part this was achieved by warming political relations with the Roh administration. Apologies were made for the shooting down of a South Korean airliner in 1983, and documentation was promised. Further apologies were expressed for Russia's role in the Korean war, and Yeltsin spoke of a new Russian diplomacy that would shift from the United States and western Europe towards Asia and the Pacific.

Yeltsin's single visit may not have transformed the atmosphere of relations with South Korea, but the signing of agreements on exchange visits by high-level military officers, and a regular sequence of high-level meetings, placed relations on a much firmer foundation than before. This new structure was further reinforced by Yeltsin's promise to cut arms supplies to North Korea, and to use what influence he had to dissuade Pyongyang from developing nuclear weapons, as well as to encourage the opening of its plants to South Korean inspectors.

Though such developments marked further successes for South Korean diplomacy, relations with the North still provided grounds for serious suspicion. Despite the signing of an accord to exclude nuclear weapons from both states, a group of armed North Korean infiltrators entered the South in 1992 – an incident that dramatized the major differences that still separated the two regimes.

Nevertheless, the difficulties of dealing with North Korea, and some slowing of investment in the Russian Federation, were largely counterbalanced by the rapid advance of Sino-Korean relations. In August 1992, diplomatic relations were opened, and a month later the South Korean president visited Beijing. Not only did this strengthen Seoul's diplomatic ties, but South Korean investment in China continued to expand rapidly. Samsung Engineering won a major order to construct a chemical plant, and agreement was reached on the building of a South Korean industrial park in Tianjin. Plans for joint ventures to build minibuses and trucks, and South Korean investments in mining and highway construction, added to the impetus of trade and investment. As in Kazakhstan, ethnic Koreans had a role in South Korean activities. It was no coincidence that much investment concentrated in northern China, where most of China's Korean community was well established.

Overall, South Korea's improving relations with Russia and China, which followed the collapse of Communism in the former, and the economic liberalization of the latter, marked the rise of a small power that could threaten no one, and whose political and economic interests were often interlinked. Japan's relations with the Soviet Union and, later, Russia provided a far less successful example of attempts to utilize economic power to achieve significant national objectives.

Russia, whether Tsarist, Soviet or otherwise, has never been a popular country in Japan. The Russo-Japanese war, the Russian invasion of August 1945 and the mistreatment of Japanese prisoners saw to that, but this antagonism has been further sustained by two aspects of Japanese policy. Japan's particularly close relationship with the United States has repeatedly made it advantageous, or apparently so, to avoid the resolution of difficulties with the Soviet Union. Furthermore, whatever the legal niceties of the dispute, the Japanese government has sought to keep the issue of the Northern Territories alive, over many years, by celebrating a Northern Territories Day. Similarly, Japanese Liberal Democratic Party (LDR) politicians have helped in the organization of petitions and support groups. To that extent, the excitement and emotion that surround this issue are partly of Tokyo's own making. Furthermore, the key recent event in this saga, and in recent Japanese-Russian relations, illustrates several of the diplomatic difficulties of this economic super-power. In April 1991 – well before the abortive coup – Gorbachev visited Tokyo with mutual expectations that this would improve relations between Japan and the USSR. To many Japanese, the issues seemed simple: the Soviet Union was in dire financial straits and would be likely to barter the Northern Territories for the promise of large amounts of financial aid. A further dimension was added to this background by the activities of the Secretary General of the LDP, who visited Moscow to talk about major aid payments, arguably with the aim of promoting his own political career, and placing his name in the pages of future history books. Conversely, the Japanese business world, which was arguably the key to any major commitment to closer relations, took a severe view of the Soviet Union, and its likely future. Not only did Keidanren and other business organizations stand firmly for the return of all four northern islands, but they showed little finesse during Gorbachev's visit. But perhaps the most interesting aspect of this key diplomatic failure was its direct link with the advancing tide of liberalization in the Soviet Union. Liberalization not only meant a more divided array of elites – with the armed forces and Boris Yeltsin clearly opposed to the loss of Russian territory – but Russian public opinion was now measurable by surveys and other modern methods. The majority of Russians opposed this loss of territory, and these voices could not be totally ignored. Thus Japan, a democracy, tended to ignore the quasi-democratic pressures inside the Soviet Union. Indeed, Tokyo often behaved as though Gorbachev commanded a Stalinist degree of personal authority. Overall, Gorbachev's visit did place the territorial issue on the Russo-Japanese agenda and made some contribution to improved relations, but unrealistic Japanese expectations, and the severity of business leaders' condemnation of the chaos in the Russian economy, made the visit appear a more serious failure than it was.

In the aftermath of the abortive Moscow coup it first appeared as though Japanese policy was achieving some success. Not only had Japanese suspicion of Soviet instability been justified, but the new Russian government appeared to demonstrate a new flexibility. One Russian official talked of linking the islands question to a US$15 billion aid payment, and Tokyo seemed more conciliatory, partly to avoid isolation when other democratic powers sympathized with the post-Soviet regime. This apparent convergence of diplomatic attitudes was reinforced in September 1991, when Boris Yeltsin sent a conciliatory letter to Tokyo clearly linking territory to aid, but emphasizing the need to prepare and shape public opinion.

Soon after, Tokyo softened its financial stance and offered Russia US$2.5 billion in credit to add to other democracies' gestures of emergency help. The following year saw Japanese-Russian relations develop new complexities which, in part, reflected the political instability that characterized the new Russian state. Formally, Japan's position appeared to be strengthened: during the summer, France and Germany gave their support to Japan's cause, and the G7 meeting also urged a settlement of the territorial dispute. But such formal support counted for little when set against Yeltsin's domestic difficulties and the increasingly nationalistic tendency of Russian public opinion.

In April 1992, Russia talked of a gradual solution to the problem. In May there were plans for the drafting of a peace treaty by a Russo-Japanese committee, but in July Yeltsin made a particularly dramatic speech. Referring to his planned visit to Japan in September, he declared: 'Our economic cooperation must not depend on a political solution to the question of the Kurile islands.' Presumably with his domestic critics in mind, he declared that Japan had not 'invested a cent, a half dollar or even a half yen in Russia', and drew attention to the dramatic and historic attempts Russia was making to reconstruct her economy. Relations were hardly helped by the reported statement of Shin Kanemaru, the vice-president of the LDP, to President Bush that the Russians were 'underhand and liars and that helping the Russians was as good as throwing money out of the window'.

By now the two foreign ministries were preparing to publish rival collections of documents to justify their respective claims. Russia did reduce her forces on the controversial islands and made arrangements for selected Japanese to visit them without visas. But these gestures were forgotten amid this bitter public debate. Relations were also damaged by a further troublesome issue – accusations of corrupt behaviour by a Russian diplomat in Tokyo. At the same time, small steps taken by businessmen indicated that economic cooperation was possible. Nissho Iwai discussed participating in a gas development project in Asiatic Russia, and a Russian fishing enterprise seemed close to establishing a venture in Hokkaido, but strong personalities, emotions and the islands continued to be at the centre of debate. This was overwhelmingly clear in September 1992 when Yeltsin abruptly cancelled his visit to Tokyo. This may well have been the last step, since parliamentary and public opinion in Russia, not least the population of the Northern Islands, opposed any dramatic concession. A Yeltsin visit would have been likely to end in failure, and arguably further damage the delicate tissue of Russo-Japanese relations. But for the Japanese, this sudden cancellation seemed at best a quasi-insult confirming the views of those who saw Russians as fundamentally unreliable. Yet another start was necessary, with no particular grounds for optimism. In the aftermath of this quasi-disaster, Russians talked again of the possibility of transferring two of the four islands, and by October this suggestion had been rejected by Japanese officials.

For both sides, these unfortunate encounters produced very little, but Russia's need for aid, and Japan's need to maintain some effective relationship when South Korea's relationships were improving, meant that relations had to be relinked. By the beginning of 1993, Russo-Japanese talks returned to some of the same themes that had preoccupied negotiators from the beginning of the Gorbachev era – debts/loans, trade and the possibilities of economic assistance – for neither side had gained much by recent debates and, arguably, the increasing publicity given to the territorial issue had made other, more structural, cooperation difficult to advance.

Yet to dwell on this aspect of post-Soviet Japan is to neglect factors that have been far more fundamental to recent Japanese diplomacy. Despite Japan's interest in Yeltsin's Asia, this is only one of many diverse and often greater interests. Not only does China represent a more immediately promising environment for Japanese investment, but so do Thailand, Malaysia, the United Kingdom and the United States. Furthermore, if the Northern Islands represent a sensitive issue for Japanese prestige, even more important are such issues as maintaining a Japanese at the head of the World Health Organization, or Japan playing a major role in the UN High Commission for Refugees or performing a quasi-military role in sweeping mines from the Gulf.

The improvement of relations with South and North Korea – whether the issue be the treatment of the Korean minority, South Korea's trade deficit or the danger of North Korea's nuclear ambitions – constitutes an important rival to the issue of Russian relations. And beyond all these is the central issue of relations with the United States, which may still benefit from a cool attitude towards Russia, and the non-existence of particularly close relations. In other words, although Japan's world-wide interests demand some involvement in the future of Russia, any policy dominated by commercial thinking is likely to regard Russia as a less than central issue in Japanese diplomacy. Nevertheless, Japan has potentially much to offer, perhaps in expertise rather than money, for it is organization that is crucial to improvement of production distribution to the Russian economy.

If Russo-Japanese relations have seen conflicts based upon a lack of trust and confidence, relations between Beijing and Moscow have seen an improvement based upon the relegation of ideology and the promotion of economic ties. It is easily forgotten that 1989 saw Gorbachev's visit to Beijing which normalized inter-party relations. If China was humiliated by demonstrations during Gorbachev's visit, she was even more troubled by the international reaction that followed. Yet the régime survived during 1991, when economic as opposed to political liberalization brought greater trade and an all-time peak in foreign currency reserves. Joint ventures with foreign companies multiplied during the same year. In 1991, European leaders visited China and further contributed to the régime's political recovery. The Asian Development Bank also helped, and in March 1991 Beijing's confidence was reflected in a US$730 million loan to Moscow. This, along with talks to settle details of the eastern sector of the Russo-Chinese border, all indicated that China sought to end support to the Soviet Union, however much its policies differed from Beijing's.

For China, the collapse of the USSR was a profound shock that did more than simply contribute to her sense of isolation. The consequent creation of independent states in central Asia threatened further problems with the possibility that minorities on the Chinese side of old frontiers might seek to join their compatriots in independent states. However, by November 1992, initial shocks had been overcome and China embarked on a foreign economic and political policy that exuded confidence.

In Seoul, China sought to soften criticism of North Korea's nuclear policy by calling for dialogue rather than pressure, while China's foreign minister also used his time in Seoul to discuss industrial cooperation with major companies. A more vivid symbol of normality was the growth of a remarkably free border trade between Russian and Chinese citizens in Manchuria. Tinned meat and a wide variety of Chinese clothing crossed the border into the new Russia. Within this cooperative atmosphere, talks on reducing border forces received encouragement. When the Russian foreign minister visited China, economics rather than politics were clearly dominant. China now expressed interest in acquiring Russian scientists who were no longer needed in defence industries. Furthermore, talks on the supply of advanced Russian fighter aircraft for the Chinese air force reached an advanced stage, as did broad discussions on the import of Russian military technology.

By December 1992, the earlier suspicions of the post-Soviet government in Russia had almost disappeared, and Yeltsin made an official visit to Beijing. By this time, Russian leaders were paying tribute to China's economic achievements. Arkady Volsky, leader of Russia's Civil Union, stated that 'China has been able to feed more than a billion people on its own. We must study their methods.' Similarly, Yeltsin praised China's 14 years of economic reform, stating: 'I had considered the Chinese people to be extremely regimented under the Communist Party yoke ... I am now convinced that there is no such regimentation, the standard of living is increasing. There are goods and foodstuffs in the stores.' The success of Yeltsin's visit was clear from the signing of 24 joint statements, documents and memoranda – including issues of military cooperation and space and nuclear development. Yeltsin stated: 'We are now entering a new stage of de-ideological relations.'

For Russia, China presented an attractive market for the one high-tech Russian product of international quality, namely arms. China signed contracts for US$1 billion-worth of military equipment and Yeltsin agreed to cooperate in all areas of military science.

China now bought fighters and the S-300 missile system. In addition, Russia agreed to grant China a large loan in order to build a nuclear power station. Both Russia and China accepted each other as super-powers seeking stability and economic development.

Barter trade was now expanding, growing by 20 per cent per year, and authorities believed that Russian arms exports would reach US$2 billion by 1994. A new secret trend in China's foreign relations was particularly striking. At the height of the Cold War, Western commentators often saw Chinese in south-east Asia as possible Communists. Yet by 1993, an opposite trend was noted. Capital from Chinese communities in south-east Asia was aiding capitalist developments in the People's Republic. Now even Taiwan was making some contribution to the mainland economy. In a world of high technology – ironically – such traditional factors as geographical proximity and social and cultural links were increasingly aiding economic development in north-east Asia. Minority communities – whether Korean or Chinese – were proving creative rather than subversive in the post-Soviet era. Information and training remain major problems, and diplomatic underrepresentation may be another.

In responding to these rapid changes, Europeans face many difficulties. Europeans should be able to cooperate in their response, by creating new EC missions or by creating bi- or tri-national offices. Post-Soviet east Asia may be less political than in the past; but education, and diplomatic data-gathering, remain essential for any successful economic activity in the rapidly-changing context of post-Soviet Russia and its neighbours.

8 Japan and east Asia

The impact of economic links

Glen D. Hook

INTRODUCTION

Japan's post-war relationship with other parts of east Asia has been fraught with difficulties, some arising from the legacy of Japanese imperialism and aggression, as symbolized by the attempt to create the 'Greater East Asia co-Prosperity' sphere; some arising from the post-war settlement, with Japan locked into one side of the Cold War confrontation as a result of signing the US-Japan security treaty, along with the San Francisco Peace Treaty, in 1951; and some arising from the nature of the post-war economic links forged between Japan and its neighbours, with Japan as the first economic success story of the region, joining the wealthy nations of the world, in the North instead of the South.[1] The American goal of making Japan a bastion against Communism, which helped split the region along Cold War lines, called for the rebuilding of the Japanese economy and its reintegration into the Cold War, global capitalist system. At the same time, the major 'hot wars' in Korea and Vietnam boosted Japan's rate of economic growth. As a resource-poor, rapidly-growing economy, cut off from China, Japan became dependent on the region's developing capitalist countries, and benefited from the wars that raged wherever Communism mounted a challenge to the emerging capitalist order. In this sense, the problem of North-South disparities was from the start intertwined with Cold War political and economic considerations in the east Asian region.

In the 1950s, the payment of reparations, which were in the form of products and services rather than cash, enabled Japanese companies to secure a niche in the east Asian capitalist economies. Investment was focused on natural resources, as in the development of the Sumatran oil fields, so that south-east Asia came to replace China as Japan's resource base. Japan has continued to depend on the region for natural resources such as tin (99 per cent), natural rubber (99 per cent), natural gas (49 per cent), timber (42 per cent), copper (33 per cent) and oil (18 per cent) ('Keizai' Henshubu hen, 1988: 163). In the 1960s, loans and investments in east Asian textile industries provided Japanese companies with access to cheap labour. From the early 1970s, moreover, these emerging multinationals made large-scale foreign direct investments (FDI) in other east Asian economies, in the wake of the rise in the value of the yen. For with the Smithsonian agreement of 1971, the Japanese yen was revalued by nearly 17 per cent to 308 yen to the dollar, thereby bringing to an end the fixed exchange rate of 360 yen to the dollar established in 1949, and making Japanese exports less competitive. Following the breakdown of the Bretton Woods system, and the move to the system of floating exchange rates in 1973, Japanese companies took advantage of the higher value of the yen to invest overseas. At home, they implemented cost-cutting, rationalization and stream-lined management. The goal in both cases was to maintain competitiveness for Japanese goods in an increasingly competitive global economy.

Moving production overseas helped Japanese companies successfully to overcome the first major rise in the value of the yen in the 1970s. In the 1980s, they again faced the question of how to deal with another major revaluation of the yen, when after the G5 Plaza Agreement of 1985, the attempt to stabilize and effect an orderly depreciation in the price of the dollar led to a rise in the value of the yen, which by the Louvre accord of 1987 was generally trading in the range of 140–160 yen to the dollar. After the Plaza Agreement, Japanese companies made a major new round of investments in other east Asian economies. These investments have been crucial to the growth of a new regional division of labour. At the same time, Japan's economic success brought calls for it to play a more active political, and perhaps even security, role internationally. By the early 1990s, as seen in its involvement in Cambodian peacekeeping operations, Japan had begun to carve out a new political and security role, as well as maintaining a major economic role in the region.

THE PLAZA AGREEMENT

The Plaza Agreement was of major significance in promoting the further internationalization of the Japanese economy. This agreement can be viewed as part of a global capitalist restructuring aimed at resolving the double deficit in the United States, with the US in that year becoming a debtor nation for the first time in 71 years, running up a deficit in external net assets of US$111.4 billion, the largest in US history. By 1988 the deficit had ballooned to US$532.5 billion. At the same time, Japan's surplus continued to grow, moving from US$129.8 billion in 1985 to US$291.7 billion in 1988. Similarly, in trade, Japan continued in surplus throughout the 1980s, rising from US$46 billion in 1985 to US$82.7 billion in 1986, then dropping to US$64.3 billion in 1989. The trade surplus is now running at around US$50 billion. The United States has continued a trade deficit – that with Japan dropped from US$51.8 billion in 1988 to US$43.4 billion in 1991, but a higher deficit was expected in 1992 (Rekishigakukenkyukai 1991). The trade conflicts between the US and Japan, which had brought economic issues to the centre of the political agenda in the 1980s, were addressed by policy adjustment on the global level, as seen in the G5 Plaza Agreement, indicating the extent to which Japanese investments in east Asia and elsewhere were linked to this global restructuring.

As in the 1970s, Japanese companies adopted a number of strategies to maintain global competitiveness, including cost-cutting and the development of new products, especially high value-added products. At the same time, the increase in the value of the yen against the dollar and other currencies, and low domestic interest rates, triggered a 'push effect' on Japanese companies, encouraging them to invest abroad to remain competitive. A boost in overall FDI followed: compared with the previous year, there was an increase in FDI of 82.7 per cent in 1986, 49.5 per cent in 1987, 40.9 per cent in 1988 and 43.6 per cent in 1989 (Moriaki 1992). By 1989, Japan had passed the US and the UK to become the world's number one in FDI, although investments declined in the early 1990s, with a 15.7 per cent decrease in 1990 compared with the previous year (Moriaki 1992). Japanese FDI came to US$158.5 billion, a drop of 13 per cent on 1991 (*Financial Times* 15 June 1993). Asia, especially China has received much of this recent investment.

This move overseas, as a result of the rise in the value of the yen as well as the continuing trade conflict, especially with the US, has brought about a realignment on an international scale, involving the east Asian NIEs as well as the ASEAN. The investments made by Japanese companies in the NIEs in the 1980s centered on Hong Kong and Singapore: from 1980–9 the greatest number, as well as the largest monetary amount of investments, was made in Singapore and Hong Kong, followed by South Korea and Taiwan, with investment in Hong Kong concentrated in non-manufacturing areas such as finance, insurance, service and real estate; in Singapore it was spread across both manufacturing and non-manufacturing; in South Korea it was mainly in services; and in Taiwan it was concentrated in manufacturing, especially in electrical appliances (*Keizai* 1991: 56–8). In the case of ASEAN (excluding Brunei), the greates number as well as the largest monetary amount of investments were made in Thailand and Malaysia, followed by Indonesia and the Philippines, with investment in Thailand concentrated in manufacturing areas such as electrical appliances, machinery and textiles; in Malaysia it was concentrated in electrical appliances and electronics, as suggested by the presence of Japanese companies such as Matsushita, Sony, Japan Victor and Fujitsu; in Indonesia it was mainly in resource industries such as mining, oil and natural gas; and in the Philippines it was focused in mining (*Keizai* 1991: 58).

These investments have helped shape the division of labour between Japan, the NIEs and ASEAN. This division has tended to be based on the location of low value-added, labour-intensive products, or products using standardized technology, first in the NIEs and then ASEAN, and hi-tech, capital-intensive production processes in Japan (*Keizai* 1991: 69). This has led to an increase in cross-border, intra-company trade, on the one hand, and an intra-company division of labour on the other. At the same time, as both large as well as small and medium-sized enterprises have been crucial to the increase in trade and investment activities in the region, the division of labour between Japanese companies at home has also been reproduced abroad.

ECONOMIC SUCCESS

The economic success of Japan, followed by the Asian NIEs and, most recently, members of ASEAN, has been achieved in the context of the liberal trading order. Indeed, access to foreign markets, especially the United States, has been crucial to the success of Japanese FDI in east Asia. In the 1980s, therefore, a trilateral relationship took shape, involving Japan as a supplier of capital and technology, other parts of east Asia as a production and product supply base, and the United States as an absorber market. As a production and supply base, the region could at first be used to avoid the trade tensions plaguing US-Japan relations, because even though many export items were produced by Japanese companies or joint ventures, they did not originate in Japan. It was out of concern over the imbalance in Japan-US trade, and a desire to avoid exacerbating US-Japan trade friction, that Toshiba introduced an action programme aimed at boosting imports and expanding overseas production (Katsuaki 1992). By 1989, Japan's FDI in ASEAN had surpassed investment in the NIEs, whereas the NIEs, with the contribution of external demand to economic growth becoming a minus, started to rely on internal demand from growth. The NIEs therefore made some movement away from a trilateral relationship, with the US as the absorber, towards a bilateral relationship, with the home market and other NIEs as the absorber and Japan as the supplier. In this way, along with the economic development of the region, east Asian domestic markets have come to act as absorbers of higher-priced consumer products.

Accordingly, the increase in Japanese production activities in the NIEs and ASEAN did not lead to a major increase in the NIEs, exports to Japan. Overall, between 1985–90 a slight upswing occurred in exports from the NIEs (including Singapore) to Japan, from 10.0 per cent to 11.2 per cent, with the main increase registered by South Korea. In the same period, a decrease occurred in exports to the United States, from 34.8 per cent to 27.6 per cent. A major expansion occurred instead in intra-NIEs exports, up from 6.9 per cent to 12.2 per cent, suggesting a change in the consumption patterns in the NIEs (*Keizai* 1991: 70). In the case of ASEAN, however, Japanese companies moved the less sophisticated part of their consumer electronics industry to ASEAN countries, especially Malaysia, and to some extent Thailand. Reflecting this, trade between Japan and ASEAN increased in the 1980s, with an over 40 per cent boost in trade with Japan in 1987, 1988 and 1989 (Ohata and Urata 1993: 91). During this period, Japan became an attractive market for consumer goods manufactured in ASEAN.

At the same time, however, the sheer magnitude, rapidity and diversity of investments in ASEAN in the late 1980s is striking, with a downturn in investment following the overall decline in Japan's FDI in 1990 and particularly 1991. In the case of Thailand, for instance, Japanese investment was the highest of all the ASEAN countries in 1990, with a total of over US$1,154 million, compared with only US$48 billion in 1985, Japan being the top overseas investor. This fell to just over US$807 million in 1991, behind Indonesia's US$1,193 million and Malaysia's US$880 million. Given that, on average, each investment was only around half the size of individual Japanese investments in Singapore, this suggests the important role played by Japan's small and medium-sized companies and Japanese affiliates in Thailand. Indeed, the size of capital investments in ASEAN, which tends to be about one quarter that of investments made in the United States, suggests the prominence of these companies in the region (Ohata and Urata 1993: 122–4; Jetro 1993: 521). In 1990, and again in 1991, manufacturing investments made up around three-quarters of overseas investments in ASEAN (excluding Singapore) by small and medium-sized enterprises (Moriaki 1992). There are, of course, large companies present in both the car and electronics industries: the car giant Toyota, for instance, has a joint venture in Thailand for producing commercial vehicle diesel engines, which are exported to both Malaysia and New Zealand. In addition, Mitsubishi is involved in a joint venture producing the Saga for the Malaysian domestic market, and has exported the Proton to the United Kingdom and elsewhere. In the electronics field, Sony Siam Industries has, since 1988, produced colour televisions, videos and audio equipment in Thailand, and Sony Video produces VTRs in Malaysia (Ohata and Urata 1993: 130). The growing importance of the local supply of components to other manufacturers as a motivation for investment in ASEAN is suggested by the president of Toshiba, which from the early 1990s started operating a second semiconductor plant in Thailand, having earlier built one in Malaysia: 'With just our Malaysian factory we could not fill Asian demand [for semiconductors]. We advanced into Asia not because of the cheapness of labour but because our customers are in Asia' (*Asahi Shimbun* 7 January 1993). The continued importance of Thailand for future investment is suggested by a survey carried out by the *Nihon Keizai Shimbunsha*, where executives chose Thailand as the number one country for investment up to the year 2000 (Ohata and Urata 1993: 123).

The diversification in the type of Japanese investment in the region in the late 1980s and 1990s, which points to a complex division of labour, is illustrated by the decisions taken by Matsushita. In Malaysia, Matsushita produces and sells consumer electrical goods such as colour TVs, fridges and vacuum cleaners, and acts as a production base for air conditioners. Approximately 70 per cent of the parts required in the production process are produced or acquired locally. In addition to the production of these consumer durables, in 1989 Matsushita set up management headquarters for Asia and the Middle East in Singapore. Further, in 1991, Matsushita established a research and development centre for air conditioners in Malaysia. Thus, not only production but also management and research are being located in the developing parts of east Asia

(*Toyokeizai* 22 May 1992: 108). The Matsushita example suggests the difficulty of charactizing the relationship between Japan and the NIEs and ASeAN as solely a vertical division of labour, with Japan exploiting cheap labour and resources.

Finally, it is nonetheless important to note that, despite the increase in Japanese investment and the relocation of production facilities, the region still remains an important source of raw materials for Japan, with imports from south-east Asia having increased from 18.3 per cent in 1975 to 25.1 per cent in 1989. Indeed, Japanese investments in the ASEAN countries have continued to include resource extraction and processing, with a total investment of US$17 billion in the period 1951–89, US$9 billion of which was resource-oriented. In this sense, resources from other parts of east Asia are still essential for Japan's economic well being.

Economic bloc?

The tremendous increase in the amount of Japanese investment in east Asia has led to calls for closer ties between Japan and other economies in the region, on the one hand, and fears of a regional economic bloc on the other. This suggests that the functional economic links between Japan and other parts of east Asia, strengthened after the Plaza Agreement, have created an environment where talk of an economic bloc or economic zone takes on more substance. One of the problems, however, is that many of the economic links developed in the 1980s – especially after the decision at the twentieth anniversary of ASEAN in Manila to pursue economic growth by giving a key role to foreign capital – are not necessarily autonomous links between members of ASEAN, or between ASEAN and other east Asian economies, but are rather links between or within Japanese multinationals. In this sense, Japanese companies can be expected to play a crucial role in any economic bloc or zone in the region. Of the proliferation of proposals, the Asia-Pacific Economic Coooperation Forum (APEC) proposed by Australian Prime Minister Hawke in 1989, and the East Asia Economic Caucus (EAEC) proposed by Malaysian Prime Minister Mahathir in 1990, deserve most attention.

In contrasting these two proposals, the first can be said to be rooted in the Cold War economic and political framework, as socialist or former Communist governments were inititially excluded from membership. At the Seoul meeting of APEC in 1991, however, the 'three Chinas' – the People's Republic of China, the Republic of

China (Taiwan) and Hong Kong – were allowed to participate. This points to the crucial role the dynamics of east Asian economic growth can play in breaking down political barriers: APEC offers a forum which the United Nations – having ousted Taiwan and excluding Hong Kong – cannot provide. Given the threat to regional stability posed by the escalation of any conflict amongst these three, their inclusion in APEC shows how regional bodies like APEC may gradually come to take on a wider role than economics. The main aims of APEC, however, are economic: to push forward with the liberalization of farm products based on the Uruguay Round, and to maintain the liberal trading order; to carry out training of the work force; to promote investment; to maintain the dynamism of growth, and so on.

In a sense, the EAEC can be viewed as a challenge to APEC, as well as to the EC and the north American Free Trade Agreement (NAFTA). Not being originally rooted in the Cold War framework, it includes the leading capitalist (Japan) and Communist (China) states as well as the 'other Chinas' and the Indochinese states. Unlike APEC, however, it does not include the United States. The aim is to press forward with free trade in east Asia in order to promote economic development, making the GATT Uruguay Round of importance for EAEC, too. As it does not include the United States, however, opposition has been voiced both within and without ASEAN, especially by US political leaders (*Toyokezai* 22 May 1992: 38–9). The opposition of the United States, which led to a downgrading in the original naming from 'group' to 'caucus', brought to the surface the latent conflict between east Asia, on the one hand, and the United States and Europe on the other, which had been obfuscated by Cold War structures. The proposal by Malaysia also seems to point to a greater confidence that, despite its historical legacy, as discussed below, Japan can play a more prominent role in the region. Indeed, for Malaysia, with a population of over 30 per cent ethnic Chinese, Japan can be viewed as a balance to the other main power in east Asia, politically as well as economically. For Japan, however, outright support of EAEC could unravel the balance it has tried to maintain between being a 'member of the West', cooperating closely with the United States and other Western powers, and an Asian power, with vital interests in the region.

Accordingly, of the two proposals, the Japanese government has been supportive of APEC rather than EAEC; yet Japan's participation in the latter is seen to be essential for its success. The crux of the problem is that both east Asia and the United States are important economically to Japan. Splitting the Asia-Pacific region is not in Japan's interest, as a foreign ministry official states: 'The splitting of Asia-Pacific should be avoided' (*Nihon Keizai Shimbun* 12 January 1993). Thus, instead of taking a lead role, as Prime Minister Mahathir had hoped, the Japanese government has made use of the lack of consensus among others in the group to resist being proactive. Then Prime Minister Kaifu Toshiki set the tone when he declared on his April 1991 visit to Malaysia: 'I would first like the debate to be completed in ASEAN. When it is settled as an ASEAN proposal, I would like to investigate whether to participate or not' (*Gaiko Jiho* March 1992: 12). As well as the competition from other concepts of economic cooperation, the possibility for rivalry between Japan and China, and political opposition to Japan's dominance of such a grouping remain as impediments to the realization of EAEC.

In his recent visit to a number of ASEAN countries, as discussed below, Prime Minister Miyazawa Kiichi was unwilling to support the idea of EAEC, preferring instead to strengthen APEC activities. Crucially, Miyazawa would not put relations with the US at risk. 'In order for NAFTA and the EC not to become a fortress,' he argued, 'it is important for Asia-Pacific to continue as an open region (*Asahi Shimbun* 15 January 1993). But this did not preclude the possibility of cooperation in the economic development of Vietnam, as Prime Minister Mahathir suggests: 'The reconstruction of the Vietnamese economy is indispensable for the stability of the peninsula, and we wish to continue in the future to cooperate with Japan in this' (*Nihon Keizai Shimbun* 15 January 1992). The Japanese prime minister's goal seems to be to avoid any move that could be seen to promote an economic bloc in the region, as this may provoke protectionism, which will be disadvantageous to Japan. In line with the recommendations of the Council set up by Miyazawa to think about Japan and Asia-Pacific in the twenty-first century, whose report was issued in December 1992, regional integration should be neither exclusionary, nor conflict with GATT nor harm a third party's interests (*Nihon Keizai Shimbun* 12 January 1993). In this respect, Japan remains unlikely actively to support EAEC.

Finally, mention should perhaps be made of the Asean Free Trade Agreement (AFTA) and the ASEAN post-ministerial conference. AFTA commenced in January 1993, with the aim of reducing tarifs to below 5 per cent amongst members of ASEAN by the year 2008, in order to bring about a major expansion in trade and investment.

This, too, can be viewed as a response to the EC and NAFTA, but progress is expected to be slow, especially as, in contrast to the EC, where intra-regional trade is over 60 per cent, ASEAN intra-regional trade has dropped from 18.6 per cent in 1985 to 14.4 per cent in 1991 (*Nihon Keizai Shimbun* 11 January 1993). Indeed, although all ASEAN countries were expected to act together to reduce tariffs on 1 January 1993, only Singapore did so, removing tariffs of 1–2.5 per cent on chemical products and clothes. In the background, of course, are Japanese companies, which have been called the 'main player in the shadows of AFTA' (*Nihon Keizai Shimbun* 11 January 1993). From summer 1993, for instance, Nissan will produce a small, multi-purpose 'ASEAN strategic car' especially for the south-east market, based on a regional division of labour involving Thailand, the Philippines, Malaysia and Taiwan, with Nissan wanting to 'in the future concentrate the production of parts in each country centering on AFTA and accelerate the horizontal division of labour' (*Nihon Keizai Shimbun* 11 January 1993). This suggests Japan will continue to play a key role in the region, even if AFTA's goals are slow to be realized.

As far as the ASEAN post-ministerial meeting is concerned, this is becoming increasingly important as a forum for discussions of issues of concern not only to the members of ASEAN, but also to the United States, Japan and the EC, who are in the near future expected to be joined at the meeting by Russia, China, Vietnam and Laos. Although the post-ministerial conference does not represent anything more than a first step, it may well develop over the years into a forum for a multilateral dialogue on political and security issues, which is lacking in the region. The more positive stance of the Clinton administration towards multi-lateral dialogue should enhance the importance of this forum (*Far Eastern Economic Review* 15 July 1993: 23).

THE MIYAZAWA DOCTRINE

Prime Minister Miyazawa, in his speech on Japan-ASEAN cooperation in Bangkok on 16 January 1993, and in his Administrative Statement to the Diet on 23 January 1993, outlined what has become known as the 'Miyazawa Doctrine'. In his speech, Miyazawa moved away from the tendency of previous Japanese leaders to focus on economic issues, and brought up Japan's political and indeed security role in the region, proposing contributions to peace and stability in the region and the world by furthering Japan-ASEAN dialogue on politics and security; promoting an open economic system and economic development; and enhancing democratization, human rights and other universal human values. Although the prime minister did bring up the question of the infringement of human rights by Indonesia in East Timor, when he met with President Suharto, the main thrust of his speech was on politics, economics and security, with a forward-looking emphasis on future cooperation based on a recognition of the 'diversity' of Asia. The goal now seems to be to build closer political and security, rather than purely economic, links with members of ASEAN (*Nihon Keizai Shimbun* 13 January 1993).

The same theme reoccurred in the prime minister's administrative policy speech to the Diet after his return (*Asahi Shimbun* 23 January 1993). The position taken by the prime minister in his visit and in his speech to the Diet contrasts with previous visits by Japanese prime ministers. On these occasions, the incumbent has tended to express regret for Japan's past actions, and to promise aid. Miyazawa, too, reiterated the promise not to become a 'military big power' and to maintain the US-Japan security treaty and the presence of US troops in Japan, suggesting Japan's continued need to mollify Asian concerns about its role in the region (*Asahi Shimbun* 26 January 1993).[2] At the same time, however, the end of the Cold War and the move towards a new international order is providing the Japanese government with an opportunity to play a bigger political and security role, as symbolized by Japan's participation in United Nations peace-keeping operations in Cambodia. Moreover, in attempting to clear the way for President Suharto, the incumbent head of the non-aligned movement, to attend the G7 meeting in Tokyo in July 1993, following the precedent set by Soviet Premier Gorbachev at the 1991 London summit, Miyazawa has taken on an active political role. In the end, however, Suharto was unable to address the summit itself, although in a pre-meeting with Prime Minister Miyazawa he was able to press the developing world's case (*Financial Times* 6 July 1993). Japan will require the support of ASEAN and other east Asian countries in its attempt to play a more powerful international role, just as it needs their support in securing a permanent seat on the United Nations Security Council, as well as the support of the Western powers in giving Asia a larger voice at Western-dominated meetings.

LEGACY OF WAR

The dynamics of Japanese investment in east Asia, and the call to strengthen relations between Japan and its neighbours, ineluctably spills over into the question of how Japan's legacy of imperialism and aggression will affect the future of the region. Despite attempts by the Japanese government to ameliorate anti-Japanese sentiment, suspicion of Japan remains in some of these countries, both on the governmental and popular levels. This surfaced in South Korea at the time of then-Prime Minister Kaifu Toshiki's visit, when several hundred people protested. Moreover, with the eruption of the 'comfort women' issue in August 1991 (this being the euphemism deployed during the war for the mainly Korean women forced into prostitution with Japanese soldiers), the legacy of the war has continued to dog Japan's relations with South Korea and its other east Asian neighbours (*Far Eastern Economic Review* 18 February 1993: 32–7). The imbalance in trade between Japan and South Korea, for instance, can be linked to the legacy of colonialism and the war: at present, imports from Japan are closed out of 258 'important diversification items' established by the South Korean government (Bernard and Ravenhill 1992: 17).

The legacy of imperialism and war has meant east Asian countries have been suspicious of Japan playing a larger political and security, as well as economic, role in the region. This surfaced at the time of the debate on sending Japanese troops to participate in United Nations peace-keeping operations in Cambodia. At the time, Prime Minister Kaifu found it necessary to visit Asian neighbours in an attempt to gain their understanding for Japan's despatch of troops – made easier with the promise of economic support. Although suspicion remains over Japan's goals, these have waned in some quarters with the ending of the Cold War, as Prime Minister Mahathir declared: 'I don't think Japan will become a military big power' (*Asahi Shimbun* 17 January 1993).

Finally, the recent emphasis on the 'diversity of Asia', as seen in Prime Minister Miyazawa's speech in Bangkok, is in stark contrast to the wartime emphasis on the 'unity of Asia'. As has been pointed out, however, the government's present call to 'look to Asia' may be nothing more than an updated version of the old theme, 'Asia is one', which regarded east Asia as 'a resource base' (*Asahi Shimbun* 27 January 1993). So long as such a nuance exists, fear of a new edition of the Greater East Asia Co-prosperity Sphere, which denied the diversity of Asia, will leave many in east Asia suspicious of Japan's motives.

CONCLUSION

This brief overview of the economic links between Japan and other parts of east Asia suggests how Japanese companies have been affected by changes in the global economy. The need to remain competitive has forced many companies to move some of their production facilities offshore and invest in both the NIEs and ASEAN. Needless to say, one of the motivations for moving offshore was cheaper labour costs. This helps to explain the shift away from investment in the NIEs to ASEAN in the 1990s, as labour costs have risen in the NIEs. At the same time, however, the increasing number of Japanese manufacturing plants based in the region makes location, per se, important to Japanese suppliers, as in the case of Toshiba's location of its new semiconductor plant in Malaysia. This suggests that the move overseas by Japanese companies is not neces- sarily driven by the desire to use 'cheap Asian labour'. At the same time, the establishment of both management and R&D centres in the region points to the complexity of the division of labour now developing between Japan, the NIEs and ASEAN. The extent to which this will complement the vertical division of labour as a permanent, not temporary, phenomenon will be crucial to the future relationship between Japan and the other economies of east Asia.

Moreover, although Japanese companies have played the lead role in linking Japan and other parts of east Asia, these functional links have spilled over into the political arena. It is precisely as a result of these close economic ties that the breakdown of the Cold War structures has allowed Japan to play a more important role in the politics and security of the region. At the same time, however, in order for Japan to be fully accepted in this new role, it needs to come to terms with two legacies: the Second World War and Japan's occupation of other Asian nations. At the moment, however, the legacy of the war is off-set by the legacy of the occupation: the 'revival of Japanese militarism' (the legacy of the war) is seen to be kept in check by the US-Japan security treaty (the legacy of the occupation). As outlined in the 'Miyazawa Doctrine', any new role for Japan in the region is envisaged alongside the maintenance of the alliance with the US. Thus, pressure from the United States, as well as consideration of national interest, suggest a continued reluctance on the part of Japan to support the proposed EAEC. In the end, the dynamics of Japan's economic relations with east Asia may be enough to undermine the remaining suspicion of Japan as a result of its wartime legacy, but not enough to call into question the fundamentals of the US-Japan alliance relationship. In this sense, the ending of the Cold War has not yet enabled Japan to come to terms with the legacy of the occupation.

Finally, the extent to which Japan's role in Cambodian peace-keeping will herald in a new military role in the region remains to be seen. Although domestic opinion is now much more supportive of Japan playing some sort of military role in the world than at the time of the outbreak of the Gulf War, many Japanese remain apprehensive. At the same time, many of Japan's east Asian neighbours, especially those with memories of Japanese imperialism and aggression, continue to harbour doubts about a militarily proactive Japan. In this sense, the legacy of the war can be expected to continue to influence the development of relations between Japan and its east Asian neighbours.

Notes

1 The term 'east Asia' is used here to denote the Asian NIEs (Hong Kong, Singapore, South Korea and Taiwan) and the five main members of ASEAN (Indonesia, Malaysia, Singapore, the Philippines and Thailand, excluding Brunei), Singapore is counted as an NIE unless otherwise stated. The socialist/capitalist economies of China, North Korea and Indo-china are omitted unless otherwise stated.
2 The Council on Japan and Asia-Pacific in the 21st Century sees the maintenance of the alliance with the US as the basis for Japan not to become a military super-power.

Bibliography

Bernard, M. and Ravenhill, J. (1992) 'New Hierarchies in East Asia: The Post Plaza division of Labour', Working Paper, Research School of Pacific Studies, Australian National University.

Jetro, H. (1993) *Sekai to Nihon no Kaigai Chokusetsu Toshi*, Tokyo: Jetro.

Katsuaki, O. (1992) 'Denki Kikaikogyo no Kaigaishinshutsu to Shinryakute-kiteikei no Shinten', *Keizai*, October: 40–54.

Keizai 1991, 'Higashi Ajia keizaiken to Nihon' (symposium report), December.

'Keizai' Henshubuhen, (1988) *Kaigai Shinshutsu no Jittai*, Tokyo: Shinnihon Shuppan.

Moriaki, T. (1992) 'Kokusaika Senryaku to Tenbo – Nihon no Kigyo o Chushin ni', *Gendai Nihon Shakai* 7: 136.

Ohata, Y. and Urata, S. (eds) (1993) *ASEAN no Keizai, Nihon no Yakuwari*, Tokyo: Yuikaku.

Rekishigaku Kenkyukai (1991) 'Tenkanki no Sekai to Nihon', *Nihon Dojidaishi* 5: 229–30.

9 The rationale for strategic planning in the Asia-Pacific region
Implications for european corporations

Foo Check Teck

INTRODUCTION

This chapter follows up on a recent *Long Range Planning* article (Foo *et al*. 1992) on the strategic planning process within the Asia-Pacific region. Its purpose is to develop some insights into the role of strategic planning in major ASEAN corporations. This is done through appreciating the nature, context and performance of these organizations. Empirical findings relating to the benefits, problems and contributions of strategic planning are then discussed. Drawing on these analyses, some implications are suggested for European management.

Since Ansoff's early work (1965) on corporate strategy, there has been an interesting stream of empirical research studies of strategic planning in major corporations in the West (for the US, Ringbakk 1969, Ang and Chua 1979; for the UK, Taylor and Irving 1971, Denning and Lehr, 1971, Grinyer and Norburn 1974, Bazzaz and Grinyer 1980, Higgins and Finn 1977, Higgins 1981, Bhatty 1981; for Germany, Strigel 1970). Capon *et al*. (1980) raise the little-explored perspective of strategic planning research – the international diffusion of Western approaches to corporate strategic planning. It is useful to ask whether, in this West-East transmission of corporate strategic planning practices, the corporate experience of strategic planning in the Asia-Pacific region is similar to that in Europe? Are there gaps between theories and practices of strategic planning (Martin 1979)?

Western corporate experiences of strategic planning during the 1970s and early 1980s are particularly relevant as a basis for comparative analysis, since some of the industrializing countries in the ASEAN region (e.g. Singapore) can be said to be at a similar stage of national economic development today. It is possible that strategic planning approaches as defined in the US may, in the process of their implementation by European corporations, undergo some refinement or even transmutation as a consequence. This may be due to fundamental cultural differences in management. For instance, Foo (1992) found differences between Eastern firms (Singapore-owned) and Western firms (mainly European- or American-owned) in the 'molecular' structuring of their productivity improvement efforts. This is despite the fact that all the firms studied were operating within the same national context of Singapore – a country often described as being too 'Westernized'! Thus, despite the fact that the English language is so commonly used in Singapore, in terms of organizing strategies, the indigenous Singaporean approaches are more 'soft' that those of foreign-owned, mostly Western firms, which are defined as 'hard' or highly *strategy-driven*. This suggests the value of empirical studies.

Empirical research seeking to encompass a much wider geographical spread, such as the ASEAN nations (Singapore, Malaysia, Thailand, the Philippines, Indonesia and Brunei), should prove to be of even greater value since it will capture the rich cultural diversities in Asian management. European corporations that are seeking to fuel their growth by tapping the dynamic, fast-growing economies in the Far East will naturally be keen to examine the strategic planning process in major, publicly-listed ASEAN corporations. By definition, strategic management deals with the long term. Thus, top European management needs to be able to cooperate at a strategic level with its Asian counterparts. Better Western insight into Asian strategic management means companies will be able to reap the benefits of coadaptation of strategies.

The ASEAN experience

Foo *et al.* (1992) discussed aspects of the strategic planning process found to operate within ASEAN corporations. The basic conceptual model of strategic planning that underpinned this study is derived from Grinyer 1971. The rational, systematic characteristics of the *traditional* planning process are obviously part of the managerial process in these publicly-listed corporations. This does not, however, mean that these corporations are necessarily overly rational in their managerial approaches (Lindblom 1959). Another common feature of the ASEAN corporations is their orientation towards goal-setting and formality. Formality is seen in the development of comprehensive, written plans especially for functional areas such as marketing, finance and operations. Also, there is the expectation of growing investment in the strategic planning process, in terms of financial and human resources; the use of qualitative, quantitative and computing techniques; and greater involvement of managers in the process.

Even more interestingly, in parallel to this coordinated, monitored and controlled process of strategy implementation, ASEAN management also emphasize *ad hoc* strategic decision-taking. A paradoxical 'tight/loose' quality characterizes the ASEAN approach to strategic management in large corporations. Indeed, it may even be argued that Asean management sees the formal strategic process as enabling flexibility rather than diminishing it, since the strategic planning process (which leads to an explicit formalization of goals, strategies, task and resource allocations) should facilitate a more fine-tuned, more quickly coordinated adaptation of strategies to changes in the external environments. This quality of management is especially valuable for very large organizations operating in rapidly changing economic environments. However, some questions remained unanswered. For instance:

- What are the profiles of those corporations that responded to the chief executive and senior manager instruments?[1]
- How effective are these corporations in terms of goal achievement? Do they operate in highly predictable environments?
- How do these corporations compare with the others in the same industry? What are some of the benefits and problems experienced?
- What are the contributions of strategic planning to strategy-making? Does strategic planning contribute to goal achievements?

This chapter tries to fill these gaps and provide a more complete picture of strategic planning in this important part of the Asia-Pacific region.

THE PROFILE OF ASEAN CORPORATIONS

Table 9.1 provides an interesting profile of the ASEAN corporations, including characteristics of respondents (chief executives and senior managers).[2] As can be seen, chief executives fall within a wide age range (31–70 years). Interestingly, most of these were taught in English at school. The mean age for the senior managers is around 41 years. In terms of response rates, Singapore is the highest with

Table 9.1 Profile of ASEAN sample

Respondents' profile		
Chief executive officer	Age range = 31 to 70 years	
	English in schools = 79.3%	
Senior manager	Mean Age = 41 years	

Pattern of response		
Overall ASEAN response	24.7%	(n=109)
Singapore	43.9%	(n=43)
Malaysia	18.2%	(n=31)
Thailand	24.1%	(n=20)
Philippines	17.6%	(n=13)
Indonesia	11.8%	(n=2)

Distribution by international standard industrial code of overall responding sample (n=109)	
Financial services	10.1%
Banking	10.1%
Construction and services	8.3%
Trading	11.9%
Hotels	5.5%
Agriculture	8.3%
Mining	4.6%
Food, textiles and paper	11.9%
Chemical	12.8%
Metals and minerals	6.4%
Machineries	10.1%

Organizational characteristics (1985)*		
Age (number of years)	30	(n=98)
Number of employees	1611	(n=21)
Annual sales (1985)	US$81,268,000	(n=83)
Total assets value	US$468,727,000	(n=74)
Annual net profits	US$4,747,000	(n=79)

Key financial ratios (1985)*		
Return on sales	7.8%	(n=79)
Return on assets	5.1%	(n=65)
Return on equity	4.2%	(n=55)
Equity to assets	43.0%	(n=69)

*For some companies, these data were not available

43.9 per cent, the lowest being 11.8 per cent. In terms of country compositions (n=109), Singapore is the largest (n=43), followed by Malaysia (n=31), Thailand (n=20), Philippines (n=13) and Indonesia (n=2). Most industries are represented, with the chemical industry figuring most prominently (12.8 per cent), followed by food, textiles and paper (11.9 per cent), trading (11.9 per cent), financial services (8.3 per cent), banking (10.1 per cent) and machineries (10.1 per cent). Construction and services (8.3 per cent), agriculture (8.3 per cent), metals and minerals (6.4 per cent), hotels (5.5 per cent) and mining (4.6 per cent) are also present in the total ASEAN sample. Such a diverse sample in terms of industries as well as countries implies that the findings here have the added attraction of general applicability across a wide range of contexts.

The other interesting characteristics of the sample are also reflected in Table 9.1. Most organizations are well-established (30 years, n=98), with a sizeable workforce (1611, n=21) and assets (US$ 468 million), and significant sales volume (US$ 81 million, n=83), and are making profits (US$ 4.7 million). In terms of profitability, these are generally healthy as reflected in the different measures of return on sales (7.8 per cent, n=79), return on assets (5.1 per cent, n=65), and return on equity (4.2 per cent, n=55). From a capital perspective, there are moderate levels of debt with equity to assets at 43 per cent (n=69).

In interpreting the empirical findings on aspects of strategic planning, it is important for readers to bear in mind these organizational characteristics, obtained from secondary sources.[3]

GOAL PERFORMANCE AND ENVIRONMENTAL CERTAINTY

Goal performance context

In order to put the strategic planning systems of major ASEAN corporations into context, it is useful to have some insights into their current situations.

Are these organizations already achieving their goals at the time of the survey?

From Table 9.2, it is obvious that these are goal-achieving corporations. Indeed, more than half (50.6 per cent) claim to have achieved more than their quantitative goals Some are even claiming that their quantitative goal achievements are *significantly above what is set* (13.8 per cent). Less than one-quarter of those surveyed are underachieving in terms of quantitative goals (21.8 per cent). Most surprisingly, the ASEAN corporations find the superior achievement of qualitative dimensions of goals to be more difficult. This is seen in the lower per centage of those claiming that qualitative goal achievements are *above what is set* (29.5 per cent, cf 36.8 per cent)

Table 9.2 CEO perceptions of goal performance context (percentage)

	Quantitative goals	Qualitative goals
Significantly above what is set	13.8	2.3
Above what is set	36.8	29.5
As is what is set	27.6	46.6
Below what is set	20.7	20.5
Significantly below what is set	1.1	1.1

as well as being *significantly above* (2.3 per cent, cf 13.8 per cent). Such a perspective is additionally reinforced by a marginally higher proportion of corporations claiming to achieve qualitative as compared with quantitative goals (78.4 per cent versus 78.2 per cent). These findings suggest that the achievement of qualitative goals *significantly above what is set or expected* are more difficult. Perhaps, due to their very nature, qualitative goals are more illusive and the extent and level of their attainment more difficult to determine. The results suggest that the interaction between quantitative and qualitative goals is an interesting phenomenon meriting further research.

1 Why do organizations such as those in the ASEAN region experience such difficulties?
2 Is this mainly a problem of lack of measurements of the qualitative goals?
3 Will the quantification of these qualitative goals make any difference?

Some background understanding of the nature of the goal achievement context in these firms is useful, since these results have important implications for strategic management consultants. Strategic planning processes and techniques need to evolve towards helping organizations to achieve qualitatively defined goals.

Environmental certainty context

One role often cited for strategic planning in the literature is to help the chief executive officer (CEO) cope with environmental uncertainty. This explains the technical orientation of traditional models of strategic planning towards the rise of forecasting techniques or scenario generation. Despite the rapidly changing nature of the ASEAN economies, CEOs through their responses have painted a broad picture of predictable environments (Table 9.3). More than half of the sample described their resource environments as *predictable to a large or very large extent*: funds (68.1 per cent), manpower skills (67 per cent) and materials (59 per cent). The competition environment is also seen by more than half of the sample to be just as predictable (58.4 per cent). As for the other environments, the proportion of the sample that felt these environments to be largely predictable remains quite sizeable, at above 40 per cent – technological (47.7 per cent) demand (45.5 per cent)and regulatory (43.2 per cent).

These findings seem to reflect the consequences of having implemented strategic planning processes. For example, CEOs may, through the application of forecasting techniques or the generation of alternative scenarios, perceive their environments to be more predictable. It is equally possible that the role of strategic planning as a coordinative, direction-setting device may help ASEAN CEOs to cope better with sharp, unexpected changes in their environments. But environmental unpredictability still remains as one of the major problems (see later discussion) encountered in strategic planning. It is thus possible that although the implementation of strategic planning may have made significant contributions to managing uncertainty and change, environmental unpredictability from unexpected sources still remains a major difficulty.

Given the above analyses, it is now possible to appreciate better the empirical findings on the associated benefits and problems of strategic planning. Also, when discussing the role of strategic planning, it is useful to bear in mind these organizational characteristics.

COMPETITIVE POSTURING

To appreciate the type of organizations that constitute the ASEAN sample, perceptions are captured from the senior managers over a wide range of 'competitiveness posturing measures' (perceptually relative to the corporation's industry). These 'competitiveness postures' are those often emphasized in strategic management literature. The external market-related, competitiveness postures captured include aspects on the product (range, pricing, quality) and market diversification. Internal posturing when competing is seen in the emphasis placed on strategic planning, corporate integration (through promoting corporate identification), new technology application and innovations in product development. Table 9.4 provides detailed statistics for each of these. Although the detailed percent-

Table 9.3 The degree of predictability within each environment to which the corporation is exposed (percentage)

	Demand environment	Competition environment	Technological environment	Materials	Resources availability Manpower skills	Funds	Regulatory environment
None	–	1.1	2.3	4.8	2.3	1.1	1.1
A little	12.5	10.1	6.8	10.8	4.5	4.5	19.3
Some	42.0	30.3	43.2	25.3	26.1	26.1	36.4
Large	30.7	44.9	42.0	49.4	53.4	54.5	39.8
Very large	14.8	13.5	5.7	9.6	13.6	13.6	3.4

Table 9.4 Comparing with the norm within the industry (percentage)

	Product range available	Competitiveness of prices	Quality of product	Emphasis on strategic planning	Promotion of corporate identity	Application of new technology	Diversification into new markets	Innovativeness in product development
Very much less than average	–	1.2	1.2	2.4	2.3	3.6	5.9	3.5
Below average	3.5	3.5	2.3	12.9	14.0	8.3	17.6	9.3
Average	24.7	38.4	26.7	38.8	26.7	26.2	35.3	34.9
Above average	49.4	41.9	46.5	35.3	32.6	42.9	36.5	41.9
Very much above average	22.4	15.1	23.3	10.6	24.4	19.0	4.7	10.5

ages may vary across the individual measures of competitive postures, there are interesting patterns in these findings. In general,
these are organizations that tend to emphasize more than the industry on a wide range of competitiveness measures. Indeed, when
competing, more than one-fifth of the sample claim their organizations to be *very much above average* in the following aspects: product
range (22.4 per cent), product quality (23.3 per cent) and promotion
of corporate identity (24.4 per cent) – with almost 20 per cent for
the application of new technology. The corresponding sample statistics for the *above industry level* emphases are: product range (71.8
per cent), product quality (69.8 per cent), application of new technology (61.9 per cent), price competitiveness (57 per cent) promotion of corporate identity (57 per cent), and product innovation
(52.4 per cent).

   What is most surprising, is that strategic planning (45.9 per
cent) lags behind all these competitiveness measures in terms of
above average industry emphases. There remains some possible
scope for an enhanced role for strategic planning as a competitive
tool among these publicly listed corporations. This expectation must,
however, be tempered by the finding that almost 85 per cent of the
sample are either *average or above industry* in their emphases on
strategic planning. Another interesting implication is suggested by
these findings, namely that even the large, long-established, publicly
listed ASEAN organizations are utilizing, in parallel, processes other
than formal strategic planning in developing their competitive pos-
ture. This finding reinforces the discussion earlier (Foo, *et al.* 1992)
of a role for the *ad hoc* incremental processes in organizations
(Quinn 1980).

BENEFITS AND PROBLEMS OF STRATEGIC PLANNING PROCESS

A broad range of benefits are enjoyed as a result of implementing
strategic planning within the ASEAN corporations. Consistently,
more than half of our sample reported having benefited to a large
extent in direction-setting, enhanced corporate behavioural
responses and effects on the organizational culture (Table 9.5). The
most enduring quality that strategic planning is able to bring to bear
in organizations is *a sense of purpose and direction* (81.3 per cent)
with the formally written plan as a guide (71.1 per cent). There is
also an enhancement of corporate behavioural responses in terms
of proactivity (66.1 per cent), awareness of external developments

Table 9.5 Benefits of formal planning

	Direction		Awareness of external developments	Corporate behavioural response			Corporate culture	
	Value of plan as a guide	Sense of purpose & direction		Evolving timely strategies	Corporate reactive capability	Corporate proactive capability	Creates team spirit	Shared values & philosophy
None	–	–	–	1.7	1.7	1.7	3.4	3.4
Little	6.8	6.8	6.8	16.9	8.5	8.5	16.9	11.9
Some	22.0	11.9	28.8	22.0	28.8	23.7	27.1	33.9
Large	50.8	50.8	45.8	42.4	44.1	49.2	42.4	39.0
Very large	20.3	30.5	18.6	16.9	16.9	16.9	10.2	11.9

(64.4 per cent), reactivity (61 per cent) and the evolving of timely strategies (59.3 per cent). Besides these, corporate culture also gains in terms of team spirit (52.6 per cent) and the emergence of shared values and philosophy (50.9 per cent). The experience of such a wide range of benefits may explain the expected, and growing, investment in strategic planning systems.

ASEAN corporations are seen to be experiencing problems in implementing strategic planning processes. One major problem encountered is an unpredictable environment – almost half of the sample (48.3 per cent) find this to be so to a large extent (see earlier discussion) (Table 9.6). This lends some support to the argument that a major role for strategic planning in ASEAN is in helping organizations cope with uncertainty. More than one-third of the sample seems to face problems with inadequate published statistical data (33.4 per cent) and too much paperwork (33.9 per cent). Corporations in ASEAN find it necessary constantly to revise and update their strategic plans possibly and this is quite associated with the need to cope with changing, uncertain environments. This gave rise to the growing perception of the problem of too frequent reviews (25.9 per cent). Such frequent changes may have led some to realize the limitations in the applicability of strategic planning tools. As much as 44.8 per cent of the sample cite this as a problem to some extent. The ASEAN corporations also experience human problems in implementing strategic planning, although these are less pressing. For instance, strategic planning is perceived as not fostering entrepreneurial skills (37.9 per cent), and as generating too much rivalry (35.1 per cent).

The above discussion highlights the types of benefits enjoyed, and the problems encountered, by ASEAN corporations in implementing strategic planning. The next section looks at the role of strategic planning especially in terms of coping with environmental changes, CEO strategy formulation, identification of SWOT (corporate strengths, weaknesses, opportunities and threats) and contribution to goal achievements.

THE ROLE OF STRATEGIC PLANNING

Table 9.7 provides descriptive statistics of the contributions of strategic planning in helping ASEAN corporations cope with environmental change. The major areas where strategic planning can be said to be effective (to a large extent) are funding (57.3 per cent), manpower skills (55.1 per cent), demand (55.1 per cent) and compe-

Table 9.6 Problems associated with formal planning

	Unpredictable environment	Inadequate published statistics	Planning tools impractical	Too much paperwork	Too frequent revisions	Generates too much rivalry	Does not foster entrepreneurial skills
None	–	1.8	15.5	1.7	8.6	22.8	20.7
Little	10.3	14.0	39.7	25.4	36.2	42.1	41.4
Some	41.4	50.9	34.5	39.0	29.3	22.8	31.0
Large	32.8	24.6	10.3	28.8	20.7	10.5	6.9
Very large	15.5	8.8	–	5.1	5.2	1.8	–

Table 9.7 CEO assessment of strategic planning system capability to help the corporation cope with environmental changes (percentage)

	Environment				Resource availability		
	Demand	Competition	Technology	Regulation	Material	Manpower	Funds
None	2.2	3.4	3.4	5.6	2.3	3.4	3.4
Little	9.0	7.9	12.4	16.9	20.5	10.1	12.4
Some	33.7	34.8	42.7	48.3	37.5	31.5	27.0
Large	47.2	43.8	38.2	24.7	33.0	46.1	46.1
Very large	7.9	10.1	3.4	4.5	6.8	9.0	11.2

tition (53.9 per cent). This is remarkable, since the persons surveyed are the CEOs themselves. And where the test is for 'some contribution' other than a major role, then the contribution of strategic planning is seen to be even more wide-ranging. Over 80 per cent of the CEOs claim strategic planning to have made at least some contribution to demand (88.8 per cent), competition (88.7 per cent), manpower skills (86.6 per cent), funding (84.3 per cent) and technology (84.3 per cent). For the remaining types of environmental change surveyed, the percentages claiming strategic planning to have made some contribution are only slightly lower – regulatory changes (77.5 per cent) and changes in material environments (77.3 per cent). Based on these findings, strategic planning can be said to have helped ASEAN corporations to cope with the changes that emanate from a broad range of environments.

The direct contributions of strategic planning processes to aspects of strategy formulation and implementation are even more interesting and reassuring for strategic management scholars. The extent to which strategic planning has contributed to CEO's formulation of corporate strategies, SWOT (strengths, weaknesses, opportunities and threats) identification and goal achievement is shown in Table 9.8. Nearly all the CEOs (over 90 per cent of the sample) claim strategic planning has made some contribution to their formulation of corporate strategies (94.2 per cent), to the corporate achievement of goals (quantitative 94.4 per cent and qualitative 90 per cent) and to the identification of corporate strengths (97.8 per cent) and weaknesses (96.6 per cent). As for identifying external opportunities (89.8 per cent) and threats (82 per cent), the percentages remain substantially high. If the most critical role for strategic planning is to help CEOs shape corporate strategies, then clearly ASEAN CEOs have found obvious justification for implementing the process. More than three-quarters of the ASEAN CEOs surveyed (75.8 per cent) share the view that strategic planning has helped to a large extent. An equally important reason for continuing with strategic planning is its contribution to quantitative goals. Again, more one-quarter of the CEOs (75.3 per cent) affirm that strategic planning has contributed to a large extent. Strategic planning is, however, less effective in helping ASEAN corporations achieve qualitative goals (54 per cent claimed it was effective to a large extent).

The picture that emerges is one in favour of the continued practice of strategic planning. ASEAN corporations seem to heed well the advice of Halpern (1984) in 'Strategic Planning for the Future'.

Table 9.8 Assessment of strategic planning performance* (percentage)

| | Strategy | SWOT identification | | | | Achievement of goals | |
	Strategy	Strengths	Weaknesses	Opportunities	Threats	Quantitative	Qualitative
None	0.0	1.1	2.2	3.4	3.4	2.2	2.2
Little	5.7	1.1	1.1	6.7	14.6	3.4	7.9
Some	18.4	33.7	32.6	30.3	24.7	19.1	36.0
Large	60.9	51.7	48.3	49.4	48.3	58.4	46.1
Very large	14.9	12.4	15.7	10.1	9.0	16.9	7.9

*The extent to which strategic planning activities are perceived to help in strategy (strategic decision-making), identifying SWOT and helping in achievement of goals

There is none of the pessimism currently prevalent in the practice of strategic management (Hurst 1986). Interestingly, even as far back as 1971, Ringbakk painted a less than optimistic future for formal strategic planning processes. There are obviously differences in perception of the utility of strategic planning. We should ask what are some of the possible implications of these empirical findings for the management of major European corporations?

IMPLICATIONS FOR MAJOR EUROPEAN CORPORATIONS

First, in terms of cooperation with the major corporations in ASEAN sharing the above characteristics, a possible approach to business collaboration is to evolve a shared philosophy of a planned yet flexible approach to strategic management. This implies the importance of cross-cultural understanding of strategic management styles.

Besides exposure to work in an Asian environment, some insights can be gained via the literature. For instance, a reading of texts such as Sun Zi's classic *Art of War* can provide valuable insights into Chinese strategic business thinking. Also, ancient Chinese works such as the *I Ching* or the *Book of Changes* often stressed the mutability of worldly, external developments. Sustaining strategic momentum (Miller and Friesen 1980) is an integral part of the strategy process.

Second, it is important to have a more contextualized, contin-gently-based perspective of management. Empirically-based research works on strategic management, such as Grinyer *et al.* 1980, 1986 and 1988, should be extended to the analysis of Asian corporations in their own contexts. For instance, unlike the situation in Britain or the US, trades unionism in Singapore is often associated with a variety of productivity improvement practices (Foo 1991a; 1991b). In the same manner, formal strategic planning activities are seen to be very much part of the fabric of the managerial process in major ASEAN corporations. This is despite the fact that the traditional mode of strategic planning may be *passé* in the West.

Third, given the continued relevance of strategic planning pro-cesses in the Asia-Pacific region, top management in European corporations should think twice before scrapping formal planning entirely. If European and Asian firms are to collaborate, it may be useful to engage in strategic planning exercises involving senior managers from both sides. Participation in such activities should help to foster better mutual understanding and a longer-term strategic perspective on collaborative business. If such activities are held prior to the formal establishment of collaborative partnerships, they should help both sides to gain better insights into their respective strategic approaches. For instance, the lack of statistical data bases in Asia means that the approach to strategy formulation is likely to be more intuitive. Typical textbooks such as Steiner and Miner 1977 do emphasize the intuitive elements in strategy formulation (p. 92). Both sides will appreciate how the other 'senses' changes in the environment (Norburn and Grinyer 1973/4). Also, such active participation may engender a more 'culturally adaptive' approach in management (Keesing 1974), and possibly to shared expectations (Cyert and March 1964), 'theories in use' (Argyris 1978), 'recipes' (Grinyer and Spender 1979), or 'strategic capabilities' (Porter 1985). It may even be possible to shape a mutually satisfying balance-of-power structure (MacMillan and Jones 1986; Pfeffer 1981) to ensure the long-term survival of any collaborative efforts.

Notes

1 Foo *et al.* 1992 provides a profile of corporations that responded to the corporate planner instrument.
2 The profile given here relates to companies that have responded to the chief executive and senior manager instruments. Of these, a smaller subset of companies also responded to the corporate planner instruments, and their profile is given in an earlier paper (Foo *et al.* 1992).
3 Corporate data derived from *Asia's 7,500 Largest Companies* published by ELC International, 1983 and 1985 editions.

Bibliography

Ang, J. S. and Chua, J. H. (1979) 'Long Range Planning in Large United States Corporations – A Survey', *Long Range Planning* 12, April: 99–102.

Ansoff, H. I. (1965) *Corporate Strategy*, New York: McGraw-Hill.

Argyris, C. (1978) *Organizational Learning: A Theory of Action Perspective*, Wesley, MA: Addison-Wesley.

Bazzaz, S. A. and Grinyer, P. H. (1980) 'How Planning Works in Practice – A Survey of 48 UK Companies', *Long Range Planning* 13, 4, August.

Bhatty, E. F. (1981) 'Corporate Planning in Medium-sized Companies in the UK', *Long Range Planning* 14, 1.

Capon, N., Farley J. U. and Hulbert, J. (1980) 'International Diffusion of Corporate and Strategic Planning Practices', *Columbia Journal of World Business* 5–13.

Cyert, R. M. and March, J. G. (1964) *A Behavioural Theory of the Firm*, Englewood Cliffs, NJ: Prentice-Hall.

Denning, B. W. and Lehr, M. E. (1971) 'The Extent and Nature of Corporate Long Range Planning in the United Kingdom: I', *Journal of Management Studies* 1: 145–61.

Foo, C. T. (1990) *A Cross-sectional Study of the Interrelationships of Strategic, Contextual and Performance Variables*, Unpublished Ph.D. thesis, University of St Andrews.

—— (1991a) 'Does Unionisation Lead to Corporate Changes in Productivity Practices – Insights from Singapore', *International Journal of Human Resource Management* 2, 2: 221–6.

—— (1991b) 'Union Presence and Corporate Productivity Practices', *British Journal of Industrial Relations* XXIX, 1: 123–7.

—— (1992) 'Culture, Productivity and Structure: A Singapore Study', *Organisation Studies* 13, 4: 589–609.

Foo, C. T., Grinyer, P. H. and McKiernan, P. (1992) 'Strategic Planning in the ASEAN Region', *Long Range Planning* 25, 5: 80–92.

Grinyer, P.H. (1971) 'The Anatomy of Business Strategic Planning Reconsidered', *Journal of Management Studies* 8, 2: 339–50.

Grinyer, P.H. and Norburn, D. (1974), 'Strategic Planning in 21 UK Companies', *Long Range Planning* 7, 4, August.

—— (1975) 'An Empirical Investigation of Some Aspects of Strategic Planning', *Journal of the Royal Statistical Society* Series A, 138, Part 1: 70–97.

Grinyer, P.H. and Spender, J.C. (1979) 'Recipes, Crises and Adaptation', *International Studies of Management and Organisation* IX, 3: 113.

Grinyer, P.H. Al Bazzaz, S. and Ardekani, S.Y. (1980) 'Strategy, Structure, the Environment and Financial Performance in 48 UK Companies', *Academy of Management Journal* 23, 2: 193–220.

—— (1986) 'Towards a Contingency Theory of Corporate Planning: Findings in 48 UK Companies', *Strategic Management Journal* 7: 3–28.

Grinyer, P.H., McKiernan, P. and Ardekani, M.Y. (1988) 'Market, Organisational and Managerial Correlates of Economic Performance in the UK Electrical Engineering Industry', *Strategic Management Journal* 9: 297–318.

Halpern, R. S.(1984) 'Advice to Researchers: Strategic Planning for the Future', *European Research*: 60–6.

Higgins, J. C. and Finn, R. (1977) 'The Organisation and Practice of Corporate Planning in the UK', *Long Range Planning* 10 August: 88–92.

Higgins, R. B. (1981) 'Long Range Planning in the Mature Corporation', *Strategic Management Journal* 2: 235–50.

Hurst, D. K. (1986) 'Why Strategic Management is Bankrupt', *Organisational Dynamics* autumn: 5–27.

Keesing, R. (1974) 'Theories of Culture', *Annual Review of Anthropology* 3: 73–9.

Lindblom, (1959) 'The Science of Muddling Through', *Public Administration Review*, 19: 79–88.

Macmillan, I. C. and Jones, P. E. (1986) *Strategy Formulation: Power and Politics*, Saint Paul, MN: West Publishing Co.

Martin, J. (1979) 'Business Planning: The Gap between Theory and Practices', *Long Range Planning* 12, 16.

Miller, D. and Friesen, P. (1980) 'Momentum and Revolution in Organisational Adaptation', *Academy of Management Journal*, 23: 519–614.

Norburn, D. and Grinyer, P. (1973/4) 'Directors without Directions', *General Management* 1, 2.

Pfeffer, J. (1981) *Power in Organisations*, New York: Harper Business.

Porter, M. E. (1985) *Competitive Advantage*, New York: Collier Macmillan.

Quinn, J. B. (1980) *Strategies of Change: Logical Incrementation*, Homeward, IL: Richard D. Irwin.

Ringbakk, K. A. (1969) 'Organised Planning in Major US Companies', *Long Range Planning* 2, 1.

—— (1971) 'Why Planning Fails', *European Business* spring.

Steiner, G. and Miner, J. (1977) *Management Policy and Strategy*, New York: Collier Macmillan.

Strigel, W. H. (1970) 'Planning in West German Industry', *Long Range Planning* September: 9–15.

Sun Zi (1989) *Art of War*; Facsimile translation of 1910 edition, edited by L. Giles, Singapore: Graham Brash.

Taylor, B. and Irving, P. (1971) 'Organised Planning in Major U.K. Companies', *Long Range Planning* 3, 4, June.

10 Time and strategic action
The Japanese case

Michael Hay and Jean-Claude Usunier

INTRODUCTION

This chapter presents a way of analysing an organization's temporal identity. Central to this approach is our belief that an organization's sense of time is revealed through action and, specifically, through its approach to strategic planning. A framework is developed showing levels of strategic planning and their cross-cultural variability, especially in relation to Japanese temporal culture (*makimono* time). Strategies pursued by international banks from the US, the UK, Germany and Japan illustrate how a strategic time perspective reflects the temporal cognitive styles prevailing in a particular culture. We further show the influence exerted by the constituencies to which an organization is beholden, the definition of performance criteria, and their reinforcement through human resource management policies.

A central proposition of this chapter is that Japanese corporations and Japanese banks operate with a culturally specific conception of time, which shapes their strategic planning process. The Japanese banks, for instance, have quickly achieved notoriety within the world's club of international banks. According to *The Banker*, in March 1988, twelve Japanese banks ranked among the world's largest, of which the top five overall were Japanese. Japanese banks have concentrated on acquiring market share, at the expense of short-term profitability. Their internationalization has been fairly rapid: from 1977 to 1987 they increased their Europe outlets (branches, subsidiaries and offices) from 307 to 741 (Gupta 1989).

According to global banking consultant Steven Davies: 'Time was never articulated as a major aspect', by Japanese banking executives (Davies 1989). Therefore, an understanding of managers' concepts of time depends on an analysis of their strategic action and the ways in which this *reveals* a view of time.

Japanese banks and Japanese companies are stereotypically long-term in outlook, and can afford to be so, given their lower capital costs and ownership structure. This is typically contrasted with the short-term orientation of Western, and especially US, organizations, driven as they are by the pressures of quarterly reporting to stockholders, and by the financial markets. However, it seems that the reality is more complex. Hayashi (1987) develops a view of Japanese time (which he calls *makimono* time) as contrasted with Western patterns of time. The Japanese appear to be fundamentally present-oriented, with specific ways of relating the future and the past to the present. US organizations, on the other hand, are culturally future-oriented, while their management is short-term oriented. Indeed, not only does their basic temporal culture influence their strategic actions, but their very concrete reporting systems also influence their temporal culture. That is why this chapter supports a view that time *is not external to action* but rather internal, or mixed with it. This is particularly true of strategic action.

Rarely, however, does management pause to consider the origin, nature and impact of the assumptions that it makes about time. Such assumptions are deep-seated and taken for granted. Indeed, the meaning of time itself is seemingly self-evident. Is there any need, therefore, to discuss its nature or to consider how it impinges upon the way in which managers plan, decide what to do or measure the results of their action? Our answer is, emphatically, 'yes'. In this chapter we shall show why this is the case and outline ways of addressing this question. We will focus on how cultural time patterns (US, English, French, German and, more generally, Western as opposed to Japanese patterns) influence the ways and means of strategic management in a particular industry: the global banking business.

Just as managerial action takes place in and through time, so time, or rather particular concepts of time, are embedded in and exemplified by action. Time can be said, in a sense, to be *in* action; a view of time, albeit implicit, underpins and informs every action a manager takes. The purpose of this exploratory research is, in broad terms, to examine how concepts of time influence and shape the practice of strategic management. Moreover, the intention is to develop a cross-cultural analysis of what we might call temporal meaning or temporal culture. But in approaching this issue we start not with explicit, articulated views or images of time but rather with strategic action and strategic planning. We look to action and to a range of different activities to reveal prevailing concepts or images of time.

Our interest is, first, in the way in which action discloses a sense or understanding of time, second, how that sense of time differs across cultures, and third, how differing concepts of time influence managerial action. How do these concepts give shape and substance to, for example, planning horizons, budgeting periods, performance measures, or decision-making processes? By comparing essentially similar organizations (in terms of their sphere of activity, size and market position) within the banking industry, operating in different parts of the world (Japan, Germany, the UK, the USA) we hope to trace both the cultural roots of differing views of time and the impact that these have upon the way in which a business operates.

The purpose of this chapter, therefore, is to formulate the research issues as clearly as possible; to set these issues briefly in the context of other relevant research; to outline an initial framework for analysis and, on the basis of this, to formulate a set of preliminary propositions derived from interviews with top banking executives, and from the relevant literature. We will explore organizational time rather than individual time (although there are inevitably close links between the two) (Bluedorn and Denhardt 1988). We will emphasize temporal orientations[1] – past, present, future – and especially the latter, in the context of its capacity to foster strategic vision and the ability to design strategic intent. Present-oriented organizations are also studied, in the context of how such an outlook can foster the relevant implementation of broad mission statements.

TIME AND STRATEGIC PLANNING: A FRAMEWORK FOR CROSS-CULTURAL ANALYSIS[2]

Strategic planning as a time-bound process

Time is *the* dimension in which strategic planning takes place. Strategic plans are grounded in the past, developed/implemented in the present, and targeted to the future. The planning process itself, which is frequently cyclical, typically gives rise to time-bound plans embodying a linear view of time – that is, as a line joining the past, present and future. The traditional planning process is heavily loaded with a normative Western view of 'linear separable' time (Graham 1981) in which time is assumed to be:

- external to and separable from action and events;

- measurable;
- a scarce and therefore valuable resource;
- best represented in linear form; this line is directed toward the future; a point on the line (for the present) separates the past from the future;
- divisible into slices (of any size).

This time pattern is typically Western, and even though the Japanese may sometimes adhere to it, especially in their relations with Westerners, it seems that they do not generally conceive of time in this way (Hall 1983), being less preoccupied with the scarcity of time, and less used to its 'sliceability'.

Consider for a moment the elements of which a strategic plan is usually made up: forecasts (of sales, market share, income, etc.); scenarios encapsulating expectations as to how the market, customers and competitors might change and evolve; objectives and milestones to be reached by a specific time; key steps to be taken, and their sequence; budgets and other yardsticks against which progress, over time, may be measured. All of these elements are developed over linear separable time, usually in a planning or budgeting cycle that specifies timetables for the preparation, evaluation, approval and implementation of different components of the plan. Other aspects of time suffuse every aspect of both the planning process itself and the products of that process. Strategic planning has seasons (cyclical time), and particular times of the year in which it 'gets done' (event time, procedural time). [3] The products of the strategic planning process (the plans, forecasts, budgets and new initiatives) are circumscribed in time. And, of course, the managerial action to which planning gives rise is scheduled, timetabled and evaluated over time. Strategic planning, seen as a process, or as a set of identifiable 'products' and resulting actions may in a sense be said to be 'saturated' in time.

Moreover, strategic planning itself addresses another fundamental organizational and temporal issue: synchronization. Ideally (in a normative linear separable view of time) the preparation, submission and assessment of plans should occur in an orderly, coordinated manner in which each of the key activities in the process is properly synchronized. To be effective, the activity of planning itself requires management and coordination over time. Hence the carefully structured, clearly laid-out planning timetables found in so many Western companies – timetables that set dates and deadlines by which key elements in the process must be completed. No sooner has one annual planning cycle been completed than another, or so it seems, begins. And of course the outcome of this activity, the product of the planning cycle, is a set of time-bound and time- related documents which typically comprise forecasts, budgets, statements of resource allocation, timetabled objectives and milestones.

In part at least, the function of planning is to reduce the uncertainty of the future. Planning aims to bring the future closer to the present; to prepare an organization for the future by giving it some sort of guide to the future. As we shall show later in this chapter, *makimono* time fulfils a similar function: that of bringing the future closer to the present. Much of planning represents an attempt both to find out about and in some respects to forecast or predict the future; the assumption is that we may, through planning, be able to discover things about the future, to create a workable image of the future and thereby reduce our uncertainty – and anxiety – when confronting it.

Forecasting, which forms a part of many strategic plans, could be said to constitute an attempt to create the history that is to come. Forecasting gives shape and structure to an imagined history. In so doing it represents an attempt, in a sense, to capture the future for the present. Or, to paraphrase the psychologist Fraisse, planning – and particularly the forecasting component of planning – orients us to the future 'as the prospect of a conquest towards which we are advancing' (quoted in Das 1986: 42). The forecasting side of planning effectively 'closes' the future. In developing these forecasts, recourse is typically had to the past and to previous experience which, it is hoped, provides some guide as to what might happen in the future. The most typical use of the past to predict the future is provided by time series forecasting techniques (Bourbonnais and Usunier 1992). By extrapolating the observable trends of the past into the future (having, of course, modified these to take full account of our expectations of how things will change) we can link these different time horizons, thereby building a bridge between where we have been, where we are now and where we wish to get to.

Levels of strategic planning

Western managers asked to describe the meaning of 'strategic planning' will most likely invoke a mixture of different terms – vision, objectives, plans, operating plans, budgets, mission statements, etc. – the precise meaning of which is rarely clear. The relationship between these different terms or levels of strategy is also typically

Table 10.1 Time orientation, time horizons, levels of strategy, organizational needs and their temporal issue

Time orientation	Time horizons	Levels of strategy	Organizational needs	Temporal issue
Distant future	5–10 yrs	Vision	Inspiration	Uncertainty
Future	3–7 yrs	Mission/ goals	Focus	Bounded horizons
Intermediate future	2–5 yrs	Plan/ staircase	Co-ordination and synchronization	Pace
Near future	1–3 yrs	Step by step initiatives	Sequencing	Scarcity
Present/ near future	1–2 yrs	Individual objectives	Guidance	Career timetable
Present and past	1 yr	Annual budgets	Effectiveness	Feedback

unclear; hence our first task is to create some sort of ordered pattern from this tangled web.

Table 10.1 sets out a framework in which six levels of strategic planning are identified (see Hay and Williamson 1992 for a fuller exposition of this framework). The content of each level of strategic planning is summarised briefly below, and its cross-cultural validity is questioned.

That certain time periods should be associated with different levels of strategy, for example the time required to accomplish the mission, the period to which the plan relates, the length of time for which a budget runs, is scarcely surprising. A strategic planner working in a linear separable time culture would probably state that 'None of these different levels makes sense except in relation to time.'

Vision

This has two dimensions: external and internal. Strategic planning typically begins, therefore, by looking outside the firm, at the world in which it operates, then progressively moving inside to develop a vision of how the firm will evolve and what it might become in its changing environment. However, in linear separable time, vision statements themselves make full sense in the context of a particular period, even if this refers to a period of years to which the vision relates. A strategic planner working in linear separable time would probably say: 'A vision statement encapsulates, at least implicitly, a view of what we might term the life expectancy of the organization and the time available to it to accomplish its ambitions.' However, it is quite conceivable that organizations are seen by those working within them as being everlasting; a timeless vision can then be meaningful.

Mission

This constitutes an expression of purpose. The statement of mission should convey the purpose or *raison d'être* of an organization, the destination to which that purpose leads and the rationale behind it. The mission statement defines the point on the horizon towards which the organization wants to move. The mission thereby sets a boundary to the horizon; it provides a focal point on the horizon.

For people with a linear separable view of time, a timeless mission statement is unlikely to motivate individuals and capture their imagination. Conversely, for cultures which do not rely principally on linear separable time, a timeless mission statement may make full sense.

Let us take an example contrasting US with Japanese companies. At one level a mission statement defines the destination towards which the company is going; it may also define the timetable for the journey. In 1961 President Kennedy defined NASA's mission as 'achieving the goal, before the decade is out, of landing a man on the moon and returning him safely to earth'. In a similar vein Bob Millar, the CEO of the MIPS computer company defined its mission in 1987 as 'to make the MIPS micro-processor architecture the most pervasive in the world by the mid 1990s'. In 1990 the Schlage Lock Company defined its mission as 'to become the dominant lock supplier in the US by the year 2000' (Collins and Porras 1991: 42–4).

These diverse statements have in common a clearly defined aim, a deadline by which the aim is to be accomplished and, implicitly at least, a timetable for achieving it, against which progress can be measured. Such statements convey an image of the future as being closed and determinant, something over which control can, in a sense, be exercised. Implicit within this is a sense that the point at which the company now is and the point towards which it is aiming may be linked by a line – a line drawn across time which brings the future closer to the present.

Compare such statements with this: '*Yamaha wo tsubusu!*' (We will annihiliate Yamaha!) (quoted in Collins and Parras 1991: 44). Such a statement finds its echo in Komatsu's succinct mission: '*Maru-C*', or 'encircle Caterpillar'. At the time that this mission was defined, in 1970, Komatsu was one-third of Caterpillar's size, had a narrow product line, a reputation for poor quality and reliability and nominal sales outside its home market, Japan. As documented elsewhere (Hay and Williamson 1991), '*Maru-C*' was pursued relentlessly via a whole succession of programmes and initiatives geared to improving quality, reducing cost and broadening the product range.

Although oriented towards the future, '*Maru-C*' has no date or timetable attached to it. The timing of its accomplishment is open ended, as is the future in which it will be pursued. As it moves towards its goal, Komatsu will exploit new, unforeseen opportunities towards which it remains open. But the mission remains stable over time. A mission statement can be 'read', in a sense, as a statement about time or at least about the time perspective prevailing within an organization. Just as it may be symptomatic of a prevailing view of time so, too, a mission statement is profoundly shaped by the time horizon that predominates within an organization. The prevailing time perspective leaves its imprint upon a company's mission statement, shaping it in subtle ways.

Plan

If the mission expresses *what* the organization wishes to achieve, then the plan focuses on how this is to be accomplished. But the point on the horizon towards which we are aiming may seem somewhat distant. A strategic planner working in normative linear separable time would define 'good plans' as those that tackle this problem by breaking down the tasks involved into smaller, bite-sized pieces and by setting out the sequence in which these tasks or steps should be tackled. 'Good' plans also provide guidance as to the *pace* at which this sequence of steps should be taken. Any one of the defined series of steps may be quite large: for example, improving quality or reducing cost. The next level of strategy requires, therefore, that each step is broken down into specific initiatives.

Individual objectives

These are derived from the specific initiatives being pursued. Objectives provide individuals with a focus for activity; they help them prioritize what they do, decide when they do certain things, and assess how much time to allocate to different parts of their job.

The emphasis on individual objectives is also culturally relative. The assumption that implementation and goal-setting are individually based is typical of highly individualistic societies (Hofstede 1981). In collectivist-oriented societies, implementation relies on a group process, and rewards and goal-setting avoid individualization as much as possible. Linear separable time (clock time, which assumes the individual possession of a watch) is strongly related to individualism (Hofstede 1991).

Budget

Budgets capture the expenditure implications of agreed strategic initiatives; they establish the relationship between key initiatives, individual objectives and the revenue side of a firm's activity. Budgets provide one quantitative measure of progress towards the attainment of stated objectives. Emphasizing the budgeting side of planning focuses more attention on quantitative than qualitative goals. Nevertheless qualitative timeless goals (such as the zero defect philosophy of quality) may be effective in establishing the relationship between key strategic initiatives and individual objectives.

Organizational needs and the levels of strategy

Organizations, irrespective of their sphere of activity, their geographical location or their cultural identity, have to meet a similar set of needs (see Table 10.1). There is, for example, the need to elicit commitment from members and to motivate those who belong to the organization, and the need to provide individuals with a sense of purpose or inspiration that gives meaning to their activities, as well as to that of the organization as a whole – a purpose that provides a *focus* for effort. Organizations, of any size, have to coordinate the activities of individuals, departments and functions and ensure that these often diverse activities are, as far as possible, harmonized and consistent with the overall purpose of the organization. The centrifugal tendency of many organizations, the tendency for individual efforts and initiatives to pull apart rather than together, can be overcome only by careful coordination and synchronization of activities across the firm. Integral to this coordination is a set of decisions about the sequence in which initiatives should be pursued and the *pace* at which this should be done. If the desired sequence is to be followed then individuals will require *guidance* as they set priorities and make their choices between alternative courses of action. Finally, an organization needs to have some way of measuring the *effectiveness* of its activity and the efficacy of its chosen plans.

Having defined some key time-related issues in strategic planning, we move now to examine these issues in a particular setting: that of international banking. More specifically, we shall outline a set of five propositions, where the Japanese are constrasted with their European and American competitors.

TIME AND STRATEGIC ACTION IN GLOBAL BANKING

Proposition 1: Performance targets play a major role in shaping corporate and individual time horizons.

Clearly defined performance targets shape both managerial action, at the everyday level, and the time horizon within which management sees itself working, and on the basis of which its performance will be evaluated. The targets themselves, and the manner in which they are defined or measured, exerts a decisive influence. A vivid illustration of this is provided by Lloyds Bank, whose mission is defined as follows: 'Lloyds Bank's primary objective is to create value for its shareholders – by increasing the dividend and appreciation in the share price. This is the driving force behind our decisions and actions. (CEO's report 1989, quoted in Handler 1992: 34).

Having thus formulated its key objective, three specific objectives are defined:

- To achieve a net return on equity greater than 18 per cent
- To increase the dividend payout ratio
- To maintain a strong balance sheet with equity grown from retained earnings

(Handler 1992: XX)

These targets, which in themselves embody a time horizon, i.e. the financial year on the basis of which dividend payouts will be determined, have an immediate impact at the level of managerial activity, shaping the choices and decisions that are made. Thus a senior manager working with Lloyds Bank observes that:

Lloyds Bank has now adopted the principle of managing for shareholder value. It is now clear that it is extremely difficult for a project to be approved unless it can be demonstrated that it will be profitable and payback within 5 years. Historically there was a long term investment culture in which major capital investments were proceeded with very much on the basis of (a) instinctive feeling and (b) concern not to be left behind by competitors.

(Handler 1992: XX)

This is reflected in the CEO's report for 1989 (quoted in Handler 1992: 34): 'We rank each business on the basis of the shareholder value they create; each activity is viewed as a creator or destroyer of value. Businesses which consume cash and destroy value are targeted for divestment.

But competitors to Lloyds, particularly those from outside the US or UK, operate with a different principle. Creating a competitive presence in a new market by systematically pursuing volume and market share is, for example, a characteristic approach adopted by Japanese banks. Thus both Lloyds and National Westminster have found themselves losing new business in non-UK markets to Japanese banks 'on terms which would be unacceptable to us'. A senior British banker's personal experience of working in the United States, where he frequently came into direct competition with Japanese banks, confirmed him in the view that they operate with a somewhat different time horizon. He cited a number of Japanese competitors winning business away from National Westminster on terms that would simply be unacceptable to National Westminster.

Generally speaking, the performance criteria of Japanese banks reflect a concern with market share rather than immediate profits (Davies 1989; Gupta 1989). This 'non profit-earning orientation' is confirmed by several bankers. One of our Japanese interviewees argued that US banks are targeting maximum two-year profits, whereas Japanese banks target market share, which they are 'willing to buy'.

Davies (1991) insists on the fact that 'culturally the Japanese banks are "followers" '. Historically, their strategy has been to 'cut prices'. A senior manager at Lloyds Bank, who spent considerable time in Brazil, remarked that Lloyds Bank fared considerably better there than the Japanese banks. Indeed, he did not regard Japanese banks in Brazil as particularly efficient or effective, notably in terms of their risk evaluation. Being market share-oriented they tended to be less conservative about the basis on which they won new business.

However, another of our Japanese interviewees notes some changes that put a constraint on the Japanese banks' performance criteria. World-wide, there is now a standard of 8 per cent of equity ratio (Cooke Committee regulation); since Japanese banks' equity ratios were far lower, i.e. in the 5–6 per cent range in the mid- to late 1980s, they must reach this target.

Japanese banks tend to compete with other Japanese banks. Mitsubishi Bank, for instance, is described by one of our interviewees as more conservative than Sumitomo Bank. Unlike Sumitomo, Mitsubishi Bank has not become involved in fine art and real estate, risky deals that have proved to be questionable choices for Sumitomo in recent years. Mitsubishi Bank, like many other Japanese banks, focuses more on lending to industrial projects, with an emphasis on financing Japanese companies in their European FDI (Gupta 1989). Japanese banks are thus peceived as competing is against other Japanese banks, and as reliable partners of Japanese manufacturing companies expanding overseas.

As a rule, the Japanese tend to reject the 'number-crunching orientation' of quantitative performance-driven strategic thinking. For instance, Akio Morita (1991: 4) stated that:

> In Japan you will notice that almost every major manufacturer is run by an engineer or a technologist. However, here in the UK, I am told some manufacturers are led by CEOs who do not understand the engineering that goes into their products. Someone once mentioned to me that many UK corporations are headed by chartered accountants. . . . For an accountant the central concern is statistics and figures – of PAST performance. So how can an accountant reach out and grab the future if he is always looking at LAST quarter results.

There is also evidence that expansion by UK banks into overseas markets entails a redefinition of both the performance criteria by which international expansion is judged, and the time horizon over which this judgement is made. For example, a senior strategic planner at National Westminster observes that, 'if we are to build a substantial business in the Far East we will have to change our time horizons and, specifically, adopt a much longer-term perspective than that prevailing in our domestic business.'

But performance targets do not arise *ab initio*. They are a function both of a corporate mission and of an organization's constituencies

– and the expectations of the constituencies to which the company is beholden. This leads to our second proposition.

Proposition 2: Constituency time horizons shape company time horizons

As emphasized by Davies (1991), there is in some cases a 'constitutional pressure to perform quickly'. Davies defines the different constituencies to which banks in the US, Japan and Europe are responsible, thus:

- Shareholders own the banks in the US;
- clients own the banks in Japan;
- nobody owns in Switzerland and Germany;
- in France and Italy the State owns the banks.

Simplified though this observation is, it captures a fundamental point: that the constituencies to which a corporation is responsible – and the time horizon within which key constituencies operate – exert a decisive influence upon the framing of strategic time horizons.

The point can be well illustrated with a concrete example. The constituency to which Lloyds Bank is primarily responsible is unambiguously clear from its mission statement: 'to create value for its shareholders'. Of course, its other constituencies – notably its employees, customers and the communities within which it operates – are important, but there can be no doubt that the shareholders are paramount. We do not take issue with this. Rather, the important point is this, that corporate constituencies themselves operate within a particular time perspective; they too have clear, time-related expectations that a company has to meet.

Compare the position of Lloyds Bank with that of its competitors in Europe and elsewhere. For instance, Davies (1989: 112) argues that: 'In markets like Japan and Europe, considerations such as national interest, market positioning and the presence of non-stockhholders institutions will play a more vital role than that of the stockholder value.'

What is of interest is the way in which the time perspective prevailing within a company, and that of its key constituency, interrelate; how they interact with each other and, specifically, the degree to which the constituency time horizon shapes that of the corporation. In much of the literature this issue finds expression in the debate about short-termism. It should be emphasized that we are not primarily concerned with this question, or with the issue of whether or not short-termism is in fact a reality. The examples that follow illustrate aspects of the short-termism debate, but our interest is in the relationship between different time horizons and the way in which a company seeks to reconcile these.

A good example of the tensions involved is provided by Dr Peter Williams, Chairman and chief executive of Oxford Instruments:

> Six-monthly reporting to one's shareholders – or quarterly even in the USA – requires as favourable a portrayal of satisfactory results as circumstances allow, even in difficult times as at present. But the real world which we inhabit as businessmen is somewhat different; Newtonian physics teaches us that things that go up do (occasionally) come down, the time scales of business plans do not run neatly in little six-monthly packets.
>
> (Williams 1991: 3)

Williams then goes on to argue that while he has no quarrel with the mechanisms by which the stock market values a company's shares, his

> calm objectivity over stock prices masks a fear that a manager with an eye on the fluctuations in his company stock price is not focusing his full energies and attentions on the prime objective of creating true long term wealth for the shareholders.
>
> (Williams 1991: 5)

For the chief executive this creates a dilemma: he needs to meet the expectations of his key constituency, the stock market, while simultaneously investing in and strengthening the company's long-term strategic position. Hence Williams' observation that:

> schizophrenia might be the best description of the state of mind of many a CEO – can we afford to invest in this or that in the current year and take an earnings hit? If we do not, will our competitors steal a march on us?
>
> (Williams 1991: 3)

Compare this with the situation confronting Dr Peter Grassmann, group executive of the Siemens Medical Engineering Group – a company that is, in many respects, analogous to Oxford Instruments. In Germany, Grassmann observes,

> the focus on short term profit taking is traditionally different and less emphasised. This is not to say that profits don't matter in Germany. Just as everywhere else they are seen as a necessity

for survival. However, it is generally accepted that profits are 'hidden' and invested in the future and to know that pay-back can take time.

(Grassman 1991: 4)

And the reason for this difference is to be found, in Grassmann's view, in the relative power of the different constituencies to which a company such as Siemens is responsible. Ownership and influence go together. Thus in Germany approximately 39 per cent of a company's shareholding is typically held by other companies, 20 per cent is held by private shareholders and the remaining 20 per cent by foreign companies or individuals. The proportion held by pension funds and other institutional investors is small. The conclusion that Grassmann draws from this is clear:

> The structure of control of German companies – the strict division of duties between the supervisory board and the managing board – coupled with the voting power of banks and the cross holding of shares between companies contribute much to stability and a longer term approach of German business.
>
> (Grassmann 1991: 13)

But this does not mean that a company such as Siemens is not concerned about creating value for its shareholders – quite the contrary. An integral part of the Siemens mission is 'to generate sustained high earnings as a condition for assuring the future of the company and increasing the value of our shareholders' investment' (Grassman 1991: 17). Siemens sees itself as responsible to shareholders, but the composition of its ownership structure influences the time horizons within which it is operating and in relation to which its performance is judged. This may well change as the percentage of shares owned by foreign shareholders and by institutional investors such as pension funds and insurance companies increases. The effects of this development are already apparent:

> Investors expect us to provide disclosure and explanation of our business development and prospects in line with international standards. Interim reports are increasingly being used as a tool for market valuation, however one may personally regret this increasingly short term view based on quarterly financial data.
>
> (Grassman 1991: 21–2)

A vivid illustration in the banking context of the impact that ownership – and particularly a change of ownership – has upon the time horizon within which a bank operates is provided by the experience of Morgan Grenfell following its acquisition by Deutsche Bank. Asked to define the most distinctive feature of the new owners, a senior Morgan Grenfell director provided a succinct summary:

> time is the most important part of their ethos. What is of interest is the manner in which this 'ethos', which is recognized to be different from that of Morgan Grenfell, is communicated. It is quite different from American bankers, who are 'paranoid' about quarterly earnings. Deutsche Bank's time horizon is rather subtly imposed now. Management at DB is 'technocrats who feel tremendous responsibility'. They value pride in performance. But there is no divorce between ownership and control.
>
> It [Deutsche Bank's temporal culture] leaks around; it is not expressed, being implicit rather than explicit, and therefore never really 'said in meetings'. It is a very gentle influence from Deutsche Bank. But they make it known that they take a long term view. Their message is mostly: 'Do your work in a very competent way.

It seems that, relative to US banks, Deutsche Bank is perceived to adopt a longer view. Much the same is held to be true at Dresdner Bank or at Swiss Bank Corporation, or, more generally German and Swiss banks. This creates problems of interpretation for their competitors. As a British banker observes: 'We have difficulty in assessing their plans ... they never speak about shareholder value.'

These diverse examples illustrate our fundamental proposition, namely that constituency time horizons shape company time horizons. Implicit within this proposition is a series of key points, which may be summarized as follows:

- Ownership structure is a key determinant of the constituency that is deemed to be critical.
- Constituencies have their own time perspective.
- These time perspectives may be different from those prevailing within a company.
- The time horizon of the dominant constituency shapes the time perspective within which the business operates and on the basis of which it makes key strategic decisions.
- Corporate and constituency time horizons may be very different and in conflict with each other.

214   *M. Hay and J.-C. Usunier*

Proposition 3: Strategic time perspectives are strongly related to human resources management styles.

In the United States, and to a lesser extent in Europe, mobility is the best way to a successful career path. Organizations see mobile managers as a necessary resource for promoting change. Human resources are largely individualized. Careers are built on personal intent, not necessarily on organizational needs and intents. This obviously reduces the time horizon of managers, since they always make choices in the full knowledge that, at any moment, they could shift to another organization. Therefore individual long-term perspective and organizational long-term perspective are not really synchronized.

In Japan, as compared with the US, the managerial market favours career path with a lifetime employment perspective (Lane and Kaufman 1991). University graduates pass company exams after their graduation, and favour large companies.[4] An individual employee's long-term perspective can be hoped to fit perfectly with that of the organization. Loyalty is favoured: it is assumed that over time there will be a balance (in the long run) between what is given to and what is received from loyal employees. In the United States, a relationship of reciprocity is favoured: reward for effort must come relatively quickly. As outlined by Davies (1991): 'Japanese banks invest heavily in people. They are prepared for the long term.'

European countries lie somewhere in between. Quasi-lifetime employment does exist in the banking business. Managers are expected to stay for fairly long periods.

The global banking business is constantly confronted with the dilemma of whether to hire specialists or generalist managers (Davies 1989). Banking used to be a generalists' world, but the increased complexity of some banking business segments now calls for specialists, with bonus scheme compensation. Naturally, Japanese banks have a tendency to prefer generalists – loyal members of the organization, who are, in a sense, organizational rather than professional specialists.

The generalist orientation of Japanese bank managers, and their long-term commitment to their organization, makes change difficult, as emphasized by one of our Japanese interviewees:

> People in the [Japanese] banks are not driven by a particular achievement in a specific job; they have to consider highly what was done before. We [Japanese bank managers] always consider the sequence between the past and the future. Dramatic change

is possible only from the outside. But continuity is very important. It is difficult to change things drastically.

Therefore we need specialists or consultants from the outside. Japanese banks hire some outside specialists for their technical abilities such as securities business or money market. Japanese banks hire Anglo-Saxon specialists to improve their competencies.

According to Davies (1991): 'The Head Office in Tokyo still reluctantly adapts to these new-fangled Anglo-Saxons.' Such *gaijin* may experience some frustration since they are considered as 'lemons to be squeezed'. It seems that imported specialists are not recruited, treated or promoted in the same way as Japanese employees.

Thus it seems that Japanese organizations – including the banks – are not change-driven but more continuity-driven by their human resource management system. Paradoxically, however, this continuity builds in fact on continuous change, and does not favour the status quo.

Proposition 4: Strategic time perspective is directly influenced by differences in temporal cognitive styles across cultures

A naïve view of Japanese temporal orientations would lead one to assume that the Japanese are future-oriented. In fact, Japanese business specialist Robert Ballon argues that the Japanese are neither future- nor past-oriented. On the contrary, he indicates that the Japanese are present-oriented, and very much focused on the here and now (quoted in Hayashi 1987). Hayashi explains the difficult attempt to find cross-culturally equivalent terms by asserting that: 'Many kinds of Japanese behaviour are extratemporaneous' (Hayashi 1987: 2). Hayashi explains further what he calls '*maki-mono*' time. The Japanese tend to posit the future as a natural extension of the present. Their view of time is basically cyclical; one explanation for this is their Buddhist beliefs that the souls of the dead are reincarnated in new-born babies, in an eternal cycle: 'In Japanese cultural time, the past flows continuously toward the present and also the present is firmly linked to the future. In philosophical terms, we might say the past and the future exist simultaneously in the present' (Hayashi 1987: 10).

The linear separable model of time, as found in Western cultures, does not, then, predominate in Japan. Continuity is central to Japanese concepts of time, just as the notion of discontinuity is

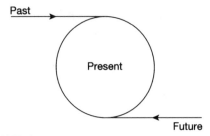

Source: Hayashi 1987: 9

Figure 10.1 Japanese *makimono* time pattern

central in Western models of time. As Hayashi states: 'A Japanese definition would say "the present is a temporal period that links the region of the past with the world of the future" '. (Hayashi 1987: 18).

This notion of continuity, as well as that of 'the arrow of the future' targeted towards the present, are central to the *makimono* time pattern (Figure 10.1). As one of our Japanese interviewees remarked: 'We always consider the sequence between the past and the future.'

Thus, an orgnization's temporal cognitive style invariably influences its strategic perspective, both in terms of its vision (an organization's ability to create an effective picture of the future) and its mission. Both must be clear enough, long lasting, and broad enough to allow for their proper interpretation by those in charge of implementing the strategy on a daily basis.

This broad vision and associative type of cognitive mental scheme is described by Akio Morita:

> The true visionaries who can really capture technology and use it to chart the future course of industry are what I call 'technologists'. By technologist I am referring to those rare individuals who have a wide understanding of science and engineering, as well as a broad vision and true commitment to the needs of society.
>
> (Akio Morita 1992: 4)

Japanese society may be said to favour associative communication (see Glenn 1981) as opposed to abstractive communication. In associative cultures people deal with all matters associated with a particular event, and consider their environment in great detail. They do not rely on general principles or abstractions, and are quick to see connections between disparate facts. Abstractive cultures, however, adopt a more fragmented approach, and only subsequently relate their 'evidence' to a particular issue. They tend to relate facts to theoretical explanations, to measure and verify. In associative cultures there is an insistence on the inseparability of the basic elements of a situation, especially reality; and this is particularly so in Japanese culture, where 'little or no theory [is] being developed, or only very cautiously elaborated, with all kinds of excuses and apologies' (Galtung 1981: 834).

This opposition between associative and abstractive cultures has been confirmed in the case of Japanese banks. They have a gift for creating a strategic vision and for defining corporate mission. According to Davies (1991), 'when McKinsey (which exemplifies an abstractive approach) advises large US banks in their strategy they appear as "conceptual thinkers". On the contrary, the Japanese tend to be very pragmatic, tradition-oriented and "part of a great system" '.

Proposition 5: The Japanese planning systems follow international standards

Planning systems are widely perceived as the core of the strategic management process. Since the time horizon of a plan is clearly defined, it would appear that a strategic plan is the obvious measure of the time horizon of an organization. Formal planning systems are relatively standard across cultures. Strategic management textbooks generally all offer the same kind of normative statements about planning (first break down tasks, then set out the sequences in which these tasks should be tackled). Planning corresponds normatively to Western linear separable time (Graham 1981). Our interviews confirmed that Japanese banks basically operate with essentially the same planning format as that of European and US banks: 'Japanese banks have a three-year planning format' (Davies 1991).

The ability of the Japanese to combine several models of cultural time is emphasized by Hayashi (1987: 8): 'The average Japanese follows neither a linear model nor a pure cyclic model.' The Japanese have been historically good learners of foreign cultures: 'Japanese are receptive to new and exogeneous cultures, which they blend harmoniously with their own historical legacy' (Hayashi 1987: 8). This is true of foreign time patterns, which they are able to adopt when interacting with Western partners (Hall 1983). As Hall states: 'The Japanese are polychronic when looking and working inward, toward themselves. When dealing with the outside world . . .

they shift to the monochronic mode.' The Japanese can move from one time model to another, depending on the situation and people involved, thereby using different types of 'operating cultures' (Goodenough 1971). It may be said, therefore, that they work with a dual concept of time that is both Western – as evidenced by their ability to work with linear separable formal planning, and by their capacity to meet delivery dates – and Japanese (*makimono* time).

We would argue that these two models of time are differently employed in the strategic planning context. In framing the overall vision, mission or 'strategic intent' (Hamel and Prahalad 1989) of the organization, it is clear that *makimono* time is a dominant influence. When it comes to the detailed implementation of a strategic plan, and the need to synchronize activities over time, a Western linear separable model is deployed to good effect. Thus, care must be taken not to interpret the time horizons invariably embodied in formal planning systems as representing the sole strategic time perspective of an organization.

Conclusion

Throughout this chapter a central proposition has remained implicit, namely, that to understand an organization fully, and to make sense of its strategic choices, the mission that it pursues and the plans that it adopts, it is necessary to elucidate its temporal culture – a culture that finds clear expression in the particular time horizon within which an organization operates. This chapter has presented one way in which an organization's temporal identity may be analysed, through the examples of Japanese *makimono* time and the global banking business. Central to this approach is our belief that an organization's sense of time is revealed through action and, specifically, through its approach to strategic planning and the evolution of a strategic time perspective. A strategic time perspective is a reflection of the temporal cognitive styles prevailing in a particular culture; the influence exerted by the constituencies to which an organization is beholden; the associated definition of performance criteria, and its reinforcement through human resource management policies. Identifying these different influences is a prerequisite of understanding an organization's strategic time perspective. Understanding this perspective is of itself fundamental to appreciating fully how an organization operates, the choices that it makes, and the strategies that it pursues.

Appendix 10.1

TIME AS A MANAGERIAL TOPIC

Time as a central concept in the social sciences

Psychologists have long asserted the centrality of time to an understanding of the individual. George Kelly, for example, observed that:

> If man exists primarily in the dimensions of time, and only secondarily in the dimensions of space, then the terms which we erect for understanding him ought to take primary account of this view. If we want to know why man does what he does, then the terms of our whys should extend themselves in time rather than in space.
>
> (quoted in Das 1986: 50)

In much the same vein Karl Mannheim argued that, 'the innermost structure of the mentality of a group can never be as clearly understood as when we attempt to understand its conception of time in the light of its hopes, yearnings and purposes' (Hassard 1991). As with man, so too with managers and organizations. Time is a fundamental dimension of every organization. To understand an organization – and the differences between organizations (both within and between national cultures) – we need to grapple with and appreciate the ways in which time is viewed, the meanings that are attached to it, the uses to which it is put and the time frames within which the organization operates. To fully grasp the complexity of an organization we must develop what Weick has called 'an exquisite sense of time' (quoted in Clark 1985: 39).

In areas as diverse as philosophy, economics, mathematics, physics, anthropology, history, literature, psychology and sociology there is a vast literature on time.[5] The centrality of time to an understanding of man and society has long been recognized by some sociologists who, following Durkheim and Mauss, accord time a pivotal role in their work (Pronovost 1989; Adam 1990). More recently there has been an explosion in the number of studies of what might be called 'social time' by historians, ethnographers and cultural anthropologists. But, as Bergmann has noted, the abiding sense that time is a neglected topic is a reflection of the fact that these diverse enquiries are rarely interconnected. As Bergmann goes on to argue, despite the proliferation of time-related enquiries a major gap still remains:

> time sociology lacks above all empirical studies in which the time aspect is the main theme ... empirical material is essentially only available where related disciplines such as anthropology or psychology have developed it ... the study of time structures of social subsystems is among the most urgent tasks for a sociology of time
>
> (Bergmann 1992: 82)

Time in the organizational and strategic literature

Turning to the management literature we find a somewhat similar picture. Again, the image portrayed is one of comparative neglect: 'students of organization and management theory have until recently paid relatively little attention to the topic of time' (Bluedorn and Denhardt 1988: 299). But, as with sociology, so too with the management field, care must be taken not to overstate the deficiency. This is not the place for a full review of the literature but certain strands of managerial research in which time plays a central role should be singled out. For example: the temporal dimensions of consumer activity, particularly at the individual level (such as shopping behaviour) have been studied (Alreck 1976; Hawes 1980; Jacoby *et al.* 1976); inter-departmental conflicts revolving around competing time horizons have been observed (Lawrence and Lorsch 1969); considerable attention has been paid to the so-called 'time span of discretion', which refers to the time period over which an individual works without direct intervention by a superior (Jaques 1964; 1976; 1982); building on the notion of time as a scarce, limited resource, much work has been done on time budgets, time management and allocation, time and motion studies, critical path analysis and so forth. More recently, time has been identified as a major source of competitive advantage, particularly in terms of the elimination or reduction of time in key areas such as new product development and the speed of competitive response (Stalk and Hout 1990).

In the domain of strategic management there have been attempts to measure, at the individual level, what is termed the 'future time perspective' or orientation of individuals; i.e. a measure of the extent to which individual managers have a 'near' or 'distant' future time perspective and the impact that this has upon preferred planning horizons (Das 1986; 1991). Also at the individual level, there is growing interest in the differences between individuals in terms of their preference to do one thing at a time (monochronism) as compared with simultaneously engaging in a number of different activities (polychronism). Assessing individuals on this so called M/P scale has been done in specific sectors (Kaufman *et al.* 1991; Bluedorn *et al.* 1992) and across different cultures (Usunier and Valette-Florence 1991).

Underpinning this particular strand in the research is the belief that an understanding of these individual and cultural differences is a prerequisite for the successful transaction of business across cultures (Usunier 1991). The ability to avoid what we might term temporal clash is, exponents of this view would argue, an essential element in being able to manage effectively in an international arena. Working beyond the limits of individual time orientations, some have endeavoured to extend this work on monochronic/polychronic scales to the organizational level, and to relate it to other aspects of an organization's culture (Bluedorn 1991).

Notes

1 On dimensions of time-related behaviour, see Kaufman *et al.* 1991 and Usunier 1991.
2 A review of the literature on time as a managerial topic is given in the Appendix.
3 See, for instance, Graham 1981 on cyclical, event and procedural time.
4 In Japan, the very large sector of small and medium-sized companies, sub-contractors, retail and service companies, does not offer lifetime employment schemes.
5 For a fairly complete review of the literature on time and organization, see Bluedorn and Denhardt 1988; on time and consumer behaviour, see Bergadaà 1991; and on time and business, see Usunier 1991.

Bibliography

Adam, B. (1990) *Time and Social Theory*, Cambridge: Polity Press.
Alreck, P. L. (1976) 'Time Orientation and Behaviour', unpublished Ph.D dissertation, San Diego State University.
Bergadaà, M. (1991) 'The Role of Time in the Action of the Consumer', *Journal of Consumer Research* 12, December: 289–302.
Bergmann, W. (1992) 'The Problem of Time in Sociology', *Time & Society* 1, 1: 81–126.
Bluedorn, A. C. (1991) 'Time and the Competing Values Model of Culture: Adding the Fourth Dimension', Working Paper.
Bluedorn, A. C. and Denhardt, R. B. (1988) 'Time and Organizations', *Journal of Management* 14, 2: 299–320.
Bluedorn, A. C, Kaufman, C. F. and Lane, P. M.(1992) 'How Many Things Do You Like to Do at Once? An Introduction to Monochronic and Polychronic Time', Working Paper.
Bourbonnais, R. and Usunier, J. C. (1992) *Pratique de la Prévision des Ventes*, Paris: Editions Economica.
Clark, P. (1985) 'A review of the theories of time and structure for organizational sociology', in *Research in the Sociology of Organizations*: 35–79.
Collins, J. C. and Porras, J. I.(1991) 'Organizational Vision and Visionary Organization', *California Management Review*, Fall: 30–52.
Das, T. K. (1986), *The Subjective Side of Strategy Making: Future Orientations and Perceptions of Executives*, New York: Praeger.
—— (1991) 'Time: The Hidden Dimension in Strategic Planning', *Long Range Planning* 24, 3: 49–57.
Davies, S. I. (1989) *Managing Change in the Excellent Banks*, London: MacMillan.
—— (1991) Interview with Steve Davies (DIBC), June.
Fraisse, P. (1984) 'Perception and Estimation of Time', *Annual Review of Psychology* 35: 1–36.
Galtung, (1981) 'Structure, Culture and Intellectual Style: An Essay Comparing Saxonic, Teutonic, Gallic and Nipponic Approaches', *Social Science Information* 20, 6: 817–56.
Giddens, A. (1987) 'Time and Social Organization', in *Social Theory and Modern Sociology*, Cambridge: Polity Press.
Glenn, E. (1981) *Man and Mankind: Conflict and Communication between Cultures*, Horwood, N.J.: Ablex.

224   M. Hay and J.-C. Usunier

Goodenough, W. H. (1971) 'Culture, language and society', Modular Publications 7, Reading, MA: Addison-Wesley.

Graham, R. J. (1981) 'The Role of Perception of Time in Consumer Research', *Journal of Consumer Research* 7: 335–42.

Grassmann, P. H. (1991) 'Time and Corporate Ownership: The View From Germany. How Long Term Do Industrial Corporations in Germany Act?', Stockton Lectures, London Business School, May.

Gupta, J. (1989) 'International Development of Japanese Banks: The European Perspectives', in Reijo Luostarinen (ed.) *Dynamics of International Business*, 15th Annual Conference of The European Business Association, Helsinki: 1376–410.

Gurvitch, G. (1964) *The Spectrum of Social Time*, Holland: D. Reidel Publishing Co.

Hall, E. T. (1983) *The Dance of Life*, Garden City, NY: Anchor Press/Doubleday.

Hamel, G. and Prahalad, C. K. (1989) 'Strategic Intent', *Harvard Business Review*, May-June: 63–76.

Handler, S. A. (1992) 'The Emphasis on Value-Based Strategic Management in UK Companies', *Journal of Strategic Change* 1, 1: 19–37.

Hassard, J. (1991) 'Aspects of Time in Organization', *Human Relations* 44, 2: 105–25.

Hassard, J. and Pym, D. (1990) *The Theory and Philosophy of Organizations: Critical Issues and New Perspectives*, London: Routledge.

Hawes, D. K. (1980) 'The time variable in models of consumer behaviour', *Advances in Consumer Research* 7: 442–7.

Hay, M. G. and Williamson, P. J. (1991) 'Strategic Staircases: Planning the Capabilities Required for Success', *Long Range Planning*, 24, 4: 36–43.

—— (1992) 'Good Strategy: the View from Below', Working Paper, London Business School.

Hayashi, S. (1987) *Culture and Management in Japan*, Tokyo: University of Tokyo Press.

Hofstede, G. (1981) *Culture's Consequences*, Beverly Hills, CA: Sage Publications.

—— (1991) *Culture and Organizations: Software of the Mind*, London: McGraw-Hill.

Jacoby, J., Szybillo, G. J. and Berning, C. K. (1976) 'Time and Consumer Behaviour: An Interdisciplinary Overview', *Journal of Consumer Research* 2: 320–39.

Jaques, E. (1964) *Time Span Handbook*, London: Heinemann Educational Books.

—— (1976) *A General Theory of Bureaucracy*, London: Heinemann Educational Books.

—— (1982) *The Form of Time*, London: Heinemann.

Kaufman, C. F., Lane, P. M. and Lindquist, J. D. (1991) 'Exploring More Than 24 hours a Day: A Preliminary Investigation of Polychronic Time Use', *Journal of Consumer Research* 18, December: 392–401.

Lane, P. M. and Kaufman, C. F. (1991) 'The Role of Time in Strategic Renewal', presented at International Strategic Management Society Conference, Toronto, Canada.

Lauer, R. H. (1981) *Temporal Man: The Meaning and Uses of Social Time*, New York: Praeger.

Lawrence, P. R. and Lorsch, J. W. (1969) *Developing Organisations: Diagnosis and Action*, Redding MA: Addison-Wesley.

McGrath, J. E. (ed.) (1988) *The Social Psychology of Time: New Perspectives*, Newbury Park, CA: Sage Publications.

McGrath, J. E. and Kelly, J. R. (1986) *Time and Human Interaction: Toward a Social Psychology of Time*, New York: Guildford Press.

Morita, A. (1992) ' "S" does not equal "T" and "T" does not equal "I" ', The First United Kingdom Innovation Lecture, Department of Trade and Industry, London, February 6.

Pronovost, G. (1989) 'Current Sociology', *The Journal of the International Sociological Association* 37, 3.

Settle, R. B., Alreck, P. L and Glasheen, J. W. (1978) 'Individual Time Orientation and Consumer Lifestyles', *Advances in Consumer Research* 5: 315–19.

Stalk, G. and Hout, T. M. (1990) *Competing Against Time: How Time-Based Strategies Deliver Better Performance* New York: Free Press.

Usunier, J. C. (1991) 'Business Time Perceptions and National Cultures: A Comparative Survey', *Management International Review* 31: 197–217.

—— (1992) *Commerce entre Cultures*, Paris: Presses Universitaires de France.

Usunier, J. C. and Valette-Florence, P. (1991) 'Personal Value Systems and Temporal Patterns ("Time-Styles") Exploratory Findings', paper presented at the Workshop on Value and Lifestyle Research in Marketing, European Institute for Advanced Studies in Management, Brussels.

Williams, P. (1991) 'Time and the City: Short Termism in the UK – Myth or Reality?', Stockton Lectures, London Business School, February.

11 Human resource management in foreign companies in Japan

Philippe Debroux

CHANGE IN THE STRATEGIC POSITIONING OF JAPAN

While attention was focused in the 1980s on the expanding presence of Japanese companies abroad, US and European firms, followed by a growing number of Taiwanese and South Korean companies, were steadily increasing their direct investments in Japan. The economic slowdown starting in 1991 probably marked the end of the 'rush to Japan' and the beginning of a profit crunch for all businesses operating in Japan, including those set up with foreign capital.

Nevertheless, FDI should continue to grow, albeit at a slower pace than in the 1980s, reflecting the dramatically changing position of Japan within the strategies of Western, and increasingly also Asian, multinationals. Japan is not only an important market for many products, but also a country where a resource-based strategy can be implemented in a large number of industries. Many new technologies are now originating from Japan, making it necessary to have rapid access to them. Japan is also a country where, in some fields, product development processes are very advanced. Therefore, a growing number of foreign companies believe that a timely access to technology, to potential partners and to the market requires a permanent and active presence to develop R&D activities, and to take advantage of Japan's capabilities in engineering and high technology development, while establishing and controlling existing and new distribution channels. Moreover, the complexity of the market access process, and of Japanese business practices, creates the necessity for continuous nurturing of regular contacts with the public authorities and with the world of trade and industry, where information is exchanged, new projects are discussed and the regulations of the future are devised.

DIVERSIFICATION OF THE MARKET ENTRANCE MODE

The last few years have seen a large increase of investment in R&D. This is especially noticeable in the fields of electronics, pharmacy and chemistry, where a number of facilities have been established during the last 15 years. Large companies such as Eastman Kodak, ICI and Digital Equipment have enlarged their research facilities. Ciba-Geigy opened an R&D facility in the biotechnology field in 1990. Hoechst has been carrying out basic research for five years in Japan. By the end of 1993, Texas Instruments expects to have about 350 researchers at Tsukuba. Glaxo also began working on new facilities there in autumn 1992, with 100 people, and expects to have up to 250 people in the near future.

In the service industries, some foreign banks, life insurers, securities firms and advertising companies have recently closed their offices in Japan due to high rents and the deterioration of the business environment at the end of the 'bubble economy' era.

However, a large number of financial institutions who had invested with the liberalization process have enlarged their activities. Salomon Brothers and Morgan Stanley can now be considered as players in the same league as the large Japanese securities firms. Taking advantage of the diversification of demand and of the loosening of regulations, newcomers such as Virgin or Toys 'Я' Us are successfully developing new channels. They will probably be followed by other large retail chains in specialized markets. While foreign entries in most business fields are slowing down, the information services field is still going strong. Although computer-related information systems operations account for the lion's share of information services, this sector also includes numerous examples of companies trying to introduce lines of business that have succeeded in the USA and Europe, such as overseas television programme sales (NNBC Ltd), and credit card registration services (Credit Card Sentinel NTT Ltd).

Many companies recognizing the limits of agreements with local agents and importers are implementing a marketing strategy on their own. In the car industry, European makers such as BMW, Volvo, Benz, Volkswagen and Peugeot created subsidiaries in the 1980s in order to set up their own marketing and sales policy. In the well-established chemical and pharmaceutical industries, too, there is a growing trend to consolidate activities and to eliminate old joint ventures or tie-ups in order to establish independent business lines and contingent alliances with multiple partners. To give a few examples, in addition to streamlining business operations and strengthening the firm's management base, Shell Kosan KK took over Shell Kagaku KK to establish the company's position as the Japan operation of the Royal-Dutch Shell group; Bayer Yakuhin Ltd dissolved its sales collaboration with Takeda Chemical Industries Ltd in April 1990, while Sandoz did the same with Sankyo Co. in October 1991; Upjohn relinquished all its old ties and is now ready for new partnerships on a new basis.

At last, despite all the remaining mainly non-regulatory obstacles, there is a growing number of foreign firms taking total or partial control of Japanese companies. The trend is noticeable in the chemical and pharmaceutical fields, even if the deals remain very modest by international standards. In 1992, five of the 43 acquisitions involved Japanese-listed companies. They included Sansui, Atsugi Unisia and Ebara, which are listed on the first section of the Tokyo stock exchange, and Japan Systems and JAX, which are listed on the over-the-counter market.

THE MULTINATIONALIZATION PROCESS IN JAPAN

As Japan's importance in the global strategy of Western multinationals grows, and as the latter beef up their direct presence, they are seeking an increased higher-level and more specialized local labour force to deal with the larger operations and the multiplicity of agreements, partnerships and alliances that are replacing the former, stable structure.

As these firms become larger employers, they are confronted more directly with the issues involved in the management of local employees and executives. In some ways, the problems are different but parallel to those experienced by Japanese companies in their subsidiaries in the USA and in Europe. Japanese companies in Europe and in the USA have to manage a workforce accustomed to working with well-defined patterns of management, a precise job description and a clear-cut share of responsibility as defined through the authority of the person in charge; a concept of employment commitment based on short-term expectations from both sides; meritocratic appraisal standards limited to directly work-related criteria, and a reward system considered in almost purely monetary terms.

Western multinationals, especially of the US variety, are used to operating standardized mechanisms of management and an indirect type of hierarchical control supposed to be applicable in all business environments. However, the characteristics of the Japanese labour force, and the relations with Japanese companies operating different concepts of management, often make it difficult for foreign firms to adopt without adaptation the business practices used at headquarters or in other foreign subsidiaries.

Western firms operating in Japan have to manage people used to an employment commitment founded on stable, long-term relations based on mutual trust and common expectations. This induces a predictable mix of seniority and merit where appraisal, promotion, titles and compensation are considered in a longer perspective. In Japanese companies, job descriptions are unclear and the scope of responsibility is blurred; there is often an overlapping of the managerial functions and a loose concept of the 'person in charge' for a given job. Therefore, appraisal criteria are broader and include a number of non-job related elements. Rewards are not considered purely in financial terms: titles and the social status linked to regular promotion remain paramount in the nurturing of a long-term commitment *vis-à-vis* the firm. The pivotal position in terms of decision-making, diffusion and screening of information, motivation and coordination is taken by the section chief (*kacho*), at a lower hierarchical level than the pivotal position in most foreign companies. Finally, even if there is a growing emphasis on privacy, Japan remains a society where private and company life are closely intertwined.

Even if the foreign companies in Japan have been (and in some respects still are) catalysts for change, introducing new methods in the human resource management field, it is well known that national socio-cultural elements are nonetheless extremely important and that foreign companies in any country must take such factors into consideration.

Devising an adequate human resource policy is all the more difficult since foreign companies are enlarging and upgrading their activities at a time when the Japanese management system is undergoing radical changes due to the socio-cultural transformation of the Japanese economy and to demographic trends and socio-cultural evolution, inducing new values and life-styles. There is more mobility among young workers and mid-career managers, and more women are appearing on the permanent labour market, even at managerial level. Attitudes *vis-à-vis* money, social status and the company itself are changing.

This fluidity has an impact on Japanese and foreign companies alike, and renders the situation quite complex and difficult to manage. Foreign companies and managers have to develop conceptual tools in order to devise a management system congruent with that used elsewhere, as required by the globalization of their activities and the need for strategic coherence world-wide. At the same time they have to adapt to a workforce used to a different framework, but whose requests and behaviour can be contradictory in a transitory period characterized by a diversification of social and professional values.

Characteristics of the Japanese labour market

The approximately 3,000 firms with 50 per cent or more foreign equity interest employ about 300,000 Japanese, i.e. less than 1 per cent of a labour force of over 40 million. In 1991 (Ministry of Labour 1992), of regular employees, 7.7 per cent were foreigners, holding 7.3 per cent of managerial and 21.55 per cent of full-time director positions. North American firms account for about 73 per cent of the jobs and Europeans for about 22 per cent. Around 80 per cent of the workers are in the manufacturing sector despite a surge in the new entries of service companies in the 1980s. Around 85 per cent of these firms are subsidiaries of large US and European corporations, but 90 per cent employ less than 300 and 80 per cent less than 100 employees (Ministry of Labour 1991).

Labour shortage and redundancy

On one hand the economic slowdown, and a mismatch caused by structural changes in the economy, have saddled companies (Japanese and foreign) with a white-collar surplus. Plans have been devised to cope with this through outplacement, anticipated retirement and other policies aiming to put a number of workers outside the company's formal structure, short of socially damaging large-scale lay-offs. On the other hand, labour shortages, especially of young graduates, reflect demographic trends. So the difficulties foreign companies face in meeting their recruiting objectives can only worsen, as the number of students is bound to decrease in the near future. Overall, only 18 per cent of the foreign firms declared themselves able to fulfil their quota of new graduates in 1991. The highest figure was 39.5 per cent in the finance and insurance businesses; and while 54.2 per cent of companies with 1,000 and more employees claimed to have fulfilled their quota, the figures drop to less than 20 per cent in companies with less than 100 workers (Ministry of Labour 1992).

Although the situation eased up a little in 1992, Japan is likely to face a shortage of labour in the long term. Japanese companies are reducing their recruitment but they know that in ten years time, qualified manpower will be priceless. Therefore, most remain active on the labour market to avoid any future discontinuity in their manpower structure. In this context, foreign firms cannot stay put either. But a structurally tight labour market for qualified people inevitably leads to a change in the bargaining power balance, thus to higher recruiting costs. Long-term employment with slow but predictable promotion and deferred rewards was based on a low starting compensation. However, salaries are now high at all levels, including starting salaries. Recruiting policy must be multipronged, with the use of advertisements and promotional devices, lengthy follow-up of the candidates, extensive contacts with universities and the development of a vast network of contacts generally.

Mid-career and career women labour markets

The pool of mid-career managers is increasing but remains smaller than that of new graduates, and smaller than that in other countries. Recruiting of mid-career people of managerial capability, experienced but still young (35 to 45 years old), is likely to remain quite limited in the future. Recent figures on recruitment in 1991 (Gashikei Kigyo Recruit Guide 1992) highlight the difficulties: foreign companies generally have to offer newly-entrant mid-career executives a salary of between 1 million yen (section chief) to 3 million yen (department chief) higher than that of currently employed executives of similar level. In 1991, only 35.4 per cent of the foreign companies were able to secure enough managerial-level mid-career executives (Ministry of Labour 1992). The figure in firms with more than 1,000 workers is 41.7 per cent, but drops to around 35 per cent in firms with less than 100 employees. The gap is still more acute for mid-career technical personnel: overall, only 18.8 per cent of companies were able to fulfil their quota. Moreover, increased use of older people would run counter to the policy many foreign concerns try to develop in Japan. An integration of Japanese activities into the global strategy requires the development of a corporate culture that can best be achieved through the recruitment of new graduates. This trend has already been seen over several years in companies such as IBM, Nestlé, Mobil, DEC, Philips, the large chemical and pharmaceutical companies and the financial institutions. However, it is not linear, and the pharmaceutical and chemical concerns recently increased their mid-career recruitment after a drop in the 1980s to compensate for the lack of availability of young graduates. In the finance industry, too, large foreign concerns regularly recruit young graduates, but they are in dire need of personnel able to run computer systems and with a mathematical background. Those specialists can be recruited directly from the computer industry but they come also from the Japanese ship-building, car and steel industries.

The difficulties foreign firms experience in attracting young male graduates is partially due to the perception of their small size as a career limitation. This explains the targeting of women with a high educational background. In 1989 (Ministry of Labour 1989) women in foreign companies accounted for only 4.6 per cent of all executives above section chief level. In 1992 (Ministry of Labour 1992) the overall figure increased marginally to 6.5 per cent. Although the figure remains extremely low in manufacturing (2.6 per cent), it rises to around 7.8 per cent in wholly foreign-owned subsidiaries, and to 13.6 per cent in branches. In the foreign finance and publishing industries women account for more than 10 per cent of the executives.

However, despite the fact that more women are eager to stay on the labour market, few of them achieve permanent managerial positions. The shortage of public social facilities still makes it difficult for women to run a career; only 19.8 per cent of foreign companies have a childcare system and 0.3 per cent nursery facilities. Therefore, a more effective use of women is bound to remain a marginal option for foreign firms.

The durability of the system

The existing pattern of employment, based on long-term career commitment, is still the most durable and records only marginal changes. Younger people under 30 are more mobile and do not hesitate now to leave a company after a few years with their first employer. A record 2.77 million people switched jobs between June 1991 and May 1992 (Management and Coordination Agency 1992).

One employment agency predicts that nearly three out of ten university graduates will quit within three years of joining their first company. Among female graduates, the figure jumps to 45.6 per cent . Nevertheless, young graduates from the best universities generally retain a preference for the large, well-established Japanese firms, and all the more so since Japanese companies have begun redoubling efforts to secure personnel by improving their welfare programmes and offering more challenging work. The term '*Dai-ni Shinsotsu*' ('new graduates of a second type') has been coined for those leaving their first employer early on. However, the very fact that they are still called 'new' (*shin*) graduates means that they are staying in the mainstream. After a few years and the acquisition of a marketable capability in a foreign concern (or another Japanese company), they generally return to the traditional pattern and show a preference for well-established Japanese firms for their 'real' start in professional life. They are now all the more inclined to try out a short 'adventure' in a foreign firm, secure in the knowledge that their career will not suffer, in fact quite the contrary.

Japanese people show considerable resilience in their career attitudes and behaviour. They tend to give first priority to the challenges they can expect in their work (and this is true of graduates and older employees alike), but very few of them are willing to jump at another offer just because the conditions are slightly better than in their present job. Only a very small number of them think that by changing jobs they will enlarge their opportunities and enrich their careers. Over the age of 30, there is still a stigma attached to changing company. The mobility of Japanese staff will not evolve until that perception disappears. The negative image associated with a change of job was clearly illustrated in a recent Japanese drama, '*Kabuka Zero*', on NHK (23 November 1992). The TV show pictured a top bank employee being headhunted to work for a foreign securities house, and losing his new job very quickly. The opposition he faced from his peers and family, and his own hesitations to accept the job, indicate that such practices are not yet fully socially acceptable in Japan. This lack of mobility means that only a few per cent of Japanese employees will be ready to change job for a foreign company, and these are not necessarily the best people (Busquin 1992).

ISSUES FACING FOREIGN COMPANIES AS EMPLOYERS

Image perception and preference

The young graduates

Until recently, only a handful of companies such as IBM, Nestlé or Coca-Cola appeared on lists of the most desirable places for Japanese graduates to work. Over the last few years, this picture has gradually changed. Recruiting success on campus is increasingly a function of a firm's image, size, location and maturity in the domestic market, rather than its ownership. However, there is still a gap between the way in which foreign concerns are perceived by prospective employees (especially young graduates) and the reality of human resource management in those firms. Students and companies often seem to be on parallel tracks: new graduates still tend to shun the foreign firms for their perceived instability and the 'alien' characteristics of their management style (individual responsibility and evaluation, 'dry' human relations, lack of commitment *vis-à-vis* the development of personal potential). Even among students with a good opinion of foreign concerns this is still the main reason why the majority of them do not eventually apply for jobs in those firms. Similarly, foreign firms seeking to attract Japanese personnel emphasize their long-term commitment to Japan and their Japanese-style human resource management practices, such as long-term employment, a mix of seniority and merit criteria for appraisal and promotion, and group activities. In other words, they emphasize their 'Japaneseness' more than their foreign identity, something that, conversely, tends to turn off precisely those looking for a genuinely different career pattern, and who would be ready to take the risk of entering a foreign firm.

Psychological elements remain important: Japanese students are reluctant to make long stays abroad, and fear they will be ill at ease with foreign employees because of their supposed difficulties in coping with foreign culture. If the life-employment system is increasingly rejected in principle, job security nonetheless remains very important, especially among young males. It appears that, despite their lack of global significance, staff rationalization moves in a small number of high-profile foreign firms have reinforced the latent feeling of insecurity: staff reduction in a number of (mostly US) foreign financial institutions at the beginning of the 1990s has done great damage to their image in Japan, all the more so because financial institutions were considered more secure, offering better financial and promotion opportunities and representing a high-growth, high-profile industry.

Two other surveys confirm the enduring importance of job security: One shows that about one-third of students think that a foreign subsidiary can be closed at short notice through a decision from headquarters (Nemoto 1991); the other shows that 60.5 per cent of students consider that job security in foreign firms is lower than in large Japanese corporations (German Chamber of Commerce in Japan 1991). In both cases the job security factor was a significant element.

To offset the perceived reluctance of male students, foreign companies claim to have high hopes of female students. Indeed, overall preference for foreign firms is generally regarded as higher in women than in men. Moreover, students whose foreign language ability is generally high, as is the case with comparatively more female students than male, show an appreciable preference for foreign-affiliated companies. Conversely, natural science students are comparatively bad at foreign languages and tend to shun foreign companies. The female preference for foreign firms seems also to be related to the job security factor – for women, jobs in foreign firms are more secure precisely because male students have a significantly higher interest in lifelong employment and are markedly more sensitive to a company's future (Suwa 1991). It is also clear that very few women have a scientific background, and that they are still far less willing than men to enter a managerial career. This is important at a time when foreign companies are establishing R&D facilities and strategic alliances requiring high-level technical negotiations.

One observation is valid for both males and females: the size of the home office or the international standing of a foreign firm does not compensate for the handicap of the small size of the Japan-based subsidiary. A small organization in Japan is associated with limited career opportunities. This surely reflects the fact that not only do very few Japanese students seriously consider an international career, but that most of them have only scant knowledge of the activities of Western multinationals outside Japan. This is an embarrassing situation for most foreign firms. In a narrow sense, they are indeed small entities, but the level of their activities, and their competition with first-class Japanese and foreign companies, put them in a different category to domestic small and medium-sized firms. They still need a first-class labour force.

The older generation

In the minds of the employees of foreign firms, there is a lingering uncertainty that seems to be shared by many middle-aged Japanese considering a change in their career but reluctant to try a foreign firm. They associate frequent shifts in human resource management policy with changes of business direction and organizational structure. The fast rotation of top expatriate managers reinforces the image of short-term policy and commitment. There is a feeling that snap changes in the organizational structure and in personnel policies are aimed solely at exploiting the immediate possibilities without considering the long-term effects on the company as a whole. Newly arrived top expatriates tend to hire a consultant in order to have a better idea of what is going on in the subsidiary, while local managers consider themselves perfectly able to explain the situation and to propose possible management changes without the help of an outsider. They recognize the usefulness of external consultants in introducing compensation schemes of new management tools. However, their systematic use to solve management problems is perceived by top management as a lack of confidence in the capabilities of local managers.

There is also the feeling that top management, especially the position of company president, is a foreign preserve, a false perception in the majority of cases since the percentage of local CEOs in foreign companies in Japan is far higher than that in Japanese subsidiaries abroad (see Figure 11.2). As for the rotation at the top, it is impossible to generalize because the situation is very different from company to company. In some foreign firms, mainly of European origin, a number of top expatriates stay a long time in the country, learning the local business practices and the language. In others, the rotation rate is just two or three years, and this frequent turnaround can cause confusion and inconsistency in the company's business and personnel policies. For US citizens, the five-year limit on overseas postings is mainly due to tax issues. On the whole, however, foreign firms in Japan follow practices in line with the policy followed by multinationals, including Japanese ones, all over the world.

A perception gap exists between local employees and expatriates in this respect. With some caveats (see Conclusion, p. 258), foreign firms try to localize as many functions as possible and to make use of internal resources, mainly for purposes of compensation, and to nurture a favourable corporate image. But this is often difficult in

Table 11.1 Number of years stationed/planned for foreign CEOs in Japan

Range (years)	Stationed		Planned	
	Number	%	Number	%
<1	33	18	3	2
>1<3	61	33	31	25
>3<5	38	20	51	40
>5<10	29	16	31	25
>10	25	13	10	8
Total	186	100	126	100

Table 11.2 Number of foreign expatriates in Japanese subsidiaries

Total number	%	From parent company	%	From other subsidiary	%
183	46	17	8	18	28
149	38	146	68	41	64
29	7	29	13	1	2
24	6	16	7	3	4
6	2	3	1	1	2
1		1			
1		1			
5	1	3		1	
398	100	216	98	64	100

the short term due to the rapid development of activities and the need for 'on-the-spot' expertise. In many cases, the use of external consultants is more a question of time than a deliberate policy to shun people raised in the company. One the whole, whether it is accurate or not, such a perception gap is nevertheless damaging because it creates a weak centripetal force, especially at the crucial level of middle management.

Foreign companies are also often perceived as having a higher labour turnover than local Japanese firms. However, a 1991 survey on US companies (American Chamber of Commerce in Japan 1991) emphasizes the point that with 59 per cent of the firms reporting turnover as less than 10 per cent, and 84 per cent less than 20 per cent , this view is not supported by the facts. Other statistics show that the average turnover for all industries in Japan is 20.19 per cent, with manufacturing at 16.2 per cent and finance at 23.3 per cent; in the past 10 years, only 13 per cent of the firms in the sample reported lay-offs (71 per cent of these only once); 11 per cent reported labour disputes (Temporary Center K.K. 1989). Even if these figures need to be qualified due to a number of imbalances by age-group and function in the personnel turnover in foreign firms (see below), it appears that many of them are, on the whole, in line with Japanese companies of the same category.

Management practices

Adapting to local conditions: From catalysts to conformity

In Japan, foreign companies (mainly US ones) have led their Japanese competitors in areas of human resource management, providing career opportunities for women university graduates, shorter working hours, five-day weeks, older retirement, merit-based pay, mid-career hiring, etc. To some extent, this is still true for a number of them.

NCR has employed female university graduates since the mid-1950s; nearly half the company's new graduate recruits in 1991 were women. IBM has constantly promoted female workers to technical and managerial positions at a level far higher than Fujitsu, Hitachi or NEC. At Novo Nordisk, half the basic researchers are women. Without any doubt, foreign companies are more advanced than Japanese firms in providing career opportunities for women.

In a recent survey (Temporary Center K.K. 1989), 74 per cent of the women working in foreign companies replied that the promotion system was meritocratic and gave them a fair chance of climbing to a managerial position. Only 3 per cent of those working in Japanese companies agreed with that statement. Foreign firms are currently leading attempts to reduce the annual working hours of their staff, leaving Japanese far behind. Nearly 70 per cent of foreign companies claimed that their employees worked an average of no more than 2,000 hours a year, while the 1989 figure for Japanese firms was 2,076 hours (Japan Productivity Center 1990). Currently, 88.5 per cent of foreign companies have two days holiday per week (i.e. a five-day working week) while only 11.5 per cent of the Japanese concerns have such a system (most Japanese companies still demand a day's work on one or two Saturdays out of four). Only 0.3 per cent of foreign companies have a six-day working week, while this is still the case in 32 per cent of Japanese firms (Ministry of Labour 1992).

Table 11.3 Hours worked by employees of foreign firms in Japan

Average annual hours	No. of firms	%
1,800–& less	105	20.9
1,801–1,900	132	26.3
1,901–2,100	113	22.5
2,101–2,200	32	6.4
2,201–& more	17	3.4
No answer	30	6.0
Total	502	100.0

Foreign companies are having to innovate in order to stay ahead of their Japanese competitors, who are themselves modernizing old local welfare customs, reflecting changes in life-style. Compared to Japanese companies, foreign firms were seen to show little concern for the life of their employees outside the office; hence an increasing number now offer more fringe benefits. Listed below are a few examples:

- IBM Japan, Ltd offers a 'Nice Life Plan' aimed at retired employees or people preparing to be pensioned, designed to enrich the 'second life'. It provides financial support to become involved in hobbies and other interests, including the launch of business ventures. The company pays a maximum of 600,000 yen.
- Some companies offer short holidays (half a day) through time-sharing systems, or allow for convalescence after an illness. Fuji-Xerox offers a 'family nursing holiday' of up to 12 months to nurse a sick family member. A similar programme is offered by Ciba-Geigy to both female and male employees.
- Intel offers scholarships abroad for employees' children, without any obligation for the children to join the company afterwards.
- Some firms offer individual incentives to salesmen, integrating them into world-wide schemes. For example, DEC has a 'DECathlon' award open to sales staff of all subsidiaries. DEC Japan, which has some 500 sales staff, produces 10 DECathlon winners every year. Olivetti offers a two-week incentive trip to Europe, including a visit to the Milan headquarters, for top performers.
- Texas Instruments has an annual share offer in a 'Universal Profit Sharing' programme. The scheme helps to integrate Japanese employees into the global corporation.
- A number of foreign firms are also actively philanthropic. Some

Table 11.4 Comparative situation of the welfare system

Company	Housing financing	Housing facilities	Employees' stock option	Fex time system	Half-day holidays
Japanese	89.3%	92.3%	85.6%	36.5%	38.4
Foreign	25.2%	33.6%	24.4%	30.2%	65.5

have personnel exclusively in charge of developing global and individual programmes emphasizing the corporate social responsibility of the company. They open welfare facilities in rural Japanese communities and try to make use of their own resources for volunteer activities. Some have developed holiday schemes, temporary work breaks, and evaluations and rewards for such activities, in order to involve their personnel directly.

Welfare systems in foreign companies are still inherently more of the 'flow' rather 'stock' type (i.e. health care or restaurants, rather than housing or stocks) but in 1991, 33.6 per cent of foreign companies offered home financing, and 25.2 per cent had company housing. This compares well with what Japanese firms are offering.

To be sure, many foreign companies have introduced new management styles whereby individual incentives and achievement are more strongly emphasized. Bristol-Meyers, Mars Food, DEC, and other foreign companies such as Intel or Motorola, offer fast lanes to senior management positions to young Japanese executives, which they would still be unable to find in a Japanese environment.

Having generally a more precise and clear-cut job description system, foreign firms place a strong emphasis on accountability, meritocratic compensation management, job ability and performance. A self-assessment system is applied in about 40 per cent of foreign companies while the figure is about 13 per cent in the Japanese companies (Nemoto 1988). More foreign than Japanese companies have internal job application systems, although the figures for both are insignificant.

Almost no Japanese enterprise has fixed salary ranges for corresponding jobs or ranks. The only meaningful competitive salaries are for new graduates, mainly determined by supply and demand, and by the company's profitability. Pay levels of all the higher positions are adjusted mainly for vertical balances. In some large companies (generally more than 500 employees), besides a yearly pay rise based on age, curriculum and seniority, a pay rise system has been adopted under which the weight of ability and performance increases with the grade. For instance, the relative importance of age and seniority, the content of the job and the performance level in compensation were observed as follows on a visit to a large German chemical company. The weight of the job content and level of performance increased rapidly beyond the section chief position, while the weight of the basic salary decreased dramatically. Conversely, the weight of job content and performance amounted to about 25 per cent of the compensation of a new employee, while the basic salary weight is about 75 per cent.

The system adopted by Mobil Oil, with a complex system of bargaining between employees and line managers, and a Career Development Committee acting as a central steering channel, is well known.

In a handful of interviewed companies (essentially relatively small trading firms), a strict pay-for-performance system covering the whole compensation package, including the bonus, and extending from managerial through technical to clerical jobs, had been established. For most of them, this followed a long trial-and-error process leading to the resignation of those oppsed to the system (a small minority as reported by the companies) and extensive and continuous training of the appraisees and appraisers by an outside consultant.

The formula acceptance of prevalent rules

However, for the time being most foreign companies prefer to adopt prevailing local practices in order to minimize their 'foreign' image, especially in the current transitory period when changing social norms are only just beginning to become established as part of the cultural system. Their wage structures and personnel affairs are quite similar to those of Japanese companies. Even where a meritocratic pay-for-performance system is officially adopted, it is rarely put into practice. Most foreign firms still tend to give across-the-board salary rises, and bonuses are based on the industry average and the company's performance, as in most Japanese companies. Perhaps rather paradoxially, a minimal, almost symbolic, supplementary reward goes to exceptional performers.

Such a situation is partly understandable because vestiges of the life employment system persist in the attitudes and behaviour of almost all salaried Japanese workers. Japanese companies are trying to overcome these cultural factors, and to introduce effective strategies in a new environment leading to a more contingent con-

Table 11.5 Criteria for selecting the local personnel (n=414)

Criterion	No. of companies	%
Education	200	48
Experience	278	67
Personality	238	57
Motivation	300	72
Command of English	198	48
Sex	30	7
Age	111	27
Other	31	7

cept of employment commitment. There are also changes in the value system embraced by the new generation leading to a reassessment of relations *vis-à-vis* work and the company. Nevertheless, as mentioned above, the system remains very stable. The employment concept may be crumbling in its most traditional form, but job security remains a key factor in the choice of a career. Values may be more individualistic but, save for a minority segment of the population, working in a meritocratic system with purely functional interactions and individual evaluation may be attractive only on paper. Such practices seem to remain a deterrent for many young Japanese when making their career decision.

Therefore, beyond their declared emphasis on a system based on job ability, and not on the whole personality, many foreign companies end up adopting a mixed system of recruiting, appraisal and reward that is not very different from that of Japanese companies. In our survey, the selection criteria cited as important by the greatest number of companies were motivation (72 per cent), previous experience (67 per cent) and personality (57 per cent).

Only a small number of foreign firms (one out of the 20 whose human resource managers we interviewed) had a classified range rating system not incorporating seniority, age and other elements traditionally used in the Japanese classification. In fact we noticed that most foreign companies adopting a system of job classification (the Hay system, for instance) retained a degree of flexibility, as in Japanese companies. De facto, the differences in the approach of foreign companies and Japanese companies is not fundamental but more a question of degree. The same can be said of long-term employment commitment, since the level of sackings for bad performance by foreign companies is very low, to the extent that in many cases foreign firms offer higher job security than many

Japanese companies. Although it is unavoidable to some extent, the fact that foreign firms are often caught in an in-between situation, with insufficient emphasis on special management characteristics, may lead to contradictions or restrictions in policy.

For instance, many specialized posts, such as traders and analysts, are occupied by women in foreign financial firms, although the female respondents to our survey often stated that foreign employers tended to concur with the reluctance of their older Japanese managers to appoint them to positions involving contact with clients (there are exceptions, of course). This causes a perceived restriction in the development of their career, leading to frustration and, eventually, to resignation.

Foreign firms still stress 'group' as the basis for leadership, even if the percentage of foreign firms sponsoring workshop meetings and small group activities is in fact far less than that of their local competitors. Moreover, the very fact that they tend to emphasize a traditionally Japanese collective style of management alienated them from promising young managers who expect a more challenging and meritocratic style of management from their foreign employers (see below).

As a result of vertically integrating the organization on a profit-centre basis, inflexibility is often imposed on personnel administration. Even among large-scale foreign corporations, there are many where each of several divisions in the Japanese operation reports directly to the home office. In such cases, key personnel decisions are delegated to line managers. Even if the structure and functions of the personnel department are formally similar to those of Japanese companies, the personnel administration is in fact severely restricted or ceases to exist from a total-company point of view. It may happen that one division is effecting a cut in personnel while another, quite independently, is running a recruitment advertisement. Japanese employees are puzzled by such an approach, in which investment and operations are controlled by a division rather than by the corporation itself. Moreover, such practices certainly do not help to capitalize on the advantages of a larger corporate structure.

Recruitment practices

Generally speaking, many foreign companies have difficulties keeping their core employees. As pointed out before, these employees often see only limited opportunities available for career advancement in the company, because its perceived small size places restrictions on the nature and scope of its activities. Consequently, they turn to opportunities outside the company, causing frequent personnel shortages, especially at the crucial middle management level. This, in turn, forces the hiring of replacements on an *ad hoc* basis, creating a vicious circle.

Hiring *ad hoc* mid-career people and not young graduates is a policy adopted by all multinationals when they begin their operations abroad. Foreign concerns in Japan are not exceptional in this respect. Moreover, in some Japanese industries where foreign firms have made inroads, such as financial services, there is a demand for skills that are largely independent of the prevailing style of employment and the nature of corporate organization. This encourages mid-career recruitment.

In the case of foreign companies, recruitment of mid-career personnel has often been standard practice at each level of the company, for profit-protecting reasons. Greater emphasis than in similar Japanese firms is placed on the recruitment of personnel who can be immediately operational at all levels, i.e. managerial, technical, sales and administrative. Even among firms well-established in Japan, many are not yet systematically recuiting new graduates on a regular basis (Ballon 1991). Such cases are evident in about 30 per cent of the companies in our sample: 113 out of 372 companies reported regular annual recruitment from schools and universities. The reasons given are obvious and inter-related: in many cases, the small scale of operations makes it unnecessary to hire on a regular basis; the firm's profile was often too low to attract good new graduates; newly established companies, foreign and Japanese alike, need personnel who can be operational immediately. This policy is directly linked to the size of the company, as recent figures clearly show: 91 per cent of the foreign companies with more than 200 employees, 48 per cent of those with 50 to 200 employees, but only 5 per cent of those with less than 50 employees were recruiting on a regular basis in 1991 (Ministry of Labour 1992). The same year, 20 foreign companies hired more than a 100 new graduates. In 1989 (Gashikei Kigyo, Recruit Guide 1992), 56 per cent of the personnel recruited by foreign companies were mid-career people. This figure may seem quite high but even by 1982 the percentage was reported to be very similar to that of Japanese companies with over 1,000 employees. The ratio of mid-career recruitment was about 30 per cent, i.e. lower than that of the same category.

Table 11.6 Origins of mid-career local managers (n=277)

Origin	No.	%
Other foreign company in our industry	78	28
Other foreign companies outside of our industry	56	20
Japanese company in our industry	133	48
Japanese companies outside of our industry	130	47
Other	27	10

It seems obvious, in view of the need for ready-made expertise that 48 per cent of companies recruit mid-career local managers from Japanese companies in the same industry. However, it should also be noted that, besides the use of headhunters, the increasing intra-industry collaboration between Japanese and foreign firms, for instance the car industry, has led to an increasing number of permanent transfers of Japanese executives to foreign firms under interfirm 'gentlemen's agreements'.

Considering the narrowness of the market, items 1 and 2 of Table 11.6 confirm the high level of job-hopping among foreign firms. Section 5 ('Other') included career people recruited from outside Japan. The latter are the object of mixed feelings. On one hand, they bring communication and language skills and an international outlook; on the other hand, they are often considered as out of touch with the Japanese market, and with business and social practices. Younger people, graduating from a foreign university or business school (already with a business experience in the latter case) are targeted for the same reason, although their very high expectations *vis-à-vis* foreign postings, and their above-average compensation requests, have often been problematic.

Compensation/performance appraisal

The extensive use of mid-career people in foreign concerns, from top managerial positions down to low-grade administrative jobs, may result in considerable confusion within the organization each time it occurs.

A discrepancy in compensation policies and the lack of an overall system is observed even among well-established foreign firms. Experienced managers are often offered above-average salaries. Differing degrees of urgency to fill a position, and variations in individual negotiation skills, can create discrepancies in the compensation of similar jobs, exposing the management to misunderstandings and accusations of favouritism.

Foreign firms tend to consider the department head position as the most important in operations management. There is hence a rather large gap between the pay of section chiefs and department heads. That of the section chiefs is often lower than that offered to the same grade in large Japanese companies. Moreover, foreign firms often point out that overtime work by non-supervisory staff should be considered exceptional. As a consequence, the take-home pay of middle-aged male workers is reduced just when their financial needs are highest. This erodes the unity of the workforce and hinders motivation (Ballon 1991).

Western companies' appraisals are often unsystematic but explicit (Pucik 1991). In most cases, performance reviews are conducted annually, as opposed to the Japanese practice of having at least two or three reviews per year. In a Japanese environment based on trust and collective security, employees are not appraised narrowly on a short-term basis for the achievement of a specified task. Formal feedback on performance is therefore unnecessary. Informal tips and the attribution of jobs are sufficient generally to indicate one's position in the hierarchy, whether or not one is on the fast track. In the long run, the gap between the good performers and the rest will gradually widen while remaining reasonable and balanced. Japanese people are not accustomed to face-to-face individual evaluations with immediate rewards or penalties.

Many of the managers we interviewed were still uneasy with an 'objective' appraisal procedure which could be misleading, especially when applied by foreign managers. In their view, it is difficult to evaluate properly the individual's contribution to the achievement of a given task. This leads easily to subjective judgement, which is precisely not what is sought. In fact, only a handful of top managers are appraised by foreigners, while the performance of the large majority of employees and managers is appraised by other locals. But it causes a spreading uneasiness throughout the system. Japanese executives consider themselves as working in a different cycle. This is not a situation unique to Japan but reflects a feeling common in all multinationals, and often heard in the foreign subsidiaries of Japanese multinationals: locals are supposed to stay longer in the subsidiary, and be concerned by its long-term future, while the expatriates tend to be perceived as privileging short-term results because they will not stay for more than a few years. This different perspective is perceived as causing a potential bias in appraisals.

The concept of money is changing in Japan and, with it, the relative weight of employees' expectations *vis-à–vis* monetary and non-monetary types of reward. Young Japanese people talk freely about money and are becoming more assertive in this respect. Consequently, there is also a growing awareness of the 'right' to make money through work and to get a fair share of the profit in a broad sense. Previously, Japanese workers had no frame of reference other than the salarymen of Japanese companies, but now many have been in contact with expatriates and Japanese people who have worked abroad. Therefore, the basis of comparison is wider. This is reflected in the comments made by a large number of younger Japanese respondents to our survey (those under 40) working in big, well-established foreign firms (Debroux 1992). A widespread scepticism concerning titles and promotion is observed if these are not linked directly to monetary rewards. As stated above, a number of respondents were also sceptical concerning the objectivity of an appraisal system based on individual short-term performance for a specific task. However, reflecting a debate also occurring in many Japanese firms, a majority of the younger managers (80 per cent of those under 40) favour an appraisal system with prior objective-setting and result accountability. They complain about the subjectivity of the appraisal system in their respective companies and would like them to adopt stricter and more stringent criteria of evaluation and a more meritocratic 'pay-for-performance' system. Some go further and express the view that 'the personnel turn-over is too low, the company should get rid as soon as possible of the bad performers'. They are afraid that 'too much complacency in the promotion and appraisal system will lead to a corporate culture encouraging passivity and a bureaucratic way of mind, then to the loss of the competitiveness of the firm'. Once again, this is not unlike the comments often made by young local executives working for Japanese companies in Europe and in the United States. Japanese companies abroad, and large, well-established foreign firms in Japan, have indeed so far tended to avoid lay-offs for bad performance. They try to find an adequate position for almost everybody in the global company's puzzle. However, the economic downturn of the early 1990s will almost certainly not lead to a quick return to high growth and, even if it does, strong constraints will be exerted on the local management (foreign and Japanese) to adopt stricter measures of productivity and efficiency. The pressure to impose more stringent evaluation, reward and penalty systems will come naturally from headquarters looking at the business bottom line, but seemingly also from the younger management layers inside.

Training

One important reason why foreign companies in Japan find themselves lacking in both the number and quality of employees at all times is their neglect (or perceived neglect) of long-term employee development programmes. The common practice of mid-career recruitment seems indicative of the firm's underlying attitude to employment commitment: that is, the firm buys specific skills, not potential. Since it does not commit itself to a relationship with its local employees by training them, it does not lose much even if a person quits after a short period. Among the human resource managers we interviewed, most (even in small and medium-sized firms) appreciated long-term service, although their basic system did not assume a long-term commitment on the part of the employee. There are outstanding exceptions such as Bristol Myers, NCR, IBM Japan, Mobil Sekiyu and others – pioneers in the field of training. They have well-organized and comprehensive orientation programmes for young graduates and career planning schemes to respond to the growing willingness of young people to map out their career evolution more precisely.

On the whole, however, a common complaint from our local respondent managers was that the learning environment is often neglected and stunts the growth of the individual. There is no clear career progression or training programmes for new graduates. Management awareness and capabilities in human resource matters were poorly developed. Training and motivating activities are reduced to a minimum. Local managers reported an inevitable trade-off between budgets and work load. In times of budget cuts, training expenses are not given priority. This is all the more important since the availability of a comprehensive training programme is consistently cited in all surveys as essential (Rhône Poulenc, 1991). The lack (or perceived lack) of an adequate training policy is considered as a strong deterrent to a career in a foreign firm.

Only 8 per cent of our sample of 415 companies claimed not to offer any training. On the whole, there is a strong emphasis on 'on-the-job' training (83 per cent of the companies). Moreover, 52 per cent claimed to offer technical or managerial training abroad. As foreign languages were perceived as an important source of difficulties in a large number of companies (75 per cent), it is not surprising

Table 11.7 Training programmes offered by the companies (n=415)

Programme	No.	%
On-the-job training (OJT)	343	83
Generalist-oriented training	57	14
English language programme	223	54
Technical/managerial training abroad	215	52
Technical/managerial training in Japan	153	37
Training in Japanese language, culture, business practices for expatriates	111	27
No training	32	8
Other	24	6

Table 11.8 Localization of management (n=422)

	Japanese	Expatriate From parent company	From other subsidiary	Other	J/EPC[1]	J/EOS[2]	J/EO[3]
CEO	265	118	4	10	18	1	5
Gen/Aff	379	25	-	1	6		1
Person.	376	19	-	2	1		1
Fin/Acc.	347	46	3	4	9		3
Mar/Sal.	329	31	2	4	25	1	4
Prod.	216	23	1	1	5	1	4
R&D	205	33	1	4	7	1	2

1 J/EPC=Japanese & expatriate from parent company
2 J/EOS=Japanese & expatriate from other subsidiaries
3 J/EO=Japanese & expatriate from other companies

that 54 per cent offer English language programmes for their employees.

Localization of management

Overall, 59.6 per cent of the presidents of foreign subsidiaries in Japan are Japanese; this rises to 72.3 per cent in manufacturing. A substantial 90.5 per cent of the presidents of 50/50 per cent joint ventures are locals, and even in the wholly foreign-owned subsidiaries the figure is more than 50 per cent (50.2). It is only in branches that the figure drops below 50 per cent (35 per cent) (Ministry of Labour 1992). This confirms the results of our survey shown in Table 11.8.

Indeed, the cost of the expatriates (salary, lodging, fringe benefits,

250 P. Debroux

premium, etc.) seems a heavy burden for many foreign firms in Japan, including the larger ones such as IBM. However, the issue is complex. On one hand, a company like Hoechst emphasizes the fact that it plans to reduce the number of expatriates (from 40 to 16 by 1994) not to cut costs but because it has enough experienced and high-level Japanese managers (*Nikkei Weekly* 1992). On the other hand, for the time being, the growing presence of foreign firms in Japan means longer-term stays on the part of expatriates. To cope with the broadening of the scope of activities, many companies are now reconsidering their role in a more global, long-term perspective. This follows a period in the 1980s during which rapid and comprehensive localization of management seemed to be considered as the panacea. Clearly, an increasing but still small number of firms can attract truly able new Japanese graduates, up to the early 30s, but the ability of foreign companies to hire able, experienced managers with senior management potential is still very limited. In fact, foreign firms in Japan often have an inverted pyramid of local talent in their organization, a situation not unlike that of many Japanese companies abroad. When first entering the market they were unable to hire first-class local talent. Over time, their capacity to hire able people has increased, with the result that those persons who would normally qualify for promotion in terms of age and company experience are not the highest-calibre people available. This is unfortunately a problem impossible to solve in the short term. It is possible to put a small number of very bright individuals on a faster track, but a general disregard for age and experience would put the whole operation in jeopardy.

All levels of ownership included, a majority of foreign companies have Japanese directors on the board of the subsidiary (Ono 1991). The voice of Japanese employees is therefore heard, since those directors are generally promoted internally. However, it is not possible to infer from the nationality of the president or the board members alone the degree of centralization of autonomy in relations between the subsidiary and headquarters. Moreover, many presidents are indeed locals, yet the yearly turnover in foreign firms seems to be much higher than in Japanese firms: 18.2 per cent for 4–5 per cent respectively, reflecting a seemingly greater instability in the top management in foreign concerns.

It is reported that the influence of headquarters is strongest in the following areas: recruitment and transfer of the top management, transfer pricing decisions, planning and basic R&D. This was borne out by our own findings: the influence of headquarters is

Table 11.9 Extent of influence by the headquarters of foreign companies (n=423)

Influence	No. of HQs	%
Involved in recruitment/personnel management of local personnel	72	17
Involved in financial matters of the company	245	58
Involved in product development	115	27
Involved in R&D	89	21
Involved in marketing/advertising	58	14
Overall corporate policies and strategies	284	67
Other	36	9

strong mainly in financial matters, long-term planning and strategy. The subsidiary's decision-making power is strong in human resource management (except for the desigation of top managers), production, R&D and marketing.

Manufacturing subsidiaries are moderately controlled by headquarters. This probably reflects not only the reliance on the foreign parent for product design and critical parts and components, but also the growing importance of Japanese subsidiaries in terms of new product development and technology. Business planning and financial matters are the two functions most tightly controlled; training and marketing/advertising are the least controlled, which is broadly similar to the situation in Japanese and other multinational companies abroad. However, variations are observed by company, function and nationality. Delegation is high in European companies but the ratio of Japanese top managers is lower than in US subsidiaries. On the other hand, the level of top management localization in US companies is higher, but delegation is slightly lower than in European firms. This reflects the traditionally stronger emphasis placed by US multinationals on an indirect type of control, with a widespread use of *ad hoc* manuals and a higher standardization and formalization of the procedures and reporting. This permits a localization of management in a system that nonetheless remains centralized on the whole.

HUMAN RESOURCE MANAGEMENT STRATEGY
The differentiation points

In many industries, foreign companies can no longer claim to have a technological edge and, therefore, to be in a position to offer a learning ground not available in local firms. A majority of young Japanese think that Japanese companies are technologically ahead in most industries.

Although wages in foreign companies are higher on average than in most small Japanese companies, large Japanese companies offer a higher long-term global compensation package than most of the foreign companies, if we include the large number of miscellaneous allowances, supplementing basic salary, plus the opportunity to use company lodging or to get a 'soft' loan from the company in order to purchase one's own home, etc. (Hay Group 1991).

The opportunity to work abroad is an existing but declining 'bonus' offered by foreign companies, but many Japanese companies now have foreign subsidiaries, and offer the same opportunity. In our survey, the opportunity to go abroad/work in a foreign environment was considered as a moderately important factor in choosing a foreign company as an employer (mentioned as important by 37 per cent of the respondents). Moreover, most young Japanese people are interested in relatively short stays abroad, but not in an international expatriate career, which requires long stays abroad in different surroundings.

Besides offering incentives such as a higher starting salary, shorter working hours and a more consistent application of the five-day week, the strong selling point for foreign companies remains their role as agents of change, or more precisely the importance they accord to promotion and compensation based on merit and individual performance evaluations, as well as the challenge of the job and the opportunity to specialize. In our survey, companies rightly emphasized the greater individual responsibility and freedom (57 per cent) offered by foreign firms and the opportunity to upgrade one's own professional capabilities (56 per cent) as factors attracting recruits to their door.

However, as other foreign concerns and Japanese companies compete increasingly on the mid-career market, an implicit threat is posed to the employment stability of foreign companies. To lose personnel on the way is unavoidable; the flip side of more individual expression is that employees want to have the right to use their time freely and to limit their commitment. Thus, companies should do their utmost to keep core people and develop a centripetal force around a clear identity. As pointed out above, foreign companies are subject to isomorphic pressure when they enter a different market, such as Japan's. In some cases, this is a reflection not of deliberate policy, but of daily contact with Japanese companies.

Overadaptation to Japanese practices is possible in such a context but, practically, this would mean an inevitable increase in the problem of retaining core personnel, as requests for a different kind of management would multiply year by year. The small number of young graduates having a positive image of foreign firms, and eager to choose them as employers, are looking for something different from that which Japanese companies are perceived to offer. Many are still reluctant to take risks but some may feel that their career hopes do not match what Japanese companies can deliver, and shift towards foreign firms.

It was observed in a recent survey (Sakakibara 1991) that young people choosing a foreign company as employer value the following: the opportunity to develop a specialized capability, the freedom and independence of discussion and time, the pure challenge and the entrepreneurial spirit. The 'career anchors' selected by those choosing to work for a Japanese company were: the opportunity to develop a general managerial capability, the job stability, the spirit of service and sacrifice. In other words, as expected, those selecting a foreign firm preferred a career allowing them to develop original thinking and specialized knowledge, while giving them the opportunity to control their time and work with autonomy. However, an important comment was that employees in foreign companies wished to have a still more 'foreign' system of wages and promotion. Echoing the comments made during our survey, present systems were not considered to be meritocratic enough. Strangely, workers in Japanese companies also wished to have 'foreign-style' pay and promotion systems based more on merit. Both groups were also unsatisfied with the recruitment process. People working in foreign companies wished to have a more stable, fair and transparent system of recruitment. They felt that on-the-spot mid-career recruitment lead to unfairness in promotion and rewards. On the other hand, people in Japanese companies were not against mid-career recruitment because they considered it would be difficult to develop innovation without external input.

The development of a strategy

In the light of the above data, it seems that there is a place for a gradual approach leading to a hybrid system in foreign companies that would put local personnel in a challenging position without rocking the boat.

It is difficult to generalize and discern trends because no single, uniquely foreign management style or organizational pattern can be identified, even among companies with the same country of origin. To some extent, small and large foreign companies have to cope nowadays with issues similar to those faced by Japanese companies: the difficulties of small Japanese businesses in terms of recruitment and management of the workforce, but rendered more difficult still by the lack of back-up from a larger company, low public awareness levels, a shortage of resources for recruiting campaigns, and lingering doubts as to their commitment in Japan. Local managers in small foreign firms accept their lack of job stability as an unavoidable occupational hazard. Sackings for bad performance, as well as resignations, should, they felt, be considered more or less casually depending upon the economic situation and other job opportunities. However, at the same time, 65 per cent of the respondents in firms with less than 100 employees declared that they were not likely to leave the company in the foreseeable future; moreover, they tended to rate their company significantly higher than employees in larger firms, in terms of development/utilization of skills (ratings of 2.10 and 2.65 respectively) and responsibility (ratings of 2.05 and 2.90 respectively), on a five-point scale (1=excellent, 5=poor).

On the other hand, overall, workers in firms having over 500 employees consider their job as secure as in large Japanese companies, and 86 per cent of them are not likely to leave the company in the foreseeable future. They are fairly satisfied with their pay (rating 2.04) and promotion (rating 2.50). As we have just seen, they complain more of the narrow scope of responsibility and participation in the decision-making process. To avoid bureaucratic drifting, large foreign companies try to perpetuate or revive the spirit of challenge and innovation through the development of innovative structures ('intrapreneurship' schemes, or other initiatives such as Motorola's SBU units or the venture businesses set up by the senior employees of IBM Japan) and input from outside (rehiring of mid-career managers and technicians after having recruited young graduates in the 1970s and 1980s). Like many Japanese companies, foreign firms have personnel who are unsuited to the new environment and increasingly difficult to place elsewhere within the company, while also facing difficulties recruiting the personnel they need in a labour market short on first-class young graduates and mid-career people with genuine managerial capability.

A major concern of Japanese employees aspiring to work in a foreign firm is whether their performance will be appraised according to Japanese or foreign standards. Traditionally, employees in

Japanese companies work according to a number of unwritten rules and codes which they learn through the progressive assimilation of what could be called rites of interaction (Goffman 1967). There is no respect of formal rules, to the extent that their implementation becomes a task in itself for managers. As in any organization, rules do exist but they are transmitted through an informal interiorization process of internal learning. This fosters leadership by example, and learning through interaction, so that members know exactly how to behave in their work and *vis-à-vis* their superiors and colleagues. This creates a cohesive work context and provides an environment in which responsibility is shared and job attribution is carried out without extensive use of procedures and manuals. Nowadays, however, young people tend to refuse the rites of interaction, or to pay them lip-service only. They limit and diversify their commitment *vis-à-vis* the company and spread it over other private groups. This is precisely the reason why more codification and standardization is becoming necessary in Japanese companies in the current sociocultural environment. A fortiori, this is all the more true in the management of foreign companies precisely because they tend to attract people refusing the traditional norms of attitude and behaviour. Young managers (respondents under 40) placed strong emphasis on individual task and goal accomplishment. In terms of leadership traits, the most desired type of top manager was the entrepreneur (45 per cent), followed by the coordinator and administrator (29 per cent). The mentor type is widely discarded (20 per cent), even in the case of a Japanese top management. (Debroux 1992).

Of course, differences are a question of degree. Unlike Westerners, Japanese employees are not embarrassed by collective responsibility, an overlapping of functions and a lack of explicit authority within the organization. On the flipside, we found that Japanese managers claim to be hindered by excessively clear-cut.boundaries of responsibility and authority. This could explain their reluctance *vis-à-vis* perceived potential loss of flexibility due to the use of formalized and standardized procedures and reporting. They remain generally more uncomfortable with management by manuals and procedures than do Western people. Some declared that they did not expect such limitations to their scope of responsibility when they entered a foreign firm. This shows that in a business culture in which informal contacts have a unique function, Japanese employees are expected to be particularly sensitive about the negative consequences of the lack of informal interactions inside the company.

A meritocratic plan is based primarily on the employees' belief that managers can make valid distinctions between good and poor performances; without such a belief, variations in pay rises or bonuses will not be seen as a reflection of merit, even if significant distinctions are made. In that case, it can be assumed not only that rewards will fail to function as incentives, but also that dissatisfaction will develop, especially among those who are confident of their capabilities. We have found that the association between performance and reward is not always clearly perceived. A more standardized and formalized style of management and control, and a fairer and more transparent appraisal and reward system are clearly desired. However, at the same time, a flexible decision-making system, allowing involvement when and where necessary, has to be maintained. Appraisal should be broadly defined and not systematically linked to the achievement of a specific job. A mix of meritocracy, seniority and diligence should be maintained. Some form of collective measuring should remain part of the process, and non-work related factors should not be entirely eliminated when determining salary. The Japanese orientation towards group activities is deeply rooted in the educational system, and will not disappear overnight, if ever. Most Japanese people are accustomed to participating actively in many kinds of private and public group activities. This is an asset that should be utilized positively.

While it is true that the turnover rate for personnel as a whole in foreign firms is in line with that of Japanese companies, there is nonetheless a far higher rate for managers and promising young executives. In such a context, building a major programme of recruiting and training is essential. In order to develop a grass-roots network, effective recruiting campaigns should be carried out full-time throughout the year and not only when students are looking for a job. Human resource managers report that many job offers are turned down after a promising first contact due to the lack of follow-up, which is itself due to the small resources put into the recruiting sections. Moreover, a critical assessment of the recruitment marketing and PR policies followed so far is necessary. It seems that many companies are missing their targets; they do not fulfil their quotas and end up with people who are not the best available to them.

Companies must try to develop new ways of attractin attention: they have to be present in the media, publish books, be interviewed in the press, or champion attitudes reflecting new trends. This is the case, for instance, with Volvo and its 'green' campaign emphasizing the necessity of rethinking our use (or abuse) of cars in modern society, or Andersen Consulting which frequently exposes its name in the media and publishes the Andersen Consulting Book every year. After having struggled for years to recruit adequate people, this latter company recognizes that the key to its current success has been the development of a personal connections network (Andersen Consulting 1991). It seems that students are far less affected by direct mailing than foreign companies suppose (Nemoto 1991). Japan is a society in which emphasis is placed on people-to-people contacts. Therefore, the development of 'old boy' and 'old girl' networks, diffusing information by word of mouth, is essential. Humanities students accord less importance to information from their professors than foreign companies believe (Nemoto 1991) but this is certainly not true in the case of natural science students, who are invariably accessed by companies via their universities.

Regarding the relations between the parent company and the subsidiary, the comments and criticisms we have heard from local employees and managers in foreign firms are in some respects (participation in the decision-making process, relations with expatriates) not unlike those made by their counterparts in Japanese companies abroad.

Japanese managers complain of a lack of meaningful involvement in the decision-making process and of insufficient access to information. A high level of control from the headquarters, through centralized systems of reporting and planning, is negatively viewed by executives complaining about their job autonomy and the scope of their managers' functions. Asked how they would rate their company in terms of influence in decision-making and access to information, on our five-point scale, responses averaged 3.03 and 2.89 respectively. Transparency of global group objectives and the establishment of consultative channels are thus crucial to secure good people.

Besides the appraisal issue, a small number of employees complain of the lack of expatriate knowledge of Japanese business practices, of a large psychological distance between them and the locals, and of their lack of real commitment to the subsidiary. Expatriates are perceived as uninterested in the personal development of local people, and to have a narrow and egotistical mentality. Despite such comments and the slightly negative correlation of a number of measures related to job satisfaction (especially access to information and the fairness of appraisals) with the nationality of the superior, it should be pointed out that, overall, critics of expatriates have been quite muted in our survey. Most of the respondents refuse to consider relations with the expatriates in a dichotomic way. On the contrary, experienced local executives made very positive statements: expatriates are now considered to interact better at all levels of the organization; they are more sensitive to the customers' requests and they try to get the feel of the business in the market-place, a fact that is highly valued. They are better prepared to operate in Japan than before because of their new knowledge of Japanese business practices and of the Japanese language. Moreover, their important role in transferring managerial know-how is fully recognized. Very few criticisms are made of the double-track compensation system, leading to large differences in life-style. This is considered as unavoidable in a multinational, and criticized by only a handful of the total respondents. On the other hand, more criticisms are made of Japanese senior executives recruited from another company or taken out of retirement after a career in a large company or institution: they are often perceived as out of step with the company's culture and, thus, they are not considered as suitable to represent the company outside; there are doubts about their input and the fairness of their compensation package.

CONCLUSION

Human resource management in foreign firms in Japan: A global perspective

Many foreign operations in Japan are no longer small, marginal activities, whatever the size of the office. Human resource management has therefore to be examined in a broader context, balancing the global stategy with a successful adaptation to local society. Japanese companies abroad are often accused of ethnocentricity in the sense that access to key information and decision-making power is concentrated in the hands of managers of the country of origin (Perlmutter 1974). However, it seems that there are equally few foreign companies in Japan that can truly be considered as polycentric or geocentric. In many of the latter, there are barriers to local access to decision-mking and key information; and a dual management structure similar to that found in Japanese overseas subsidiaries is not altogether absent (Christopher 1986).

Paradoxically, the short-term consequence of the integration of Japanese activities into the framework of world-wide activities is often interpreted by the interviewed managers as an increase of headquarters' control. Many foreign companies have succeeded in attracting good Japanese managers while also upgrading the under-standing of Japanese business practices and the cross-cultural aware-ness of their expatriates. Such a policy of integration into the Japanese socio-economic fabric has brought business success which looks set to continue for some of them, because not all business strategies are equally global, or need to be so. But it will probably not suffice to establish a global strategy where the subsidiary must manage problems not focused on a single country or limited to relations with a central headquarters. Global managers, both local and expatriate, must be multicultural and not experts on only one particuar environment – global companies can no longer afford the luxury of dealing with each country on a separate and sequential basis (Adler and Batholomew 1992). It has been noticed that the sharp decrease in the number of US expatriates raises some major issues for strategic management and control. In many diversified multinationals, personnel are a crucial instrument of headquarters' strategic control and the eliminiation of expatriates may affect con-trol adversely (Kobrin 1992).

Moreover, in the case of many multinationals in Japan, there is still a lack of Japanese managers with an encompassing knowedge of the world-wide organization, experienced and skilful enough to understand world issues facing the company and to work effectively with clients and colleagues from other countries. So, the strong emphasis on the 'Japaneseness' of the management of the subsidiary is somewhat worrying. Integration of the Japanese operations into a global framework requires the development of a broader style of human resouce management, and organizational capability to implement global business strategies. Japanese managers want a real process of localization and not a dummy one; they want decision-making authority, and access to strategic information corresponding to their status. This is a problem that has been identified for a long time in all multinationals and not only in Japan. The issue is to know to what extent integration of local managers into the global structure is feasible, profitable and acceptable by the concerned parties. Should they move towards the development of a large pool of international managers, interchangeable and mobile all over the world, with the risk of cultural conflicts threatening the company culture, or should they move towards a true localization optimizing local resouces and the development of points of access to the global structure. It appears that in multinationals all over the world, management localization is not a straightforward process solving all problems by giving formal authority to locals; many issues have to be considered: the requirement of the function, the relations between headquarters and the subsidiaries, and the need for a definition of the roles of the locals and expatriates. There is a mix of structural and cultural aspects that have to be taken into account.

Foreign companies accepted an emphasis on the Japanese characteristics of their organization, because of Japan's perceived management idiosyncracies. However, despite a number of outstanding successes (Yoshihara 1989), it may in some cases become an impediment to the integration of their local operations into the global structure because of a lack of identification with it and its objectives.

Some foreign companies in Japan can still be considered as agents of change in human resource management. However, quite naturally, most of them are currently inclined to follow the prevalent local practices, since they cannot escape from the fact that concepts of organizations and management vary widely across national cultures (Laurent 1983). Nevertheless, they face the fact that the pool of younger workers between the ages of 15 and 24 will start decreasing by as early as 1995. The labour shortage will particularly affect the recruitment of engineers and scientists, and will therefore hit manufacturing companies hard. In the future, most young graduates and Japanese employees in Japanese companies eager to make a career change will continue to shun them. Job security fears, and doubts about the long-term commitment in Japan, remain strong; most Japanese people are still not ready for daily contact with culturally different people, and despite their denials and an emphasis on their Japaneseness, foreign companies are still perceived as willing to impose a management style based on crude short-term performance evaualtion and 'dry', functional human relations.

On the other hand, even if they want to retain a continuity in their recruiting policy, large Japanese companies will be unable and unwilling to absorb as many new graduates as they did in the 1980s. Moreover, though it is increasing, their presence on the mid-career market will remain marginal except for some special positions. Therefore, people with good credentials will become available on the market in the coming years. The pressing need for most foreign companies will then be to secure personnel among the remaining minority of people looking for a different career anchor, and for more than simple conformity to Japanese practices. Young graduates and staff members are aware of both thepresent and potential advantages of working in a foreign company, and are able to process the balance carefully. It is the consensus of many that they will stay as long as the experience gained compensates for the disadvantages (Hughes 1991).

It is generally known that availability of opportunities is a crucial variable in individuals' decisions regarding mobility. The norm of long-term commitment to a large firm, Japanese or foreign, is supported in great measure by the lack of better opportunities elsewhere. Employees in foreign firms frequently complain of complacency, of a disregard for the meritocratic character of appraisals and promotions, and of the lack of transparency of reward systems, suggesting that the best people may well quit, leaving foreign firms with people of less ambition and drive. People tending to conform would stay, with a subsequent loss of personnel displaying individual intitiative. It is true that, even nowadays, long-term commitment to a company is certainly not a value-free, purely utilitarian choice for most Japanese people, and that there is still a stigma attached to job-hopping. However, it is now clearly more possible to get a job with a large firm (even a Japanese one in the same industry), and to achieve upward mobility through changing jobs. Mobility is a model professionally recognized in foreign companies. Therefore, there is no stigma attached to mobility if it means better working conditions and career progress. We have seen that employees are not ready to leave massively and suddenly, but there is at least a trend towards an occupational type of commitment close to that typical of Western society, and this should be taken into account.

From the comments made by managers responding to our survey, the creation of an original organizational culture, and the diffusing of the company's values, do not seem currently to be a priority in most foreign firms. Indeed, such moves would often prove difficult, in view of the different origins and experience of the employees. Nevertheless, this is despite the fact that they could find some merit in placing greater emphasis on their particularities. Little by little, the points of differentiation between well-performing companies all over the world will be based less on their nationality and their supposed conformity to local or foreign practices, than on the original characteristics of their organization. The development of a successful global human resource management policy will therefore require the avoidance of two pitfalls. A simple process of localization of management through the adaptation of local practices will be insufficient to take a subsidiary beyond the level of an average local firm, and will discourage the brightest local people. On the other hand, the necessity for globalization, and for managers attuned to the world environment and to the international activities of the company, is very real. The role of expatriates is not extinct, and they will be required in many instances in a broader role than before. However, companies should avoid the development of a dual structure placing two groups, locals and expatriates, in different worlds, with the subsequent problems of communication, misunderstanding and frustration encountered in many Western and Japanese multinationals.

Transfers of management know-how in global companies are increasingly two-way, rather than from the parent company to the subsidiaries. Reinforcement of the potential input coming from the periphery means going beyond the simple distinction between 'foreign' and 'Japanese' companies: the quality of the leadership, the motivation tools, all the elements providing the glue necessary to become a good business performer will be primordial.

Bibliography

Adler, N. and Bartholomew, S. (1992) 'Globalization and Human Resource Management' in Rugman, A. (ed.) *Research in Global Strategic Management, Vol. 3*, Toronto: JAI.

American Chamber of Commerce in Japan (1991) *Employment Practices of American Companies in Japan*, Tokyo.

Andersen Consulting (1992) *Human Resource Management in Foreign Companies in Japan*, Conference organized by A. T. Kearney, Tokyo, October.

Ballon, R. *Foreign Competition in Japanese Human Resource Strategies*, London: Routledge.

Busquin, V. (1992), unpublished MA thesis, Louvain Catholic University.

Christopher, R. C. (1986) *Second to None*, New York: Crown Publishers.

Debroux, P. (1992) 'Questionnaire of 100 Japanese Managers in Foreign Firms', Kobe University Research Project.

Gaishikei Kigyo Recruitment Guide (1992) Tokyo.

German Chamber of Commerce (1991) *Survey of Recruitment in Foreign Companies in Japan*, Tokyo.

Goffman, C. (1967) *Real Functions*, Prindle, Weber & Schmidt.

Hay Group Report (1992) *Compensation Comparison in Foreign Affiliated Companies*, Tokyo.

Hughes, D. (1992) *Zainichi Gaishikei Kigyo ni Okeru Keiei ni Kansuru Kenkyu Jinzai Kakuho ni Kansuru Chose Kekka (Research on the Management of Foreign Companies in Japan – Survey on Recruitment)* Master Thesis, Tsukuba University.

Japan Productivity Center (1990) *Report on Working Conditions in Foreign Companies in Japan*, Tokyo.

Kobrin, S. (1992) 'Expatriate Reduction and Strategic Control in American Multinational Corporations' in Pucik, V. *et al. Globalizing Management*, New York: John Wiley.

Laurent, A. (1983) 'The Cultural Diversity of Western Conceptions of Management', *International Studies of Management and Organizations*, 13 (1–2).

Management and Coordination Agency (1992) *Report on the Evolution of the Labor Market*, Tokyo.

Ministry of Labour (1989) *Report on Working Conditions in Japan*, Tokyo.

—— (1992) *Gaishikei Kigyo no Roshi Kankei Nado Jittai Chosa Kekka*

Hokokucho (Report of a Field Research on Labor Relations in Foreign Companies in Japan).

Nemoto, A. (1988) *Human Resource Management in Foreign Firms*, Soeisha.

—— (1991) 'Keiei Gakubu Zainichi Gaisheikei Kigyo no Shinotsu Saya no Kadai', seminar, Miji University.

Nikkei Weekly 6 October 1992, p. 4.

Ono, A. (1991) 'Nihon Keizai no Kokusaika to Nenkoseiodo no Koko ni Kansuru Chosa Kenkyu Hokokusho', report commissioned by the Rodo Mondai Research Centre.

Permutter, H. V. (1974) 'How Multinational Should Your Top Managers Be?', *Harvard Business Review* 52 (6).

Pucik, V. (1991) 'Japanese Managers, Foreign Bosses', *Journal of Japanese Trade and Industry*, 1

Rhone-Poulenc (1992) *Human Resource Management in Foreign Companies in Japan*, Conference organized by A. T. Kearney, Tokyo, October.

Sakakibara, K. (1991) 'Kyaria Shiko to Kanri Shisutemu no Tekigo Bunseki' ('Analysis of the Adequateness of Career Anchors and Management Systems'), *Diamond Harvard Business*, Tokyo, Feb-March.

Suwa, Y. (1991) 'Why do Students not Prefer foreign-affiliated Firms?, *Labor Issues*, spring.

Temporary Center K.K. (1989) 'Gaishikei ni Hisho toshite Tsutomeru Working Woman no Jijo to Shigotokan Chosa'.

Yoshihara, H. (1989) 'Genchijin Shacho to Uchinaru Kokusaika' ('Foreign Presidents and Internal Internalization'), Tokyo: Toyo Keizai Shimposha.

12 The homecoming of the overseas Chinese

Consequences and scenarios

Eric Bouteiller

INTRODUCTION

The People's Republic of China (PRC), especially in the southern provinces, is currently experiencing the fastest economic growth in the world. The main engine of this growth is the homecoming of Chinese living outside the PRC – Hongkongese, Taiwanese, Singaporeans and Overseas Chinese – who are delocalizing their plant and the country with capital and technology so that it may, in a few decades, overcome its present underdevelopment. What is more, the massive presence of the Overseas Chinese may also exert indirect influence on PRC internal politics. In the long term, the periphery of China may in fact become crucial to the PRC's development and modernization, after having long been the last resort for so many Chinese escaping political repression and poverty.

WHO ARE THE OVERSEAS CHINESE?

We should first define what we mean by Overseas Chinese (OC). The simplest definition is 'Chinese living outside the PRC' but the reality is in fact rather more complex. Three distinct groups are traditionally identified: the *tongbao* or 'compatriots', for example Hongkongese and Taiwanese, who are Chinese but ruled by a foreign or a concurrent government; the *huaqiao*, descended from southern Chinese migrants of the nineteenth century, living in southeast Asia in host countries who would like to integrate them progressively; and the *huayi*, who acknowledge their Chinese ethnicity, but clearly reject any idea of belonging to the PRC, for example Singaporean Chinese (Chuanli and Chunsi 1980).

The OC do not form a homogeneous or organized group. The individualism of the Chinese, their diverse geographical origins,

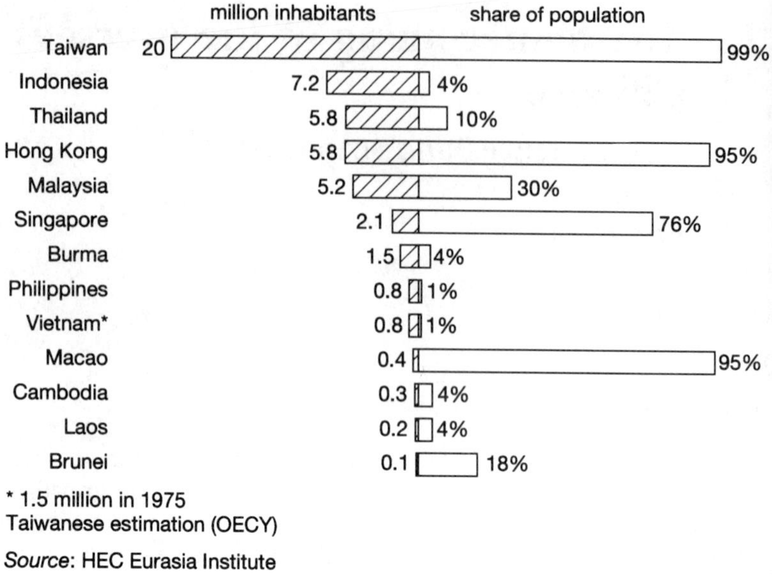

Figure 12.1 Chinese population in the Far East in 1991

social class and so on make them feel that they belong, not to one greater Chinese community, but to many different sub-communities. Moreover, many are influenced by past traditions of 'collaboration' with colonizers, and by anti-Chinese sentiment and barriers to integration in their host countries, to the extent that they may not even want to be recognized as Chinese at all. They prefer to remain discreet, and are perhaps best characterized as what might be called 'swimming ducks', paddling furiously beneath the surface, but with their heads serenely above water.

How many are they? The OC are as difficult to number as they are to define. Moreover, for political reasons, many south-east Asian countries do not recognize their Chinese minority and deny them any statistical existence. The only available data come from the PRC and Taiwan, and should be treated with some scepticism, although they will suffice as a general guide (see Figure 12.1).

What is their economic strength? The economic system of the OC is built on networks and is the best example of what we now call a borderless economy. Thus by definition there are no available classical data to evaluate their economic strength. Straightforward calculation may be the best available method, although theoretically undefendable. A 'Chinese' share of the GNP can be estimated for

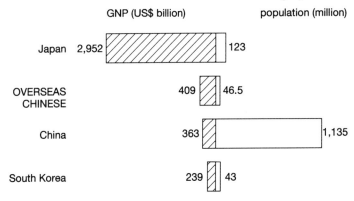

Source: HEC Eurasia Institute

Figure 12.2 Overseas Chinese and their neighbours: 1990

each OC host country, and the results simply added together (see Figure 12.2).

For countries with an almost entirely Chinese population, such as Taiwan, Hong Kong and Singapore, the Chinese share of the economy is thus estimated to be 100 per cent. Of course, this hides non-Chinese production, which is still significant in Hong Kong and Singapore. In other countries, it is impossible to define the Chinese share of the economy because the Chinese and native economies overlap. The only country that publishes official ethnic statistics is Malaysia. For other countries, the data from the PRC and Taiwan invariably overemphasize the private economy and completely hide the public sector. The Chinese are said to control 70 per cent of the private capital in Indonesia, 60 to 70 per cent of the private economy in Malaysia, plus 50 per cent of financial investments and 90 per cent of industrial investments in Thailand (Bouteiller 1992) (see Figure 12.3).

After adding the national data together, the size of the OC economy becomes clear: 50 million OC produce as much as 1.1 billion PRC Chinese. Of course, this estimate would be more precise if more sophisticated information, such as purchasing power parity data, were available, and if the Chinese shares of local economies were estimated after a careful study of all sectors concerned.

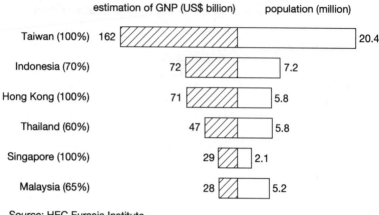

Source: HEC Eurasia Institute

Figure 12.3 Chinese population and share of GNP: 1990

WHY ARE THE OC GOING HOME?

Overseas Chinese have always maintained a special nostalgia for their respective home towns. After migrating from southern China, some have risen in just a few generations from modest coolies to major capitalists, invariably endowing their home towns with schools and impressive public facilities. As one journalist put it: 'Economic opening of the PRC meets the opening of wallets of the OC' (McGregor 1992).

Since the beginning of the 1980s, the homecoming of the OC has been increasingly profit-driven. Faced with escalating costs of production, first in Hong Kong and then in Taiwan, industrialists have delocalized massively to the PRC. At first, only labour-intensive industries were concerned, but now more and more upstream industries are also making the move. The once inviolable borders of China have been crossed by OC networks: 'The Chinese periphery combines high technology and capital to extract surplus from a low wage and increasingly accommodating quasi-capitalist PRC' (Brick 1992).

The cases of Hong Kong and Taiwan are the most mediatized. Hong Kong probably directly employs 5 million workers in the PRC. Taiwan companies may have agreed to invest up to US$64 billion at the end of 1992, according to PRC data, and the Central Bank of Taiwan puts this figure higher still, at US$10 billion (*Free China Review* 27 November 1992). But there is also Singapore. In the first six months of 1992, Singaporean investments totalled US$494 million, against a total of US$896 million for the entire period 1979–91.

The PRC's development strategy during the 1980s focused on its agricultural sector, and let individuals take the initiative. Industrial reforms then skirted around the problematic state sector and focused on opening up other sectors, such as rural collectives. But the most important action has been to allow foreign investment matched by the OC through the opening of the southern coast of the PRC, the 'hometown' region of the OC. Today, the OC finance at least 75 per cent of the 28,000 PRC enterprises with significant foreign equity.

To summarize, the homecoming of the OC brings what China most needs: capital, technology and connection to the world economy. Thus, China has witnessed exceptional growth. From the 1940s to the 1980s, China's population almost doubled without increasing its per capita productivity; but if China now continues at its present rate of growth, then by the beginning of the twenty-first century its GDP per capita will equal that of Taiwan – a total GDP of over US$13 trillion, larger than the combined GDP of the US and the EC in 1990.

However, the homecoming of the OC is not only beneficial. One side effect is the shifting of the US trade deficit within Greater China away from Hong Kong and Taiwan, to the PRC itself. The delocalization of Hong Kong and Taiwanese plant to the PRC has moved the shipment origin of their products. Now the PRC has to deal with the US deficit created by Hong Kong and Taiwanese companies (see Figures 12.4 and 12.5).

ECONOMIC LOGIC VERSUS POLITICAL LOGIC

China's opening up is highly visible in much of its affairs, but its political life remains under tight control, as witnessed in Tiananmen Square in 1989 and, now, in Chinese reaction to the reforms proposed by Hong Kong's democratizing Governor, Chris Patten. Besides being the main engine of China's development, can the OC also help to overcome political stagnation?

Overseas Chinese influence PRC politics in many, sometimes very subtle, ways. The first is, of course, through their investments, contributing to economic development and to the resulting change in perception of the Chinese Communist Party's legitimacy. Chinese people identify with the Party today less as a symbol of the nationalist struggle against foreign powers, and more as a symbol of eco-

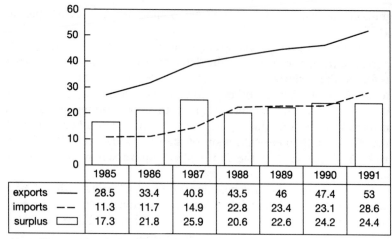

	1985	1986	1987	1988	1989	1990	1991
exports —	28.5	33.4	40.8	43.5	46	47.4	53
imports – –	11.3	11.7	14.9	22.8	23.4	23.1	28.6
surplus ☐	17.3	21.8	25.9	20.6	22.6	24.2	24.4

Note: China, Taiwan and Hong Kong trade are added
Source: USFCS, HK.

Figure 12.4 Foreign trade Greater China-United States

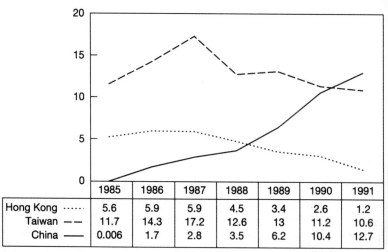

	1985	1986	1987	1988	1989	1990	1991
Hong Kong ⋯⋯	5.6	5.9	5.9	4.5	3.4	2.6	1.2
Taiwan – –	11.7	14.3	17.2	12.6	13	11.2	10.6
China —	0.006	1.7	2.8	3.5	6.2	10.4	12.7

Source: USFCS, HK.

Figure 12.5 US trade deficit with Greater China

nomic development, even wealth, although the Party itself refuses
to recognize this. Second, the leaders of the Party are changing.
More representatives from rich and opened-up provinces are being
promoted to the decision-making Politburo, as was clearly visible

during the fourteenth Party Congress. Both changes are indirectly related to the homecoming of the OC.

The second influence is the shadow impact of the OC's personal relationships with China's leaders. Some Hong Kong and south-east Asian business leaders enjoy privileged access to the leadership. Some were able to influence and limit the reaction of the Communist regime after the Tiananmen massacre. Such personal influence is further enhanced by the presence of top PRC leaders' close family and descendants living in Hong Kong or elsewhere, in direct contact with OC communities.

The homecoming of the OC may also cause Beijing to examine strategies for further modernization in China. Let us examine some more detailed scenarios.

PRC officials often cite Singapore as a model of development which they hope to emulate. They hope that they will be able to separate economic and political development, although the huge differences in size and educational levels between the two countries make this highly improbable. The Communist Party in China looks unlikely to collapse as it did in central and eastern Europe and the USSR. How, then, can the PRC reform and develop?

Another, more likely, and more pragmatic pattern for OC-influenced change in China is what might be called the 'Taiwan pattern'. In Taiwan (an increasingly rich society), reformists in the ruling party, and outside local factions such as Tangwai and the Democratic Progressive Party, all pushed for reforms, eventually creating a new and open political system which was inked into a formal constitution in 1992. Now these same elements are pushing to democratize the ruling party itself – all without changing the official ideology and institutions of Taiwan. We can summarize this as 'changing without admitting it' (Bouteiller 1993).

Let us now turn to the PRC. Economic development in the southern provinces means that local governments in the region are becoming richer and more autonomous. The Beijing government's average contribution to Guangdong province's budget, for example, has shrunk dramatically from 80 per cent in 1980 to only 3 per cent today.

This new autonomy, and the allocation of the new wealth, seems likely to foster in-fighting between local factions, either in the ruling party or outside it. The need for a more open and efficient system with some kind of official political opposition may be felt. Thus at the local level, political opening-up might evolve into a kind of parliamentary freedom. These changes could also influence Beijing and even the Central Committee of the Chinese Communist Party, resulting in a political system still quite unlike Western democracy, but nonetheless more open than at present.

This scenario is a kind of 'subversion by development'. Taiwan officials are clearly 'banking' on the contamination of the PRC political system by the homecoming of their companies and investments. The same is true of Hong Kong, where many OC are working to diffuse prosperity more deeply on the PRC mainland, although they would not see this as flagrant subversion of Beijing's authority. However, Hong Kong companies and government organizations clearly want to share some economic development with the PRC in order to block any possible retrograde moves in Beijing. The more opened-up and rich provinces there are, the harder it will be for conservatives to close the door.

WHEN WILL CHINA BE REUNIFIED?

The PRC government is resolute on the reunification of 'Greater China'. The guidelines for Hong Kong and Macao are already broadly settled, although there are still some question marks.

Taiwan is another story. Officially, mainland China and Taiwan are, of course, part of the same country, although they are virtually at war. Since 1979, the PRC has proposed several measures promoting closer integration, including a common postal service and unrestricted family, commercial and tourist relations. In the long term, the PRC proposes that Taiwan maintain its present economic and social system, and its own army ('one country, two systems', as per Hong Kong post-1997). Until 1991, Taiwan responded to the mainland's initiatives with the so-called 'Three Nos' policy. Since then, Taiwan has adopted a new policy, known as 'Guidelines for Reunification'.

What future scenarios are suggested by this present state of affairs? First, Taiwan officials refuse any reunification before the socio-economic conditions on both sides are more evenly balanced. According to them, this could take anything from one generation to 50 years.

Second, China's military threat to Taiwan should not be underestimated. If the PRC agrees to drop this threat, Taiwan would certainly accept direct links almost immediately. Taiwanese businessmen are constantly pushing for direct links. It could happen tomorrow. After the very poor showing of Taiwan's ruling party in the December 1992 legislative elections, the PRC has frequently hinted that it may change its policy towards Taiwan. For the first time, the Kuomintang won only 53 per cent of votes (not counting independent candidates).

The mainland seems to be afraid that the Taiwan opposition will be more efficient in pushing for independence. How much will the PRC concede? And when? It is too early to say, but one typically Chinese indicator is the occasional presence of Lee Kwan Yew, one of the main go-betweens for leaders of both sides, in Taiwan. His so-called 'vacations' across the straits may well be influential once the new Taiwan government's policy is settled.

THE SPLITTING OF THE PRC

The above scenarios are essentially rather optimistic, but the OC's homecoming could equally have a more negative impact. The most likely negative scenario is the splitting of the PRC into several autonomous economic regions. PRC provinces would naturally aggregate themselves following some de facto economic interdependence, such as inland transportation and port facilities. But it seems doubtful that, as was seen in the USSR, these economic regions would proclaim their independence (Goodman 1992).

The first and most important region to evolve would be southern China (with other coastal areas), linked to the world economy through the OC, enabling rapid development. Second, an inner PRC would emerge, untouched by OC networks and thus unable to attract foreign investors. With nearly 80 per cent of the country's population, this area would not experience economic growth. On the contrary, social conflicts and mass migration to the richer provinces seem far more likely. Third and last is the non-Han minority region, from Tibet to Inner Mongolia. Though very sparsely populated, this third area accounts for nearly half of the country's surface, and harbours fierce guerillas who would seek independence if their economic situation deteriorated too far.

In fact this scenario is already happening, and the resulting regional imbalances are forcing Beijing to push for new projects, in Pudong in Shanghai, and on border trading posts such as Heilongjiang or Xinjiang provinces, or even Tumen. Further projects planned include the opening up of the Yangzi River valley. Beijing has already made it clear that the OC (but also foreigners) have to help to balance economic development in the PRC.

After an investment boom in the OC's hinterland provinces of Guangdong and Fujian, OC business groups are announcing new projects deeper inside the PRC. The Gordon Wu Group has extended its highway projects from the Pearl River delta to Wuhan, far inside China; and Li Kashing will be modernizing the port of Shanghai. President Corp., the biggest agribusiness in Taiwan, has set up two multi-million-dollar factories in Beijing and Shanghai, plus a third one in Xinjiang.

Finally, what are the consequences of the homecoming of the OC for Western business? China has growth and potential, and Western companies cannot ignore what may become the single biggest economy in the world.

The first immediate concern for Western companies should be to keep abreast of developments within the OC business groups and networks, whose homecoming is opening up a huge economic hinterland. Western firms can benefit both from China's low labour costs, and its huge market.

OC enterprises will no doubt prove to be sharp competitors, but also potential new partners. European multinationals, as well as smaller companies, need OC networks in order to plug into China's potential.

Why have the OC succeeded ? According to Lee Kwan Yew, they:

> have been able to overcome the absence of a clear transparent framework of laws and the absence of an effective and open system of administration which holds the ring fairly between competing enterprises. Although some MNCs like Hewlett Packard and Philips have done well in China, they have generally found it more daunting to find their way through the labyrinths of Chinese bureacracy.

> (Lee Kwan Yew 1992)

In the long term, China may finally restructure and simplify its commercial legislation, and demystify its lines of administrative control. When this happens, the OC's comparative advantage will disappear. But until this happens, Western firms should seek to build close and lasting partnerships with the Overseas Chinese.

Bibliography

Bouteiller, E. (1992) 'The Overseas Chinese, Driving Force behind the Asian Miracle', HEC Eurasia Institute, February
—— (1993) 'Changer Sans en Donner L'impression', *Nord Sud Export*, February.
Brick, A. (1992) 'Borderless Economics Forces Change in China', *Asian Wall Street Journal* October.
Goodman, D. (1992) 'Provinces Confronting the State?', *China Review 1992*, Hong Kong.
Lee Kuan Yew (1992), Speech at the CITIC conference in Beijing, 29 September.
McGregor, J. (1992) 'Fujian Gets Boost from Overseas Chinese', *Asian Wall Street Journal*, June.
Wu Chuanli, and Wu, Chunhsi, W. (1980) *Economic Development in Southeast Asia, The Chinese dimension*, Standford: Standford University Press.

13 Translating Asian strategies into global strengths

The Philips and Thomson cases

Martin D. H. Bloom

INTRODUCTION

There are considerable changes taking place in the Asia-Pacific region, changes that will have far-reaching implications for many European companies.

A key concern is to identify the benefits that European companies receive from being in Asia. Ten years ago, Japanese specialists were suggesting that European companies not involved with Japan were missing a major opportunity. Today, the same is said of Asian countries in general.

It is also necessary to show why Asia should be given priority over other regions, eastern Europe and the former Soviet Union, or North America, for example. Despite this, every major European car company withdrew from the US market during the 1980s, retrenching into a European core of activity; this was not just for assembly, but also for exports.

I would maintain that the relevance of operations in Asia depends on two things: first, the nature of the chosen sector – as manifest in the nature of the technology and the economics of production, as well as its competitive dynamics – and second, the company concerned, especially its ability and willingness to undertake the required investments. A company's existing relations and activities in the region will also be relevant.

This chapter tackles these issues in the context of the different approaches to the region adopted by Philips and Thomson Consumer Electronics. By concentrating largely on their television and video equipment activities, and the components underpinning these, the complexity of their links with Asia becomes apparent and clearly shows that no single strategy can meet all future requirements.

Philips has had a long involvement with the region, while Thomson's connection is more recent. For both companies, it was not until the 1980s that their involvement came to have any strategic importance. Philips established its first joint venture with Matsushita in 1952, and more recently took control of Marantz in Japan and acquired 50 per cent of JVC Malaysia. Thomson started assembling components for radios and black-and-white televisions in Singapore in 1975, and has moved a substantial proportion of its world-wide production to the region. In fact, the involvement of these two companies in the region has been critical to their survival in European and north American markets, either as a source of low-cost production (whether under their own control or bought in) or as a source of component and other technologies. This latter is often not given enough weight in competitive analyses.

After separately outlining the development of the Asian activities of each of these companies, a concluding section will consider the differences between their two approaches, and assess their ability to react to the changes taking place.

PHILIPS

Philips' involvement in Asia is by far the most extensive of the two companies studied. It comprises diverse activities and encompasses a wide range of approaches. It is worth considering in some detail, though it is only possible here to give an outline of its full extent.

Some of its most important relationships in the region arose indirectly through other initiatives, as its joint venture with Matsushita (profiled below), or the Asian operations acquired through its acquisitions of such companies as GTE-Sylvania and Signetics. In the 1980s, Philips moved progressively towards a more active strategy in Asia as a whole, as the Group sought to develop its Asian activities to account for a much higher proportion of group sales.

While the Group as a whole was preoccupied with consolidation and rationalization in Europe, as well as gaining greater control over its north American operations, Asia was not ignored. Sales growth in the Asian region was faster than elsewhere in the period 1977–91. Asian sales increased more than threefold during this period, while their share of Group sales doubled from 5 per cent in 1977 to 10 per cent in 1991 (see Figures 13.1 and 13.2 and Tables 13.1 and 13.2). Even more dramatic has been the growth in deliveries from Asia, reflecting the region's importance as a supply base for Philips' markets in Europe and North America. They have experienced an almost eightfold increase, while their share of total

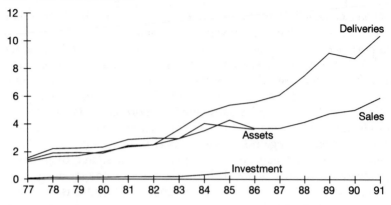

Figure 13.1 Philips in Asia
Source Philips Annual Reports 1978–91

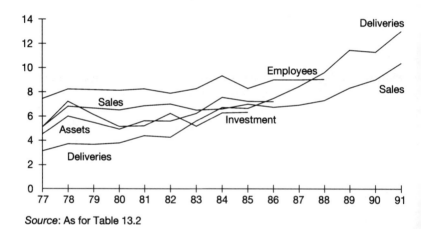

Source: As for Table 13.2

Figure 13.2 Philips in Asia (as percentage of total Philips Group activity)
Source: Calculated from data in Philips Annual Reports 1978–91

Group deliveries has increased from only 3 per cent in 1977 to 13 per cent in 1991.[1] In addition, there are significant purchases of product on an OEM basis. In 1987, for example, at a time when 8 per cent of Group output was from Asian countries, 16 per cent of total procurement was from Asia (De Jonquières 1988).

The most recent data published by Philips indicated that it had around 30,000 employees in the region in 1986, though press reports suggested a fall to 27,000 by 1988. Some tentative estimates for a country breakdown are provided in Table 13.3.

Table 13.1 Philips in Asia (billion guilders)

	1977	1980	1986	1991
Sales	1.6	2.3	3.6	5.6
Deliveries	1.3	1.9	5.4	10.1
Assets	1.4	1.9	3.5	n.a.
Investment	0.1	0.1	0.3*	n.a.
Employees ('000s)	28.4	29.3	30.0	n.a.

* = 1985
Source: Philips Annual Reports 1978–91

Table 13.2 Philips in Asia (as percentage of total Philips Group activity)

	1977	1980	1986	1991
Sales	5	6	7	10
Deliveries	3	4	7	13
Assets	5	5	7	n.a.
Investment	5	5	6*	n.a.
Employees	7	8	9	n.a.

* = 1985
Source: Calculated from data in Philips Annual Reports 1978–91

Table 13.3 Philips in Asia (employment by country)

	'000s	Year
Japan		
Matsushita Electronics (35%)	13.0	1990
Marantz Japan (50%)	1.1	1990
Singapore	6.1	1991
Hong Kong	4.0	1987
Taiwan	?	
Malaysia	>1.7	1987
Korea	?	
China	?	
TOTAL	27.0	1988

The Matsushita relationship

Of all the links that Philips has developed in Asia, that with Matsu-shita has been the longest and the most fruitful. It started on the component side, with Philips providing the technology, and has pro-gressed into finished products through licences and OEM deals for

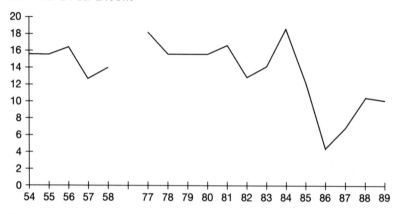

Figure 13.3 Matsushita Electronics (profits as percentage of sales)

VCRs and camcorders, the technology coming from Matsushita or its 50 per cent-owned JVC.

Konosuke Matsushita – founder of the Matsushita Group – travelled to the United States and Europe in 1951 searching for foreign technology.[2] He decided that Philips would be the most appropriate partner for this. In December 1952, Philips and Matsushita established Matsushita Electronics as a joint venture, the new company to be managed by Matsushita Electric. Philips received an initial payment of $550,000 and a 30 per cent share in the new company. After what Frederik Philips described as 'fairly tough negotiations', agreement was reached over the royalties. Philips received a 4.5 per cent technical guidance fee – rather than the 6 per cent demanded – while Matsushita received a 3 per cent fee for managing the venture. During the following 15 years, these fees were revised downwards – to 3 per cent to Philips and 2 per cent to Matsushita. In 1967, the joint-venture agreement was extended for a further 10 years, and both fees set at 2.5 per cent. The venture was again extended in 1977 and in 1987, and Philips share increased to 35 per cent.

The products handled by the joint venture have changed along with the underlying technologies themselves. Initially, production focused on light bulbs, radio valves and television picture tubes. While light bulbs and television picture tubes are still produced, the nature of these has changed. The production of monochrome picture tubes started in 1954, followed by colour picture tubes in 1960. In addition, the production of valves gave way to transistors, production of which started in 1957, and then in 1968 to integrated circuits and other semiconductors.

The venture has been profitable over the years, though less so in the second half of the 1980s. The dividends and royalties Philips has received have made a positive contribution to its operating income. In 1989–90, the dividend Philips received on its 28.7 million shares was equal to around 2 per cent of its total operating income (before restructuring). If the 2.5 per cent royalty fees still apply, the dividend and royalty income combined would be equivalent to 8 per cent of the Philips Group operating income. This is similar to the level estimated independently for 1985.[3]

The joint venture has itself become a multinational, and has production facilities for CRTs and semiconductors in the United States. In addition, Philips and Matsushita established the Philips Matsushita Battery Corporation of Belgium in 1983 to produce small alkaline batteries, and this was extended to large alkaline batteries in 1986 (*Economisch Dagblad*, 4 August 1986: 3).

The relationship with Matsushita has developed and has been an important part of Philips' strategy towards VCRs and camcorders (Bloom 1993). It also shows clearly how two companies can be extremely cooperative in some sectors while simultaneously competing fiercely elsewhere. In the early 1980s, Philips was attempting to establish its V-2000 video recorder in the face of competition from JVC's VHS and Sony's Betamax. Some initial success in Germany and Austria did not lead to success elsewhere, as JVC attempted to tie in the leading competitor to Philips in each of the three leading European markets, namely France, Germany and the U.K. Telefunken and Thorn-EMI entered a joint venture with JVC, while Thomson was stopped from doing so by the actions of the French government. Thomson's acquisition of Telefunken in 1983, and of Thorn-EMI's consumer electronics interests in 1987, made it JVC's leading partner in Europe. Thus Philips found the British and French markets difficult to penetrate, while it came under increasing pressure in the German market, where it acquired a controlling interest in its major collaborator, Grundig. Both Philips and Grundig were forced to license the VHS format, their first VHS video recorders appearing in 1984. The final decision to end production of the V-2000 was made at the end of 1985. It appears that the negotiations were intense, and that in return for stopping production of V-2000 and for marketing Japanese MSX video recorders in Europe, neither Philips nor Grundig paid a licence fee to JVC (*Electronics Times*, 20 November 1986: 20).

In 1986, Matsushita established a joint company with Robert Bosch called Matsushita Video Manufacturing Gmbh., to assemble drive systems for video recorders. This company in turn entered into an agreement with Grundig. Using technology from Matsushita, Grundig produces the video heads and both halves of the video drum and supplies them to Matsushita Video Manufacturing for incorporation into drive mechanisms. Some of these are sold back to Grundig, while others are incorporated into its German-made Panasonic video recorders (*Electronic Times*, 20 November 1986: 20).

Philips became dependent on OEM supplies from Matsushita of VHS and VHS-C video recorders for the north American market and camcorders for both Europe and North America. This was seen as a weakness, and Philips sought a strategy to overcome this. Philips decided to establish a major joint venture in South Korea with that country's largest producer of audio products, Dongwon Electronics; the intention was to produce up to 1 million video recorders a year (Bloom 1992: 52). This joint venture did not proceed due to resistance from the Korean government and from the Korean electronics companies.

Philips invested f 80 million (around $47 million) in Marantz Japan in 1986 to enable it to start limited production of video recorders. Full-scale production soon followed, along with full-scale production of VHS and S-VHS camcorders in 1990. About 90 per cent of its video production is for export. Philips' share in Marantz was increased from 50 per cent to 51 per cent in 1990, giving it majority control. Prior to that, Matsushita Electric held 1.6 per cent.

Of more immediate significance was Philips' acquisition of a 50 per cent share in JVC's Malaysian video recorder assembly subsidiary, also in 1990. This was the year after JVC had refused a request by Thomson, its partner in Europe, to establish a joint venture in Singapore. A 4.5 billion yen investment in what became Philips/JVC Video Manufacturing Malaysia enabled annual production to be increased from 300,000 to 1 million units, mostly for export to the United States.

Philips has extensive interests in several Asian markets, and is progressively expanding these as opportunities arise. Involvement with Singapore dates back to its establishment of a trading office in 1951; production of radios and PABXs followed in the late 1960s, and of cassette recorders, televisions, components and small domestic appliances during the 1970s (Hobday 1992: 23). By the early 1980s, its two most important television production facilities in the region were in Singapore and Taiwan, the latter supplying its Magnavox operations in the United States, while its acquisition of GTE-Sylvania in 1981 brought with it the television production facilities acquired by Sylvania in Taiwan in 1975 in order to supply its own operations in the United States. (Franko and Stephenson 1982: 215 and Tuner 1982: 56). Its diverse operations in the region give it flexibility. For example, in the face of trade friction between the United States and Taiwan, Philips was able to move its production of televisions for the United States market from Taiwan to Singapore.(Reuters Far East 3 June 1987).

In addition to its involvement in Matsushita Electronics, and its embryonic component ventures in China, Philips has a widespread involvement in components activities in the region, through direct sales, joint ventures and technology acquisitions agreements. Its acquisition of Signetics gave it a presence in several Asian markets. In the late 1960s, Signetics had been one of the first American semiconductor manufacturers to establish assembly operations in Korea, and by 1972 it was Korea's third largest electronics producer and the second largest exporter behind Motorola Korea. In the mid-1970s, Philips itself established a passive electronic components plant in Korea. In Taiwan, Philips is a joint venture partner in a semiconductor wafer Manufacturer, the Taiwan Semiconductor Manufacturing Company.

Philips' greatest efforts in recent years seem to be aimed at expanding its Chinese operations. Unlike Japan, who prefers to approach the Chinese market through exports – possibly due to a Chinese reluctance for Japanese investments in Chinese industrial facilities – Philips has entered into or announced a number of joint ventures for the production of colour television tubes, semiconductors, optical fibres, car radios and cassette recorders, and compact disc players. Even though Philips is possibly the largest foreign investor in China, its sales there still represent just 10 per cent of its total Asian sales, and these activities must be regarded as a long-term venture.

THOMSON CONSUMER ELECTRONICS

Thomson's approach in Asia incorporates some of the same elements as that of Philips. Nevertheless, the balance is very different, and the latter's activities overall are in some ways far more limited in scope.

Asia might appear to be relatively unimportant to Thomson Con-

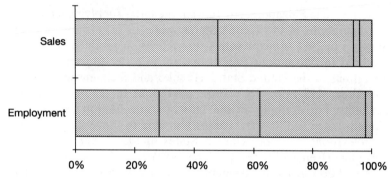

Figure 13.4 Thomson Consumer Electronics: 1990 (regional balance as percentage of total)
Source: Thomson Consumer Electronics Annual Report 1990

Table 13.4 Thomson Consumer Electronics: 1990 regional balance as percentage of total

	Sales	Employment
Europe	49	29
North America	45	33
Asia	2	36
Other	4	2

Source: Thomson Consumer Electronics. Annual Report 1990

sumer Electronics, accounting for just 2 per cent of its sales. However, the region is very definitely Thomson's most important production base (Figure 13.4 and Table 13.4). With over one third of its employees located there – in Malaysia, Singapore, Taiwan, Thailand, Indonesia and China-Thomson sees Asia as a supply source for low-cost products for sale in Europe and North America.

This situation reflects a major shift over the last 20 years. In 1974, Thomson manufactured very few consumer electronics products overseas, and exports accounting for just 9 per cent of sales mostly televisions to West Germany and Spain. A series of acquisitions in Germany between 1978 and 1983, followed by acquisitions in the United Kingdom and the United States in 1987, transformed the group out of all recognition. (Bloom . . .?) Around 90 per cent of sales now come from overseas activity.

Thomson's Asian operations have grown rapidly since it established European Standard Electronic (ESE) in Singapore in 1975 to produce radio and television components.(Savary 1992a: 30). By the early 1980s, Thomson was producing 100,000 colour televisions, mostly for local Asian markets, an activity described as 'very much an afterthought' in the context of its emphasis on European markets (Franko and Stephenson 1982: 216). ESE also had an R&D support unit. In 1986, this was upgraded, to become a specialist department employing 120, and with greatly increased expenditure (*Business Times* 19 May 1986 [Singapore]). In that year, Thomson produced around 260,000 colour televisions in Singapore (*Business Times*, 21 July 1986). Its acquisition of the television activities of General Electric and its RCA subsidiary also brought in some Asian production facilities. As part of a continuing search for sources of low-cost production of televisions, Thomson opened a small-screen television plant with an annual capacity of 1 million sets, in Thailand in 1990 and north American markets. Thomson now has around 15 plants in Asia (Savery 1992b: 30, 42–3). The only products it still produces in Europe are medium and large-screen televisions and video recorders, the latter at its joint venture with JVC. (Savery 1992: 30).

Early in 1991, Thomson instituted a four-year restructuring plan and productivity drive aimed at reducing the losses that had increased during the previous two years, and this is expected to lead to continuing emphasis on Asian production for European and North American markets.

Thomson has the capability to produce televisions and their components, and has been able to retain independent production facilities for these. In fact, several of the Japanese companies assembling televisions in Europe purchase CRTs from Thomson, including JVC.[4] Video recorders and, more recently, camcorders present a more difficult problem. As with Philips, Thomson looked to Japan for the technology. Unfortunately, it was not able to obtain more than a joint venture assembly operation, based on imported components and with little technology transfer. This is even the case with its assembly of video recorder deck mechanisms at the J2T facility at Tonnerre in France which uses parts provided by JVC.

The initial agreement with JVC in 1981 for Thomson to join the J2T consortium was blocked by the French government. Under the agreement, Thomson would have held a 25 per cent share, and video camera production would have taken place in France to supplement video recorder assembly in Germany and assembly of video-disc equipment in the United Kingdom. Thomson eventually joined the J2T consortium through its acquisition of Telefunken and, subsequently, Thorn-EMI's subsidiary Ferguson.

The J2T joint-venture highlights some of the problems arising from lack of control over components. J2T has been extremely successful in terms of volume growth and market penetration, its production of video recorders growing to 850,000 machines in 1987, and later to around 1 million. Despite that, profitability was only around 1 per cent of its sales in 1987. At that time, Thomson did not consider that the J2T plants would remain commercially viable without a continuation of duty protection. The J2T video recorder plant in Newhaven had already been closed. It has been rumoured that Thomson will have its own video recorder capabilities by the end of 1995, though this appears unlikely.

Thomson attempted to extend its relationship with JVC further. It approached JVC to suggest that they establish a joint venture in Singapore to produce VCRs. JVC declined, ostensibly because of its existing production facilities in Malaysia (*Nihon Keizai Shimbun*, 30 November 1989: 10). Thomson turned next to Toshiba, then in the process of looking to increase its output of VCRs. Under the agreement, Toshiba acquired a 49 per cent share of Thomson's Singapore-based production subsidiary, International Video Products. The two companies then invested about 1.2 billion yen for a new 30,000–square metre factory with an annual production capacity of 1 million VCRs. Production started in 1990. The products are developed jointly, but marketed separately by each partner.

Thomson semiconductor operations were separated off into a joint venture – SGS-Thomson Microelectronics – in 1987 (Bloom 1991:91–3). Thorn-EMI took a 10 per cent shareholding in the venture in 1989, on its sale of Inmos to SGS-Thomson. Both SGS and Thomson had been internationalizing their activities in the 1980s. At the time of the merger, almost all SGS production was in Malaysia, Singapore and Malta, its production in Italy and France having been reduced from 80 per cent of the total in 1980, to just 5 per cent. SGS first established operations in Singapore in 1969, and in 1984 became the first semiconductor manufacturer to establish wafer fabrication there (Hobday 1992, 12–13). Thomson also had production facilities in Singapore and Malaysia, as well as in Morocco, together with the Mostek assets it had acquired from United Technologies in 1985. In 1990, SGS-Thomson set up a joint venture with the Hong Kong-based Astec to address microelectronics applications for power conversion equipment.

These operations are of little strategic relevance to the Group; a maximum of 5 per cent of the semiconductor purchases of Thomson Consumer Electronics come from SGS-Thomson (*Les Echos* 1991:

quoted in Savary 1992b: 19). Some additional component operations are controlled through other group companies. Thus, Thomson-CSF is directly responsible for Thomson Electronics Parts Malaysia, Thomson Ferrite Asia in Taiwan and Thomson Components Asia in Hong Kong. All these were wholly-owned subsidiaries of Thomson-CSF, either directly or through its passive component subsidiary LCC. In 1991, LCC entered into a technology transfer and cross-shareholding agreement with the Japanese producer, Murata Manufacturing (*Nikkan Kingyo Shimbun* 23 March 1991: 7; *Japan Industrial Journal* 23 March 1991: 1; *Nikkei Sangyo Shimbun* 15 April 1991: 5). They will begin joint development of layered capacitors at LCC's French plant. In addition, Murata will take 10 per cent of Thomson Electronics Parts Malaysia, while LCC will acquire 25 per cent of Murata Manufacturing UK, based in Plymouth.

CONCLUSIONS

Philips and Thomson have each adopted a different combination of strategies towards Asian markets. While each industry will have its own characteristics, some of the elements they have adopted will be valid for companies in other industries. This concluding section considers these strategies in terms of their implications for global competition.

Strategies within Asia

The Asian region ultimately represents a major growth opportunity. Asian markets are expected to grow more rapidly than European and north American markets as countries in the region industrialize and move towards Western-style consumption. As this occurs, the increased integration of these regional markets will open up ever greater opportunities.

Philips has taken a positive approach to Asian markets, looking to increase the proportion of its sales in Asia to European and north American levels. While its sales in Asia have doubled from 5 per cent to 10 per cent of total Philips sales, a note of caution should be registered. It is proving extremely difficult for Philips to penetrate the Japanese market for finished products, 50 per cent of which is controlled by tied distribution by the Japanese consumer electronics companies, and production for the Chinese market is taking longer to develop than expected. More importantly, although Asian sales grew faster than those in North America and Europe between 1977 and 1991, with additional annual sales of 4 billion guilders, this was much less than the 7 billion guilders added in North America, or the 14 billion guilders in Europe. This shows the difficulty of the task ahead.

Thomson, by contrast, is relatively uninterested in Asian markets as such; Europe and North America are its key concerns. Enormous resources are required to enter a market and overcome entrenched positions, especially where it is not possible to make acquisitions, as in Japan, the most attractive of the Asian markets. More significant is its dependence on assembly joint ventures with Japanese competitors to provide the components needed for its VCR supplies. This, in effect precludes it from attacking the Japanese market, or even other Asian markets, head-on.

Asia as a springboard for Europe and North America

One key role for these Asian operations is as suppliers of low-cost products to their European and north American markets. Thomson is the largest producer of televisions in the important US market, and Philips is the third largest. Thomson has taken this strategy furthest in terms of its corporate organization, with Asia its largest production base. Nevertheless, Philips as a whole – including its semiconductor and other operations – employs around 30,000 in the region, compared to the 18,400 workers employed by Thomson Consumer Electronics.[5] Philips is moving an increasing proportion of its production to the region, as attested by the increasing share of deliveries accounted for by Asian production.

There are a number of ways in which strategies in Asia can translate back into a company's European and north American strategies. The Japanese market is often a launching ground for new products that only later enter north American and European markets. The market in Japan has tended to be more sophisticated, with consumers adopting new consumer electronics products more rapidly than in North America and in Europe. A presence of some sort is essential if European companies want to have the possibility of building volume production early enough to make profits out of their new products. It is often those companies entering a market at the beginning, thereby refining their product features and functionality, as well as perfecting their production techniques, that make the greatest profits. In addition, this enables them to reduce prices later to levels below those that are economical for latecomers. Yet the key will be access to component technologies, and here technology transfer will be significant. A presence in Japan is beneficial to enable new opportunities to be identified more readily.

In addition, the relationships that Philips initially developed in Japan, in particular, have been translated into global alliances. This is the case with Matsushita for components and for video equipment, and with Sony for audio and, increasingly, multi-media standards. Thomson has not been able to expand its relationship with JVC in Europe to create a wider alliance, and will find it difficult to benefit in the same way.

Change as opportunity

Change always provides opportunities as well as threats. In the consumer electronics industry, changes in technology and in distribution techniques are occurring. It is pertinent to consider whether the European companies are well-situated to take advantage of these changes, which include the development of High Definition Television – (stalled in Europe, but promising in the US). – as well as the implications of the acquisitions of Hollywood film studios by Sony, Matsushita and Toshiba, for control over sources of software.

Many of the changes now taking place in Asia are political – or rather geopolitical. In the same way that many European companies have been preoccupied with European markets – now including eastern European markets – so Asian companies might now become increasingly preoccupied with Asian. Korean and Taiwanese electronics producers have not emulated Japan's success in European markets and may see greater opportunities in a unified Korea or a rapidly industrialising China. While this might appear to deflect them from direct confrontation with their Western competitors, it would also give them the opportunity to build up their competitive strengths for a later assault on Western markets. The importance of Japan's large domestic market in enabling many Japanese companies to upgrade their competitive capabilities and husband the resources necessary to launch overseas expansion – sometimes including major overseas acquisitions -is greatly underestimated. Many of these companies still gain well over half of all their sales from the domestic Japanese market.

Philips and Thomson, may find themselves able to exploit greater opportunities than those provided by a rapidly industrializing China. The dangers to their Japanese competitors – or collaborators – of a television standard controlled by US corporations, combined with changes in Japanese retailing and distribution, might in some circumstances break down the dominance of Matsushita and other Japanese companies in controlling access to the Japanese market and make it more difficult for them to maintain their position in the north American market. In the past, the Japanese competitors of Philips and Thomson have appeared better able to adjust to any possible adverse changes than have Philips and Thomson, and have thus taken advantage of them. The situation may be different, with both Thomson and Philips well placed for the adoption of digital HDTV standards in the United States. Philips is also well situated to take advantage of, or adapt to, for any unforeseen changes in Asian markets, while Thomson may have enough of a foothold to reorient its Asian operations for local opportunities if the desire arose, though it has negligible brand recognition.

Since this chapter was completed, it has been announced that Philips is to withdraw from its joint venture, Matsushita Electronics, which in the present recession has been losing money. It is reported that Philips approached Matsushita proposing the sale, and is to receive more than US $1.7 billion. (Leadbetter and van de Krol 1993). It is for the reader to determine whether the analysis in this chapter is thereby faulty or whether the sale is more symptomatic of Philips' lack of coherent strategy.

Notes

1 Sales are defined as direct deliveries of goods and services to third parties in the geographical area concerned, while deliveries refer to sales by companies established within the geographical area to third parties both inside and outside that area, and also deliveries to consolidated companies outside that area.

2 Apparently, a Philips' employee in the US suggested to Konosuke Matsushita that he visit Philips in Holland (Philips 1978: 226). Nevertheless, the two companies had undertaken some business in 1937, a relationship that had been curtailed by the War. (for the background to the establishment of the new venture see Matsushita 1988: 261–64).

3 The estimates for 1985 were by stockbrokers James Capel (*Asian Wall Street Journal* 1987, 1: 7).

4 JVC is purchasing 36-in, 9:16 aspect ratio CRTs from Thomson for use at JVC Manufacturing UK in Scotland (*Nikkei Sangyo Shimbun*, 15 April 1991: 7).

5 In addition, Thomson-CSF has about 600 employees in Asia, and SGS-Thomson 1,000 in Singapore. The figure for Thomson Consumer Electronics represented a 9 per cent reduction on the previous year's figure of 20,300.

6 Other markets are also becoming more sophisticated. In Taiwan, for example, over 99 per cent of households have colour televisions (compared with only 23 per cent in 1976 and 78 per cent in 1981), while 69 per cent have video recorders. If these data are accurate, this is a higher level of penetration than in any European country (Directorate General of Budget, Accounting and Statistics Executive 1991).

Bibliography

Bloom, M. D. H. (1991), 'Internationalization Strategies of Major European and Japanese Companies', *MITI Research Institute Report* August 2–16.

—— (1992) *Technological Change in the Korean Electronics Industry*, Paris: OECD.

—— (1993), 'L'industrie Européenne de L'électronique Grand Public', in Frédérique Sachwald (ed.) *L'Europe et la Globalisation. Acquisitions et Accords dans L'industrie*, Paris: Masson.

De Jonquieres, Guy (1988) 'Management: A Two-Sided View of Asia', *Financial Times* 25 July 1988: 16.

Franko, L. G. and Sherry Stephenson (1982), 'The Micro Picture: Corporate and Sectoral Developments' in Louis Turner and Neil McMullen (eds), *The Newly Industrializing Countries: Trade and Adjustment*, London: Allen and Unwin for the Royal Institute of International Affairs: 210–17.

Hobday, Mike, (1992) 'Technological Learning in Singapore: A Test Case of Leapfrogging', Mimeo, Science Policy Research Unit, University of Sussex.

Matsushita K. (1988) *Quest for Prosperity. The Life of a Japanese Industrialist*, Tokyo: PHP Institute.

Leadbetter, C. and van de Krol, R. (1993) 'Matsushita Ends Electronics Partnership with Philips', *Financial Times* 1–2 May 1993: 24.

Philips, Frederik, (1978) *45 Years with Philips. An Industrialist's Life*, Poole, Dorset: Blandford Press.

Savary, Julien, (1992) 'Growth and Internationalisation of Thomson Consumer Electronics: A Historical Case Study', *Les Cahiers de Recherche du L.E.R.E.P* 6, Université des Sciences Sociales de Toulouse.

—— (1992b) 'Internationalisation and Competitive Challenge: The Case of Thomson Consumer Electronics', EIBA European International Business Association Annual Meeting, 13–15 December.

Turner, L. (1982) 'Consumer Electronics: The Colour Television Case' in Louis Turner and Neil McMullen (eds), *The Newly Industrializing Countries: Trade and Adjustment*, London: Allen and Unwin for the Royal Institute of International Affairs: 48–68.

14 South-east and east Asia towards 2020

Exploring an image of Asia's future

J. R. Chaponnière

INTRODUCTION

The major geopolitical changes that have transformed the world in recent years have already had a major impact on the Asian political landscape. The end of the Cold War has created new opportunities and opened new economic frontiers, the impact of which will be increasingly felt in the years to come. These transformations may offer an additional impetus to Asian countries whose growth will rely less and less on the vagaries of growth in the industrialized economies. The medium-term future of most south-east Asian and east Asian countries looks promising, but what can be ascertained beyond the millennium? How will Asia's economic geography look by the year 2020?

Before looking forward, it may be instructive to look back, and to analyse briefly the received wisdom on the future of Asia as it was presented 30 years ago.

THE FUTURE OF ASIA AS SEEN FROM A 1960s PERSPECTIVE

Today Afro-pessimism is commonplace. Virtually no one really believes in Africa's future and, as such, hardened optimists are reduced to collecting isolated success stories (such as the dynamism of the Bamilekes in Cameroon) in order to find reasons to be cheerful. Yet 30 years ago Asia was the subject of equal pessimism. Asia-pessimism, in fact, preceded Afro-pessimism.

In the late 1950s, the developing Asian countries were considered overpopulated even before the population boom occurred, and seemed doomed to suffer from famine. While campaigns were mounted to help starving Korean children, the underpopulated Afri-

Table 14.1 Asian GNP per capita: 1976 (measured in 1974 prices)

	Projected (1)	Realized (2)	(2):(1)
Taiwan	258	816	3.16
Korea	250	504	2.01
Hong Kong	488	1584	3.24
Singapore	859	2307	2.69
Philippines	459	340	0.74
India	213	139	0.65

Source: Morawetz 1975

can nations, rich in unexploited natural resources, seemed set to overcome their demographic problems.

Asia-pessimism was based on a number of factors; indeed, a brief survey of Asian countries in the late 1950s will serve to convince us that it was not entirely unfounded. Admittedly, Japan had just completed its extensive reconstruction programme, but its dynamism was without parallel elsewhere in Asia. In Seoul, American advisers were despairing of Korea's future, even though the Korean economy was already quite dynamic; in Taiwan the situation was hardly any better. In both countries, the suggestion that Confucianism might be a source of competitive advantage would have been greeted with a polite smile (it was in fact considered a further handicap). Communist China had taken its 'Great Leap forward' (1958–9) with disastrous consequences, and was on the verge of severing relations with the USSR (1960), sending all its Soviet technical advisers home. In Vietnam, Prime Minister Diem was under increasing pressure from Vietcong guerilla warfare. Thailand was undergoing another of its all-too-frequent *coups d'état* and in Malaysia, the first post-independence government had inherited a state of emergency, declared in the face of Communist guerilla attacks. Further south, Indonesia's per capita income, after ten years of independence, had dropped back to its 1915 level; one economic adviser in Jakarta wrote that Indonesia could be 'accounted the number one economic failure among the major underdeveloped countries' (Higgins 1958). The future of Singapore seemed far from rosy, too: in 1964, all but one delegate[1] of a United Nations economic mission concluded that the city-state was economically unviable, since it was importing everything, including its drinking water.

In 1960, American economist Rosentein-Rodan, a keen commentator on the future of third world countries, published economic projections concluding (among other things) that the per capita income of either Taiwan or Korea would be inferior to that of Sri Lanka, and barely 20 per cent higher than that of India by 1975 (Rosentein-Rodan 1961).[2] The future of the Philippines, where the level of education was higher than anywhere else in Asia, looked bright.

Nobel laureate G. Myrdal's work *The Asian Dilemma, an Enquiry into the Poverty of Nations* (1972), researched and first made public in the late 1960s, was clearly indicative of the general perception of Asia at that time.[3]

THE DRIVING FORCES BEHIND ASIAN DEVELOPMENT

Asia's sudden, astonishing economic development came, then, as a surprise to everyone, and has been described as little short of miraculous. The various Asian success stories are already well documented. This chapter will attempt, instead, to highlight the most salient features of Asia's economic development.

During the 1950s, natural resources were widely regarded as essential factors in a country's development. This has proved not to be the case. Resource-poor countries, such as Japan and the Asian NIEs, have become the most dynamic in the world. Indeed, resources are now often seen as unfavourable to development because they favour rent-seeking activities. However, the recent surge in manufacturing exports from resource-rich ASEAN countries has hopefully shown that natural resources do not necessarily lead to the so-called 'Dutch disease'.

Asia's first miracle was agricultural. With increased populations and limited geographical area, most Asian countries could not have reached their present level of development without the contribution of agriculture. Land reforms have contributed to a more equitable income distribution which made it easier to build internal consensus around a central growth strategy. The rapid growth of agriculture has provided vital purchasing power for the rural population, which accounts for 28 per cent of the total population of Korea, 43 per cent in Thailand and 74 per cent in China. These countries were fortunate in having a labour force eager to work and improve its skills to meet the needs of industry. Resource-poor countries have nothing but manufactures to export; but export-led growth based on manufactures has in fact proved to be the right choice both for the NIEs and, lately, for the resource-rich countries of ASEAN.

Asia is renowned for its entrepreneurship. Today, there are more than ten Korean firms among *Fortune*'s 500, and the international dynamism of Taiwan's small and medium-sized industries is well recognized. These firms are going international (Chaponnière 1992). Such entrepreneurial spirit is not the reserve of east Asian countries, Thai and Indonesian enterprises[4] have started to invest overseas, and Chinese state conglomerates are following the same course.[5] The question of state intervention is a controversial one. During the 1960s the NIEs' success was seen as their reward for the pursuance of sound economic policies (such as free trade regimes for exporters), whereas later their success was hailed as proof of successful government intervention. Leaving this debate aside it should be emphasized that these countries have been managed by high-quality governments, which have given priority to spending on education and social cohesion. Since the late 1980s the steering rule of government has gradually diminished, leaving more room for decisions at enterprise level, while trade and capital restrictions were also reduced.

The driving forces of Asian development could be said, then, to be internal.[6] Chief among them is a real sense of economic urgency ('we have to develop in order to survive') which has helped to mobilize local support. This factor is echoed in Toynbee's explanation of development. Such a conclusion may have important implications for the future of today's third world nations.

POLITICAL AND GEOPOLITICAL UNCERTAINTIES

The optimism that has replaced Asia-pessimism is now so all-pervading that the political and geopolitical problems that continue to threaten Asia's economic success are often overlooked. What are the changes most likely to occur in Asian societies? How will political successions take place? How will these nations coexist?

Economic progress and political liberalization did not go hand-in-hand, and most Asian countries are ruled by authoritative regimes. For the most part, the fundamental social changes brought about by development have not engendered the rise of a demanding working class but, rather, that of a rights-conscious middle class population.[7] This phenomenon is not confined to the relatively affluent east Asian economies, but is also to be found in the lower-income developing countries of south-east Asia. Among the symptoms of this emergence is the rise of consumerism, increasing recreational and cultural facilities, and last but not least a growing appeal for more social and political rights. Demands for political change stem from economic success and the resulting rising expectations. Authoritative regimes are being criticized by the countries' educated executive classes who, aware of international changes and conscious of their rights, find it more and more difficult to bear them.

The transition to democracy may take place as smoothly as it did in South Korea or Taiwan, or may be countered by violent repression, as in China in 1989 or Thailand in 1992.[8] Any country faced with such a situation risks entering a period of turbulence which would hamper its economic growth. And economic progress can itself have unexpected results. Fukuyama foresees Asia gravitating in two completely opposite directions (Fukuyama 1992). On the one hand, its populations may well continue to assimilate Western ideas and turn towards democracy but, on the other hand, they may feel that their success is due more to their own traditions than to 'imported' ideas, and to less liberal, undemocratic alternatives, combining the rationalism of technocracy with paternalistic authoritarianism.[9]

In addition to the uncertainties surrounding long-term social change, there are those inspired by the coming political successions, the most important of which is China's. One might well imagine that this country will succeed where the USSR has failed, by modernizing its economy while maintaining a strong political force in power. Lee Kuan Yew has been quoted in an interview, forecasting that beyond 2000, China will be governed by an authoritarian regime that will be Communist in name, and in no way different from other one-party governments. Another unknown quantity is the successor of President Suharto, who has been in power in Indonesia since 1965. The fall of his predecessor, Sukarno, was marked by the bloodshed of anti-Communist Chinese 'pogroms'; in the future, Indonesian anger may well be turned against Overseas Chinese capitalists within her borders, if the succession results in political turmoil. Such an outcome is a major source of worry for Singapore, which, like Malaysia, would suffer the consequences of any such upheavals on their doorsteps.

Let us take a brief look at the medium- and long-term geopolitical uncertainties. Asia has experienced several 'hot wars', and the progressive end of the Cold War has not created turmoil here, as it did in Europe. The Korean peninsula still faces the possibility of a suicidal move by North Korea's 'Great Leader' or his beloved son. While reunification of the peninsula seems the most likely ultimate outcome in the long term, the process could take any one of several different routes, and we should remember that 'all the great events that have defined Korea since the peninsula's partition have caught policy makers unprepared' (Eberestadt 1992). Gradual change, allowing the phased reduction of North-South disparity, is probably the best scenario for Korea; the collapse of the Northern regime, sending waves of migrants to the South, would inevitably lead to a German-style solution, which would be very costly for the South Korean economy. Korea's reunification would in any case be more difficult than Germany's, since North Korea is comparatively larger than East Germany, in relation to its neighbour, and its economy appears to be more distorted (Eberestadt 1992).[10]

Since the break-up of the USSR, the 'northern' threat to Chinese borders has diminished. Russia will not exercise much external pressure in the medium-term. However, in the long term, a Russian revival may well mean new border tensions. Beyond the uncertainties looming in 1997, a successful movement in favour of political independence in Taiwan could jeopardize the consolidation of Greater China. In the South China Sea, the progressive American withdrawal is leaving a void which China has been quick to fill, harking back to the days of the Soong dynasty, when the Middle Kingdom took great interest in these parts. And China is not alone in this. It is sometimes taken for granted that Japan will never be tempted to play the role of super-power either within or beyond the region. According to Lee Kuan Yew, the recent vote permitting the Japanese army to act outside its own borders was tantamount to 'giving a liqueur-filled chocolate to a reformed alcoholic'; the Singapore Premier has not forgotten that between 1942 and 1945 Singapore was called Syonan and that thousands of Chinese perished in Japanese concentration camps. The Kampuchean question is not resolved and numerous border problems persist as sources of potential conflict, albeit to a lesser extent than in Africa or the Balkans; counterbalancing this to a degree, we should remember that south-east and east Asian countries are virtually immune to religious conflict.

The worst scenario will not necessarily occur, and there is little reason to expect major political changes among the region's major powers. We can, then, look ahead with reasonable optimism, on the assumption that Asia's people are unwilling to throw themselves into undertakings detrimental to their economic welfare. Improvements in the standard of living have always proved to be the best antidote to war.

WHAT CAN BE SAID ABOUT THE YEAR 2025?

Long-term demographic forecasting is a hazardous science. How-ever, over a 33–year period, the margin of error is relatively small. In 2025, six of the 12 largest national populations in the world will be Asian (see Table 14.2). Some of the most astonishing surges in population growth will occur in Vietnam, whose population will then match that of Japan, and Indonesia, which may, by 2025, be twice as populated as Japan. It is possible, however, that these demographic forecasts might encourage massive migratory move-ments. Can we envisage an Indonesian population of 200 million, threatening to spill over into relatively underpopulated Malaysia, where 500,000 Indonesians are already working on a semi-clan-destine basis? Vietnam and the Philippines would surely be singled out as suitable destinations for emigration. How would east Asian countries react to these influxes, should they occur?

Of course, a burgeoning population does not necessarily bring economic power. Indeed, the former is very often the result of the latter. In 1900, at the peak of its power, Europe held no less than one quarter of the world's population. Today, the EC accounts for just 6 per cent, and by 2025 this figure will have dropped to 3 per cent, while 40 per cent of the world's population will be living in east Asian and south-east Asian countries. Moreover, Asian coun-tries will have kept a relatively young population. In 1990, the median age for the region (i.e the age that divides the population into two equal sets) was 26 (as opposed to 35 in Europe, 37 in Japan and 17 in Africa). In 2025, 66 per cent of people in developing Asian countries will be aged between 15 and 65 – a demographic structure particularly favourable to development.

These adult populations will be well prepared for work thanks to the progress made in education: Korea already has as many univer-sity students as France. Emphasis has been placed on quality as well as on quantity, as can be seen when student performance in the sciences is compared internationally. Young east Asian students obtain on average higher marks than those of several industrialized countries, testifying to the high priority given to education in Asian countries, often using extremely selective systems.

Two Asian countries will experience a significant 'grandad boom',[11] namely Singapore – where the State is having difficulty persuading its well-educated female population to have more children – and Japan, which is preparing itself for ageing (more than one Japanese in five will be over 60 in 2025). We may well imagine

Table 14.2 Forecast of population growth in Asia: 1990 and 2025 (in millions)

	1990	2025
China	1,117	1,530
Indonesia	181	280
Vietnam	82	127
Japan	124	125
Philippines	74	100
Korea (N&S)	67	94
Thailand	56	82
Burma (Myanmar)	42	70
Malaysia	18	30
Taiwan	20	26
Kampuchea	8	14
Laos	4	8
Hong Kong	6	7
Singapore	2	4
Mongolia	2	4

the Japanese overcoming this new challenge by embracing its 'grey panthers' and encouraging them to contribute to an even more productive society; however, a progressive fall in productivity and investment feasibility is a much more likely outcome. Japan might instead become to Asia what Switzerland is to its European neighbours – a rich, efficient provider of specialized financial and business products (*The Economist* 8 January 1993). The decrease of the potential labour force may redirect savings towards the more productive Asian economies. We should remember that in 1900, almost 40 per cent of French savings went abroad in search of a higher feasibility rate.

A BRIEF REVIEW OF ECONOMIC FORECASTS FOR ASIA

Economic forecasts concerning Asian countries are often inspired by the famous 'wild geese' image elaborated by Akamatsu as a model of economic progress in the region over the past four decades (see, for example, Wanatabe 1991). Japan's soaring flight has been followed by the four NIEs (whose number may be halved by 2020, with Taiwan and Hong Kong forming part of Greater China), which were in turn followed by China and the ASEAN countries, while Vietnam, Laos and Kampuchea are poised to take off.

The possibility that developing countries might catch up with industrialized countries may seem at odds with the prevailing pessimism about the future of the third world. It is an idea that has often been dismissed, for two main reasons.

Several authors have claimed that, contrary to the argument put forward by Gerschenkron with regard to Europe, 'lateness' is not an advantage. Developing countries are in fact confronted with a widening technological gap that makes it impossible for them to catch up: the spread of new waves of technology has raised the entry barriers, making it impossible to practise reverse engineering (knowledge is more opaque). The NIEs' rapid advances in high-tech industries would seem to support the 'privileged latecomers' argument, however.[12] Past experience has shown that it is not necessary to have a technological production capability in each of the major new products (associated with a new techno-economic paradigm) in order to catch up or to maintain competitiveness (Freeman 1976). What is necessary is the capability to use new technology in certain industries and to produce that part of the wide range of new products and services that is most appropriate to local conditions, resources and comparative advantage. This is what is happening in south-east Asia.[13]

Export pessimism has a very long history starting in the late 1950s. In the early 1980s the generalization of NIEs' export-led expansion was considered impossible: the international community that had recoiled before the 'Four Dragons', inhabited by fewer than 85 million people, was thought to be unable to bear the emergence of new NIEs. One decade later, we find that such generalization did not occur. However, the successful emergence of just two, very large, 'NIEs', China and Indonesia, has shown that export pessimism is not more warranted now than it was in the late 1950s. The gradual emergence of these new NIEs has opened an immense market. We should bear in mind that Korea's trade surplus finally came about in 1987, only to disappear again three years later.

Let us now consider briefly the perspective of the different countries as they appear in several recent published analyses. Barring large-scale wars or ecological disaster, the consensus is that Japan will become more powerful. Japan has predicted that its GNP will increase from 55 per cent of US GNP, to 70 per cent in the year 2000, and that it will match US levels by 2020. In 1951, Japan's GDP (in US dollars) was one twentieth that of the United States. Japan has, in fact, shown the rest of Asia that it is possible to catch up with the 'lead goose'.

Korea's prospects look bright, and increasingly so with the open-

Table 14.3 Scenarios for growth in Singapore: 1990–2020

	Pessimistic		Optimistic	
	Growth rate (%)	*GNP per capita*	*Growth rate (%)*	*GNP per capita*
1990–1995	4.4	13.3	5.4	14.0
1995–2000	3.6	15.9	4.6	17.5
2000–2010	2.9	21.0	3.7	25.2
2010–2020	2.6	27.0	3.5	35.4

*in US dollars at the end of the period
Source: Singapore Economic Planning Committee

ing of 'new economic frontiers'. The expansion of its domestic market is also of increasing importance to Korean firms. China is already South Korea's third trading partner, and the establishing of diplomatic relations between Seoul and Beijing has created a favourable investment climate for the *chaebols* which have been so far quite reluctant to invest in China.[14] South Korean firms may enjoy some advantage over Japanese firms since they are able to propose less sophisticated technology. According to the Korean Development Bank, the economy is projected to expand by an average of 6.8 per cent between 1992 and 2001. Annual growth of around 6 per cent over the next decade seems quite realistic. The targets set by the large *chaebols* would seem to support these projections.[15] If the North Korean economy does not collapse in political chaos, its gradual absorption (which may result in a decrease in the peninsula's per capita income) will open new horizons for Korean development during the first decade of the next century, and for the strengthening of its economic relationship with the CIS, as illustrated by the Tumen River delta project.

The strategic plan published by Singapore took care to pinpoint the various world-wide changes that might affect the city state's future. Among the changes considered irreversible is the decline of the US economy, which will no longer be able to exercise strong leadership in world economic affairs as it did in the post-war era.[16] Based on such assumptions, Singapore aims to achieve the per capita income level of the Netherlands by the year 2010 and, if this optimistic scenario materializes, to catch up with the US by 2030.

Singapore's optimism has spread to neighbouring Malaysia, where Prime Minister Mahatir has promised his fellow countrymen that they will join the ranks of the industrialized countries by 2020. Further north Thailand, which has never been tempted to indulge

Table 14.4 GDP in the Asia Pacific Region and Western powers: 1990 (in US$ billion and on PPP basis)

	GDP	GDP (PPP)
United States	5,392	5,391
Western Europe	7,500	6,050
Japan	2,942	2,124
China	365	2,307
NIEs and ASEAN	751	1,583
Korea	236	340
Indonesia	107	422
Thailand	80	238
Taiwan	147	193
Philippines	44	138
Malaysia	42	103
Hong Kong	60	101
Singapore	35	48

Sources: World Bank, Centre d'Etudes Prospectives et d'Informations Internationales (CEPII, CHELEM database)

in long-term forecasting or planning, may be able to progress at least as quickly as Malaysia – all the more so if Indochina does succeed in transforming itself from a battlefield into a marketplace. In such a stimulating regional environment, Vietnam will undoubtedly extricate itself from its present paralysing difficulties. Japan has already resumed its aid flow, and the normalization of Vietnam's relations with the United States should soon follow. Economic activity in southern Vietnam should regain 1975 levels within a few years, and if such dynamism spreads northwards, Vietnam should attain Thailand's 1990 level of performance during the first quarter of the twenty-first century.

Let us now turn to the 'heavyweights'. China has been described as the 'unseen giant' of Asia (*The Economist* 28 November 1992). It is an open secret that official Chinese economic statistics make no sense; according to these, China is half as well off as Indonesia and one quarter as rich as Thailand – a far cry from reality according to most observers, and explicable only in terms of the yuan devaluation, which has spurred exports and more than cancelled out China's entire economic growth in US$ since 1978. A correct evaluation of China's, or any other country's, GNP should be based on purchasing power parity (PPP) prices on a commodity-by-commodity basis.[17] Estimates of the Chinese economy, made using this method by the CEPII, make it clear that the distortion caused by

304   *J. R. Chaponniere*

the official rate is extremely large. While China's GDP in current dollar terms appears to be one-eighth that of Japan and one-twentieth that of western Europe, China's GDP measured in PPP prices appears larger than Japan's and one-third that of western Europe. After an absence from the world economic stage spanning several centuries, China has already regained its position as a large economic power. In the coming decade, we may well see an appreciation of the yuan, narrowing the gap between these two estimates.

Guandong province experienced the fastest economic growth of any region in the world during the 1980s. In close relationship with Hong Kong and Taiwan, it has grown at an annual rate of over 10 per cent , and shows no sign of slowing down. Shanghai region, the cradle of Chinese capitalism in the 1930s, is experiencing a similar rate of growth. Further north, the normalization of Sino-Korean relations has given a boost to Shandong region.This 'coastal dynamism' has gradually spread throughout China, which has seen national growth averaging 9 per cent per year during the 1980s, and more than 12 per cent in 1992 – the fastest rate in the world. This evolution has been plagued by stop-go cycles of increasing severity as the Chinese economy overheats – a process which may be about to repeat itself in the near future. China's growth will probably continue unchecked in the face of an eventual political disaster, and it will gain additional impetus from the peaceful absorption of Taiwan into Greater China, sometime during the first quarter of the next century. By then, Taiwan will have increased its GNP quite substantially. Published in 1991, the Sixth Development Plan of Taiwan envisages average growth of 7 per cent, and a generally promising long-term outlook for the island.

Indonesia, like Japan, is a densely populated island nation. Official figures undervalue the size of its economy as they do for China, The most recent World Bank report predicts a doubling of Indonesia's per capita GNP by the year 2000. Once firmly implanted among the ranks of medium-revenue countries, Indonesia's wealth of natural resources and wide market should enable it to make rapid progress.

It is interesting to compare these conclusions, from a country-to-country appraisal, with the long-term world economic scenario published by the Netherlands Central Planning Bureau in 1992, which presents a basically optimistic long-term 'balanced growth' scenario, with ecologically sustainable world economic growth of 3.5 per cent, including all regions of the world. The study also sets out a 'global crisis' scenario to counterpoint this, exploring the risks of neglecting global challenges. Two further scenarios have a distinctly regional focus. The 'global shift' scenario shows western Europe falling behind, with rigid, dirigiste economic policies dictated by nationalism. The 'European renaissance' scenario, on the other hand, sees the United States facing serious problems. A common feature of all the scenarios is the continuous and relatively undisturbed rise of the Asian economies. The projections made show a per capita income growth rate (measured in PPP) of between 2.7 per cent (the 'crisis' scenario) and 4 per cent (the 'global shift' scenario) for these countries. From these different forecasts it appears reasonable to assume that the NIEs, ASEAN and China will grow twice as fast as Japan, which will itself grow somewhat faster than western Europe and the United States. Where does this leave us three decades from now, political disasters notwithstanding?

Projections based on PPP prices[18]) paint a very different picture of the future from that to which we are accustomed. According to CEPII's projection, income levels in the NIEs may have caught up with those of the EC by the year 2000. Twenty years later, if Asia's development continues unchecked by political and geopolitical catastrophies, the per capita income of Greater China may be one-quarter that of Japan, while Greater China's economy could be nearly three times that of Japan, and larger than that of western Europe. By that time, Indonesia may have the second largest population in south-east Asia. Behind these three giants, the combined GDP of North and South Korea will amount to around two-thirds that of Japan.

ONE OR SEVERAL POLES?

The inaccuracy of previous forecasts on Asia should teach us to be cautious. If (and this is a big 'if'), it is not checked for the reasons described above, the economy of east and south-east Asia looks set to carry on rising, if only for the simple reason that it is 'so broadly based' (Kennedy 1989). As an increasing number of people in Asia reach the threshold of income allowing them to buy consumer durable goods, the impact on the regional, as well on the world economy, will be considerable.

1992 marked the five hundredth anniversary of the discovery of America – an event which could be said to have marked 'lift-off' for the Western world. Eastern Asia had until then been the most advanced region in the world, but was now overtaken by Europe. Perhaps, if history follows a cyclical rather than a linear path, Asia will once again find itself at the centre of world development and commerce.[19] Asia is, of course, multi-faceted. Will its various national identities disappear and give way to the 'huge village' envisaged by Ohmae? Will they melt away into a homogeneous Asian identity – a kind of unfocused economic 'yellow peril' in the minds of fearful Europeans? In fact, the opposite may be true. Development and the democratic process may give rise to stronger nationalistic assertions.[20] Over a million Japanese have so far bought Morita and Ishihara's book *Japan Can Say No* (a form of 'US-bashing' perhaps?). This nationalistic revival does not exclude the internationalization of firms – Asian multinationals are characterized by their strongly national infrastructure, but their extensive international contacts and networks will help them to guard against nationalism's inherent dangers. We should distrust scenarios that fail to take account of deep-seated nationalistic feelings, when we try to forecast Asia's future. This is the main objection to be made to 'nippo-centrist' scenarios, which fail to take history into account. A united and developed Korea would face one single remaining challenge, namely Japan; China, once out of underdevelopment, will be seeking to regain its lost splendour; and Indonesia (or at least, its predominantly Javanese central government) will remember the Madjapahit Empire!

Admittedly, in any consideration of the respective economic weight of the various Asian countries as measured by their GDP in dollars, Japan emerges as the regional economic leader. Such wrongly-founded evaluations give credit to the idea that the world's economic future will be built around a 'new zone of co-prosperity' revolving around Tokyo. As stressed by Van Wolferen, an Asian bloc would in itself be very unstable, since it is highly doubtful that the expanding south-east Asian economies would happily accept the subcontracting role that Tokyo's businessmen and bureaucrats have in mind for them.

The above projections based on PPP lead to a completely different picture. Instead of moving towards unipolarity, Asia appears to be moving towards multipolarity, with China and Japan as strong focal points, without exercising excess power over secondary poles such as Korea (which has traditionally enjoyed good relations with China) and Indonesia. ASEAN countries will be well connected with Greater China through the Chinese diaspora, already one of the most powerful economic forces in south-east Asia. Japan should by no means be considered either as the driving force of regional economic development, or as its inevitable future centre.

Such a non-Japan-centric view of the future differs somewhat from conventional European wisdom on Asia today. Strategic decisions should not be taken on the basis of a one-sided vision of the future based on an extrapolation of uncontested received ideas. This overall picture will naturally have consequences relative to the West's search for Asian partnerships. Linking up with a Chinese or Korean partner who will inevitably prove more demanding than a Japanese firm, is an option to be closely analysed.

Economic regional integration in Asia should be able to continue for macro-economic reasons (the more Asia's economies develop, the greater the possibilities for economic exchange) as well as micro-economic reasons (the existence of multiple networks). Such an evolution does not invariably point to the formation of a regional bloc. The rising level of intra-regional trade in Asia simply reflects the region's increased importance in the world economy.[21] On the contrary, Asia may well remain a multipolar area, with several competing poles. Today, such a perspective is generally considered as a sign of fragility in a world tending more and more towards division into major trading blocs (NAFTA and the EC). Could this perceived global trend conflict with the multipolar pattern of development in Asia? Perhaps not. Looking back to 1492, we find that subsequent European development outstripped China not because of superior capability, but because of competitive incentives. At that time, the existence of multiple, competing centres gave Europe an advantage over the unified Chinese empire, which had less incentive to look for new frontiers, and where the central government's decision was final, absolute and uncontested. While Peking prevented Admiral Cheng Ho from pursuing his voyages at the beginning of the sixteenth century, no central European authority could prevent the Portuguese from sailing. 'Divided we stand, united we fall' has been presented as an appropriate motto for the European state systems of the sixteenth century (Findlay 1991); it could equally well apply to the countries of Asia in the twenty-first.

Notes

1 The delegate in question, Professor Willemius, strongly believed in the future of Singapore, where he has acted as an adviser ever since. In 1968, Singapore was dismissed by G. Myrdal as a country with a potentially explosive population problem, threatening a mounting burden of unemployment (Myrdal 1972).
2 Some years later, Chenery estimated that the GNP of India and Pakistan would grow faster than that of Korea (Chenery 1966).
3 The analysis focused on southern Asia and made some comments concerning south-east Asian economies.
4 Unicord, Saha Union and Charone Pokphand are examples of multinational Thai companies; Liem Group is an Indonesian example.
5 As in the case of Sougang, an iron and steel company, which has recently bought a US iron and steel plant and invested in Peruvian mines.
6 Leaving aside those who have presented Asia's developments as the result of foreign firms' involvement.
7 According to South Korean social indicators, two out of three South Koreans judged themselves to be middle class in 1991. Newspaper circulation is a good indicator of this: the percentage of people reading a newspaper in South Korea and Taiwan is similar to that of the United States.
8 This transition to democracy may result in increasingly rigid social divisions and a deceleration of growth (Olson 1982).
9 Of which Singapore may be a case in point.
10 The cost of Korean unification has been estimated at anything from US$3 billion to US$10 billion per year over a ten-year period (Eberestadt 1992).
11 This process may be clearly evident in China after 2015, and the old-age dependency ratio may rise from 13 to 18 per cent in 2025. In other south-east Asia countries it is predicted to rise from 10 to 14 per cent.
12 South Korea and Taiwan stand as fifth and sixth producer countries, while in certain niches, South Korean and Taiwanese firms are among the world leaders.
14 Korean investments in China represented 0.4 per cent of cumulated foreign investment in China in 1992.
13 The other stumbling block often cited as preventing developing countries from 'catching up' is the availability or otherwise of raw materials. An

Interfutures study carried out in the early 1980s concluded that the supply of increasingly scarce raw materials need not pose a problem to the growth of the world economy until 2000. Another study extended this to 2015. The most important assumptions supporting this optimistic scenario are continual dematerialization; a switch to mineral raw materials which are in relatively abundant supply; and relatively optimistic forecasts concerning the inflows of reserves.

14 Korean investments in China represented 0.4 per cent of cumulated foreign investment in China in 1992.

15 Samsung has announced that it intends to be among the ten largest world firms, with a turnover of US$200 billion in 2000.

16 Within this trend, Singapore's strategic economic plan elaborated two major tendencies which could give rise to alternative new international orders: an 'open world' in which ex-socialist and underdeveloped countries would work together, or a 'divided world' segregated into regional blocs.

17 Exchange rates are an imperfect measure of the purchasing power of the various national currencies. Price structures vary across countries and, at best, exchange rates reflect the prices of international traded goods. The alternative is to reprice the local components of income at a uniform set of prices. PPPs refer to the number of currency units required to buy one dollar's worth of output. PPPs are a weighed average of the ratios of domestic prices to its price in some international units.

18 If we base our forecast, erroneously, on 1990 GDP figures in US$, we find that the GDP of Greater China (Hong Kong, Taiwan and China) is half Japan's weight in 2010.

19 The evolution of world powers over time has always 'gone west': Greece then Rome, then Europe, the US (from the end of the nineteenth century) and now Asia (Japan).

20 We should remember that the population of Japan or Korea is almost 99 per cent Japanese and Korean.

21 In 1980, intra-regional trade accounted for 33 per cent of total Asian trade, which in turn represented 15 per cent of world trade. In 1989, intra-regional trade represented 37 per cent of Asian trade; the Asian share of world trade had jumped to 20 per cent. Intra-regional trade divided by share of world trade had thus declined in Asia, while it rose in Europe (Frankel 1991).

Bibliography

Asian Economic Commentary (July 1992) 'Changing Asian demographics may bring forth new challenges', Merril Lynch.

Central Planning Bureau of the Netherlands (1992) *Scanning the Future: a Long-term Study of the World Economy 1900–2015*, The Hague: SDC Publishing.

Chaponnière, J. P. (1992) 'The NIEs go International', LVMH conference, Fontainebleau: INSEAD Euro-Asia Centre.

Eberestadt, N. (1992) 'Can the two Koreas be One?' *Foreign Affairs* fall.

Findlay, R. (1991) 'The Roots of Divergence: Western Economic History in Comparative Perspective', *American Economic Review* 82, 2.

Frankel, J. (1991) 'Is a Yen Bloc Forming in Pacific Asia?', *Amex Bank Review* November.

Freeman, C. 'New technology and catching up', in *Third World Revolution*.

Fukuyama, F. (1992) *The End of History and the Last Man*, New York: Viking Penguin.

Higgins, B. (1958) *Economic Development, Principles, Problems and Policies*, Woodside, CT: Constable

Kennedy, D. (1989) *The Rise and Fall of the Great Powers: Economic Change and Military Conflict from 1500 to 2000*, London: Fontana.

Morawetz, D. (1975) *Twenty-five Years of Development World Bank Publication.*

Myrdal, G. (1972) *The Asia Dilemma, an Enquiry into the Poverty of Nations*, New York: Pantheon Books.

Ohmoe, K. (1989) *Beyond National Borders*, Homewood IL. Dow Jones-Irwin.

—— (1992) *Borderless World: Power and Strategy in the Interlinked Economy*, Centerpont, NY: Fontana.

Olson, M. (1982) *The Rise and Decline of Nations: Economic Growth, Stagflation and Social Rigidities*, New Haven. Yale University Press.

Rosentein-Rodan, P. (1961) 'International aid for underdeveloped countries', *Review of Economics and Statistics* 43, 2.

Wanatabe, T. (1991) 'L'Irresistible Ascension du Pacifique Ouest', *Futuribles. NX150.*

Index

agricultural sector 9, 19, 35–6, 41, 54–5, 57, 60
appraisals 229, 245–8
ASEAN Chambers of Commerce and Industry 18
ASEAN corporations 176–9, 186–92; environmental certainty 182; goal performance 180–2; profile 179
ASEAN Free Trade Agreement 80, 168–9
Asia-Pacific Economic Cooperation Forum 2–3, 166, 167
Asia-Pacific region: definition 2–4; diversity 4–6; economic growth 6–12; economic success 163–9
Asian Development Bank 6, 152, 157
Asian economic bloc 88; emergence 77–82
Asian Free Trade Agreement 71; customs duties 80
Association of South-East Asian Nations (ASEAN-4) 2; economic history 18–19; exports 26; gross domestic product 24
Australia: capital movement 10; economic history 14–16; economic status 7; external economic deficits 10
Australia–New Zealand Closer Economic Relations Trade Agreement 15–16

barter trade 51, 52, 58, 64, 102, 159; ineffectiveness 61–2
border disputes 49
border trade 52, 54, 58, 59, 158
Bristol-Meyers 240, 248
bureaucracy 11
business opportunities 64

capital: accumulation 17, 35; stock 7
cash trade 51, 52, 58
chaebols 50, 95, 96, 98, 102, 107
Changchun Forum for North-east Asian Economic Development 116
chemical and pharmaceutical industries 228
China: economic future 303–4; economic history 19–21; economic potential 85–6, 142; reunification 272; territorial claims 142; Tumen River project 128–9; unpredictability 141–2; *see also* Overseas Chinese; Sino–Russian trade
Chinese Economic Area 46
Chinese exports 58
Chung Ju-Yung 93–4
Ciba-Geigy 227, 239
classical economists 6, 7
Cold War 45, 61, 63, 112, 160, 172
colonialism 15
'comfort women' issue 171
Communism 160
Confucianism 10–11, 39, 109
credit subsidies 9

Cultural Revolution 19, 20
cultural time patterns *see* Japanese
    time
culture values 10–11

Daewoo 102, 125, 150, 152
DEC 232, 239, 240
delivery of goods 62
Deng Xiaoping 21, 121, 149
Deutsche Bank 212–13
demographic forecast 299–300
diplomatic relations 49
distrust 61
driving forces for development
    295–6

East Asia Economic Caucus 2, 166,
    167
east Asia: economic links with
    Japan 160–73; legacy of war
    171–2
economic development 1–2; growth
    forecasts 83–5
economic dynamism 1–2, 23
economic expansion 21–33
economic forecasts 300–5
economic hinterland 105–9
economic strategies 75–7; *see also*
    Japanese economic model
economy: open 24–5, 40; sub-
    regional transformations 12–21
education 11, 39, 73
employment 74
endaka recession 23, 75, 81
exports 8, 16, 77–8; growth rate
    25–7, 40; licences 62; north-east
    Asia ratios 52–3; subsidies 9;
    volume 26–9
European companies 105, 276;
    investment strategies 135–47; *see
    also* Philips; strategic planning:
    implications for European
    corporations; Thomson
    Consumer Electronics
European economic growth 82–3
expatriates 249–50, 262

financial markets 7
financial repression 9
fiscal subsidy 9

'flying geese' 18, 72–7
foreign direct investment 15, 19, 20,
    32–3
foreign exchange 64
foreign firms in Japan: global
    perspective 258–62; human
    resource management strategy
    251–58; issues facing employers
    234–51; market entrance 227–8;
    multinationalization 228–33;
foreign trade 8–9
fortress Europe 71, 105
fortress north America 71
'four dragons' 1, 16, 301
free trade 71
fringe benefits 239–40
future: forecasts 299–307; from
    1960s perspective 293–5;
    uncertainties 296–8

General Agreement on Tariffs and
    Trade 13, 71, 167
geopolitical future uncertainties
    297–8
German companies 211–12
German reunification 82, 99
global banking 206–17
government: commitment 10, 16, 40;
    and market collaboration 10;
    policy 10
Great Leap Forward 19
Gorbachev, Mikhail 150, 155
gross domestic product 4, 5, 7;
    growth 16, 21–3, 40, 72
gross national product: Asia-Pacific
    region 1, 21, 23; China 20, 23;
    north-east Asia 47–9
growth poles 21–2, 32, 39, 40

high-tech industries 19, 98
Hoechst 227, 250
Hong Kong: economy 8; economic
    policy 7; reunification 272
human relations 11
human resource management
    213–14; *see also* foreign firms in
    Japan
Hyundai 93, 102, 125, 150

IBM 232, 234, 238, 239, 248, 250, 254
import tariffs 8–9, 102
imports 8, 60
income 1, 4–5, 24
India 86
individual trade 52, 58–9
Indochina 86–8
Indonesia: economic future 304; external economic deficits 10; food production 19
industrial sector 37, 41, 60
industrial transformation 33–9
industrialization 18, 19
inflation rate 9
infrastructure 143; bottlenecks in China 64, 85
Internal Atomic energy agency 100-1
international business/trade 29, 67–8
intra-Korean relations 49
intra-regional trade 52–4; product composition 54–61
investment 7, 19, 33, 35, 39, 81–2, 164–5; Asian strategies 146–7; direct flows 62–3, 66; in Japan 226–8; Japanese 164–6; of Overseas Chinese 270; South Korean 108–9; portfolio 33, 41; *see also* European companies; foreign direct investment

Japan: contribution to economic world order 140–1; economic centre 66–7; economic future 301; economic history 12–14; economic recovery 84; economy 1, 39; external economic surpluses 10; relations with Korea 157; ties with Indochina 86–8; Tumen River project 125–8; *see also* east Asia; economic links with Japan; foreign firms in Japan; Russia: relations with Japan
Japanese banks 207, 208, 209, 213, 214
Japanese economic model 72–5
Japanese imperialism 171
Japanese investors 81–2

Japanese labour market 230–3
Japanese Liberal Democratic Party 154
Japanese time 197–9, 217–18; and strategic action in global banking 206–17; and strategic planning 199–206
job descriptions 229
job security 234–5
joint ventures 57, 153, 165, 228, 277, 280–1, 283–6
JVC 281, 282, 285–6

keiretsu system 74
Kim Dae-Jung 93, 94
Kim Il Sung 100, 104, 121, 149
Kim Young-Sam 93, 94, 95, 96, 97
Korean economic future 301–2
Korean disease 95, 97
Korean reunification 99–105, 112
Kurile Islands 107, 155

labour force 16, 39, 41, 103, 144, 172; local 228–30; mid-career managers 231–2; shortage 230–1, 260; women 231–2, 238
Lee Kwan Yew 272,297; 'vital intangible' 8
levels of strategic planning 201–2; budget 205; mission 203–4; organizational needs 205–6; plan 204–5; vision 202–3
Lloyds Bank 206–7, 208, 209–10
local employment practice a 241–3
localization of management 249–51, 261
locations: central 143; of companies 142–3; dual approach to 144–6; peripheral 144
Lucky Goldstar 125, 150, 151

macro-economic management 9–10; 19
macro-economic policies 17, 40
makimono time 197, 198, 215, 217
Malaysia: economic future 302–3; external economic deficits 10; 'look east' campaign 18
management practices 238–51
managerial function 229

manufactured goods 16, 29–32, 41
manufacturing sector 9, 18, 37
Marantz 277, 282
market collaboration *see*
    government
Matsushita 165–6, 277, 279–82
meritocracy 11–12
military tension 149
Miyazawa Doctrine 169–70, 172
Miyazawa Kiichi 168, 171
Mobil 232, 241, 248
Mongolia 129–30
Motorola 240, 254
multipolarity 305–7

national trade 51–2
National Westminster Bank 207, 209
natural resources 5–6, 14, 16, 144,
    160–1
NCR 238, 248
Nestlé 67, 105, 109, 232, 234
New Zealand: economic history
    14–16; economic status 7;
    external economic deficits 10
newly industrializing economies 6;
    economic future 301; economic
    history 16–18; economic
    relationships 164; emergence of
    79–80
New Zealand Australia Free Trade
    Agreement 15
non-tariff barriers 74
north American regionalism 136
North American Free Trade
    Agreement 71, 105, 136, 167
North East Asia Regional
    Development Area 118
north-east Asia: definition and
    characteristics 46–9; economic
    relations 49–51; implications of
    normalization 63–8; intra-
    regional trade 51–63
North Korea: benefits from Tumen
    River project 120–22; exports 58;
    rapprochement 50, 101, 112, 117-
    18; *see also* Sino–Korean
    relations
North Korean–Russian trade 59–60
Northern Territories 154–5
nuclear technology 57, 100, 151, 152

open door policy 20, 25, 117
open economy *see* economy
Organization for Economic
    Cooperation and Development
    14
Organization for Pacific Trade and
    Development 2
Overseas Chinese: consequences of
    homecoming 272–4; definition
    of 265–8; influence in Chinese
    politics 270; reasons for
    homecoming 268–9

Pacific Basin Economic Council 2
Pacific century 2
Pacific Economic Cooperation
    Conference 2
Pacific Free Trade and
    Development Conference 2
Pacific Free Trade Area 2
pay: ranges 240–1; system 73–4
performance *see* appraisals
personnel 143; turnover rate 256; *see
    also* labour force
Philips 232, 276, 277–83; Asian
    springboard to Europe and north
    America 288; opportunity for
    change 289–90; strategies within
    Asia 287-8
Plaza Agreement 161–3, 166
political future uncertainties 296–7
political normalization 49
political risks 142
population: Asia-Pacific region 5;
    China 4; north-east Asia 47–9
post-Confucian 'collectivism' 11
post-Soviet east Asia 149–59
power shift 49
price distortions 9, 40
price wars 98
private enterprise 18, 63
product specification 62
production structure 9
property prices 143, 144
protection measures 74, 98

Rajin Sonbong Free Economic and
    Trade Zone 49, 117–18, 121
recruitment 230–1, 260–1; graduates
    233, 234–5; older generation

236–8; practices 243–5; women 235
redundancy 230–1
relations: with China 108–9; with Russia 106, 107–8
research and development 227
rewards 229
Roh Tae-Woh 93, 94, 100-1, 150
Russia: exports 57, 104; raw materials 59; relations with China 157–9; relations with Japan 154–6; relations with Korea 149–51, 152–3; Tumen River project 129

salary *see* pay
Samsung 125, 150, 152
savings 40; domestic 7, 73; growth 17; rates 7
Sea of Japan Economic Circle 125, 127
services sector 9, 37, 41
Singapore 169; economic future 302
Sino–Korean relations 151–2
Sino–North Korean trade 57–9
Sino–Russian trade 54–7
small businesses 63
socialist market economy 21
soft authoritarianism 11, 17–18
south-east Asia: contributions to international order 140–2; future of 293–307; intra-and extra-regional economic relations 135–9; location of companies 142–7; trade patterns 139–40
South Korea: benefits from Tumen River project 122–8; economic policy 7; external economic surpluses 10; financial repression 9; political changes 92–9; rapprochement *see* North Korea; *see also* Sino–Korean relations 151, 153–4
special economic zones 120, 121
stability 7, 8; trade with 60–1
state-owned enterprises 21, 63
strategic planning: ASEAN experience 178–9, ASEAN corporations 179–80; benefits and problems 186–9; competitive posturing 184; environmental

certainty 182; goal performance 180–2; implications for European corporations 192–3; role of 189–92
structural transformation 33–9
supply-side factors 26

Taiwan: external economic surpluses 10; fiscal subsidy 9; pattern 271; reunification 272
technology 11, 66, 98; sharing 98–9
Texas Instruments 227, 239
Thailand: capital movement 10; external economic deficits 10; economic growth rates 7
Thomson Consumer Electronics 276–7, 283–7; Asian springboard to Europe and north America 288; opportunity for change 289–90; strategies within Asia 287–8
three-country triangle 53
Tienanmen Square massacre 149, 269
time: in organizational and strategic literature 220–1; in social sciences 219–20; *see also* Japanese time
tongbao 265
Toshiba 164, 165, 172
trade: balances 72–3; extra-regional relations 139; intra-Asian flows 77; intra-regional relations 137–9, 169; Japanese 78–9; between the two Koreas 102–3; types 51–2; *see also* north-east Asia
training 248–9
Tumen Economic Development Area 118
Tumen River area 53, 54, 112–15
Tumen River Area Development Programme 50, 51, 104, 109; benefits and potential problems 120–30; emerging concept 115–20; future prospects 130–1
Tumen River Area Management Company 131
Tumen River Economic Zone 118

United Nations Development
   Programme 51, 104, 119
university graduates 233, 234–5
US-Japan security treaty 172
USA 81, 83, 136, 137; multi-lateral
   dialogue 169; trade policy 84
USSR 20, 112; disintegration 149

value-added 37–8, 40, 41
Vietnam 86–7; economic future 303
Volkswagen 67, 228
Volvo 228, 257

wages *see* pay
welfare systems 240
Western companies 146–7
Western Europe regionalism 136–7
women: career opportunities 232,
   238; recruitment 235
world: economic growth centre
   82–8; economic order 140;
   economic power 1; economic
   slow-down 140

Yeltsin, Boris 107, 150, 153, 154